I0755802

Refuting Antisemitism: Dismantling the Stereotypes, Canards, and Tropes of Jew Hatred

Dr. Jeremy Havardi

Refuting Antisemitism:
Dismantling the Stereotypes, Canards, and Tropes of Jew Hatred

Dr. Jeremy Havardi

Academica Press
Washington

Library of Congress Cataloging-in-Publication Data

Names: Havardi, Jeremy (author)
Title: Refuting antisemitism : dismantling the stereotypes, canards, and tropes of jew hatred | Havardi, Jeremy.
Description: Washington : Academica Press, 2026. | Includes references.
Identifiers: LCCN 2025945984 | ISBN 9781680533903 (hardcover) | 9781680533910 (e-book)

Contents

For the great enemy of truth is very often not the lie – deliberate, contrived and dishonest – but the myth – persistent, persuasive, and unrealistic.
— John F. Kennedy

Tell me what you accuse the Jews of – I'll tell you what you're guilty of.
— Vasily Grossman, *Life and Fate*

Introduction

We live in an age beset by irrational thinking. Conspiracy theories and pseudoscience have a growing popularity, especially among the young, and are being disseminated faster than in any previous era in history. It seems part of common knowledge that we are being lied to by big government, by our scientific institutions and by the media, and that we are poorly served by our 'experts.' Within this framework, 9/11 is a big lie, Islamist terror attacks are false flag operations by the West and a hidden cabal controls the financial system. These forms of irrational thinking are far from the preserve of fringe organizations; they have a ready audience of millions. They are spread online at the speed of a mouse click, often at the behest of a deluded influencer whose twisted endorsement serves a growing appetite for counter-cultural narratives.

The last few decades have also seen a major surge in global antisemitism. The hatred against Jews and Jewish institutions is certainly ancient but it has gained a new lease of life amid a zeitgeist that disparages facts, logic and evidence. Stripped to its basics, antisemitism is a diabolical defamation against the Jewish people, a set of calumnious condemnations about Jews past, present and future that rely on a wilful distortion of truth. But it is also a conspiracy theory about Jewish power and control over the rest of society. Indeed, its allegations could hardly be more serious: Jews are a God killing nation devoid of mercy, the betrayers of prophets, the murderers of Christian children, the cause of global pandemics, the spreaders of disease, the instigators of war and slavery, the puppet masters of financial chaos, the corrupters of culture, the polluters of racial purity and the wirepullers of political change. They are depicted as evil incarnate: a usurious, cowardly, avaricious and unpatriotic people with an insatiable lust for power and control. Their nation state, Israel, is condemned in the same hateful terms: as a diabolical, genocidal, blood thirsty and irredeemably evil nation that sows regional and global conflicts, persecutes and terrorizes its victims without reason and instantiates every political evil of the age.

Antisemitism has often been likened to a form of superstition or folklore, an analogy with a superficial plausibility. The history of Jew hatred is full of myths, tales and legends, whether that is the blood libel or the notion that Jews killed the son of God. It does appear that antisemitism, like superstition, has an oral tradition whereby these legends and myths are passed down from one generation to the next, creating a popular understanding of the world. In addition, this prejudice has influenced many products of culture, including art, architecture, poetry and music.

The problem is that an educated public can see superstitions for what they are: irrational and outdated beliefs that are not anchored in the real world and which rely on supernaturalism. By contrast, antisemites, even highly educated ones, appear to really believe what they say about Jews. Antisemitism is a belief system that informs their understanding of the world and 'explains' the things that go wrong in their lives. It is a racist *Weltanschauung*, a twisted philosophy of the world that seems entirely credible to those who embrace it. It is perhaps more a form of pseudo-intellectuality than an urban legend, though it has elements of both.

Anti-Jewish hatred is not just a threat to the Jews, nor has it ever been. It is a major scourge of any civilized society and a potent threat to the liberal, democratic order. By proposing the message that 'democracy is a sham that hides the power of the Jewish puppet masters,'[1] that the whole of society is under the control of a shadowy elite acting for their own selfish purposes, antisemitism opens the way to a form of populist politics that corrodes all standards of truth, logic and decency. It encourages the type of demagogue who traffics in dangerous ideas about foreigners or who believes that sinister forces are undermining the rest of society. It encourages people to be seduced by lazy, simplistic solutions to complex issues. Whenever people are persuaded by the idea that an economic crisis, a global health emergency, a religious conflict, a threat of terrorism or another pressing social concern is ultimately down to the Jews, they are closing their minds and their energies to the real issues confronting them. Worse, it is an open invitation to adopting hateful attitudes towards 'the other,' attitudes that all too easily spill over into violent outbursts and criminal behaviour. It is not for nothing that the White House, in its 2023 National Strategy for countering antisemitism, has said that protecting the Jewish community from racism is 'essential to our broader fight

[1] Nick Cohen, "Anti-Semitism is a threat to the West," *Spectator*, December 17, 2023.

against all forms of hate, bigotry, and bias—and to our broader vision of a thriving, inclusive, and diverse democracy.'[1]

Antisemitism, whether in fascist countries like Germany or Italy, Muslim majority states like Iran or far left dominated nations in South America, disfigures the society that adopts it and leaves it at the mercy of other forms of corrosive hatred. As such, outbursts of antisemitism are often 'harbingers of societies in deep trouble and omens that extremism and violence are imminent.'[2]

This seems to be true of nations with traditions of radical politics, the so-called basket cases where democratic norms have long been absent. But liberal democracies too have come under strain in recent years where the forces of far-right nationalism and left-wing populism have come into the ascendant. Modern European democracies are experiencing a fragile moment amid a deepening despair over the economic crisis and a clamour for populist solutions to issues of race and immigration. As mainstream political thinking has come under attack, reactionary forces like Front Nationale, the AFD, the Five Star Movement and the Sweden Democrats have gained more traction and appeal. For some, the rejection of mainstream politics goes hand in hand with conspiracy thinking and, in turn, the tendency to blame Jews, the age-old enemy, for society's current predicaments. One EU official has described antisemitism as a 'deeply ingrained racism in European society.'[3] But it is also a major problem for modern American society.

This book is about refuting the key tropes of antisemitism and does so by examining four areas: ancient and medieval antisemitism, anti-Jewish prejudice relating to Jewish character, modern conspiracy theories about Jews and political antisemitism. Ancient canards include the idea that the Jews murdered Jesus, the trope which is foundational to all western anti-Jewish prejudice; the blood libel; the notion of a Muslim-Jewish golden age and the idea of the hooked-nosed Jew. Some antisemitism proceeds from attributing undesirable characters to the Jew: avarice, lack of patriotism, cowardice and hatred of gentiles. Modern conspiratorial antisemitism includes the accusation

---

[1] U.S.-National-Strategy-to-Counter-Antisemitism.pdf (whitehouse.gov), accessed May 19, 2024.

[2] Stephen Collinson, "A new wave of antisemitism threatens to rock an already unstable world," *CNN*, October 31, 2023.

[3] Jason Burke, "Antisemitism is deeply ingrained in European society, says EU official," *The Guardian*, October 30, 2023.

that Jews dominated the slave trade, that they were responsible for world communism, that they instigated the world wars of the twentieth century and that they have attempted to dilute the white race. Finally, there is political antisemitism with its panoply of accusations against Israel: that it is an inherently illegitimate, genocidal, apartheid state that lusts for Arab blood and whose evil acts portend an unprecedented world crisis. All these myths will be refuted, comprehensively so.

The book should obviously not be taken as a defence of all Jews at all times and in all places. Such a book would be preposterous. There have been plenty of rogue Jews through the ages who have engaged in illegal, criminal and immoral behaviour. There are Jewish rapists, perverts, fraudsters, mafiosi and murderers – in short, a gallery of rogues that shame not just their own community but the nations from which they arise. None of this should be surprising. Jews are human like everyone else and, like any community, produce from their ranks a motley collection of uncivilized characters. What is illegitimate is to see a vindication of antisemitism from such behaviour.

Thus, one is entitled to attack figures like Harvey Weinstein, Bernie Madoff or Baruch Goldstein without seeing them as a typical instantiation of Jewish character. Madoff was a thief and fraudster but his was not a species of 'Jewish theft.' Weinstein sexually abused his victims but such predatory behaviour was not a preserve of rich Jewish men. Goldstein carried out a massacre of Arabs in Hebron but he was not a typically bloodthirsty Israeli. One should dislike these characters, but no more than is necessary, to paraphrase Isaiah Berlin. Antisemitism is not about disliking disagreeable Jews and it is not a 'Jewish' problem. It is about an invented or chimerical Jew, a figure with stereotypical traits who is taken to embody an entire people. It relies on a foundational antisemitic paradigm which has been built up over two millennia and which has come to infect all forms of western culture.

Some will object to this book on the grounds that it dignifies a fundamentally irrational and evil worldview. By refuting antisemitism, by debating its merits so to speak, one is giving it a veneer of legitimacy that it does not deserve. The great Zionist leader Vladimir Jabotinsky would doubtless have agreed. Writing in 1911 in response to the Mendel Beilis Affair, another instantiation of the charge of ritual murder, Jabotinsky wrote the following words that have resounded down the ages:

> We constantly and very loudly apologize… Instead of turning our backs to the accusers, as there is nothing to apologize for, and nobody to

> apologize to, we swear again and again that it is not our fault… Isn't it long overdue to respond to all these and all future accusations, reproaches, suspicions, slanders and denunciations by simply folding our arms and loudly, clearly, coldly and calmly answer with the only argument that is understandable and accessible to this public: 'Go to Hell!'?[1]

Others will say that we should not engage in a 'futile attempt to refute a myth on the basis of historical facts and statistical data,' simply because antisemitic tropes are cultural constructions that are impervious to reason.[2]

All of this makes sense if one is talking about engaging with antisemitic leaders directly. Debating with antisemites suggests an equal playing field of ideas where the pros and cons of racist tropes are pored over by both sides. But true antisemites do not argue in good faith because what guides them is not a mere intellectual or cognitive error. They are seized by an animus, a hateful passion whose expression provides various forms of emotional satisfaction.[3] Antisemites do not come to the table with an earnest desire to understand society and its ills for they have already decided that Jews are to blame. They claim moral seriousness in their accusations but it is no more than a veneer hiding altogether more suspicious motives.

Refuting antisemitic accusations in a detached manner is rather different to debating antisemites. It is about highlighting the absurdity of Jew hate without giving antisemites the additional platform they relish. It is about persuading the young that they are latching on to a preposterous and divisive ideology that will lead them to ever greater forms of hatred and prejudice. It is about warning people not to buy into a set of ideas that are divorced from reality and which strain credulity.

This book is not about persuading antisemites to suppress their passion. Nothing will shake such people from their belief that Jews control the world for sinister and nefarious purposes, or that the hidden hand of the Jew stands behind every major social and economic disaster. They fully endorse every trope, canard and cypher of Jew hatred and no amount of critical thinking will shift their perspective. This book is not aimed at such people. It is designed

---

[1] Paula R Stern, "A people as all other peoples," *Times of Israel*, January 27, 2014.
[2] Christopher Browning, "The Fake Threat of Jewish Communism," *The New York Review of Books*, February 21, 2019.
[3] Eve Gerrard, "The pleasures of antisemitism," *Fathom*, Summer 2013.

primarily to be read by all those who are, as yet, untainted by the sick ideology of antisemitism and who are open minded enough to learn more about Jews, Judaism and Zionism. For these people, antisemitism must be refuted - comprehensively, systematically and definitively. That is what this book aims to do.

Chapter 1

Theological Antisemitism

1. Jews killed Jesus

The Charge

The foundational calumny against the Jewish people is that of deicide, the notion that the Jews murdered the son of God and now bear eternal responsibility for his death. The myth, which was propagated by countless church leaders, preachers and theologians in many countries over an equally large number of centuries, served as the basis for two millennia of faith-based persecution, prejudice and violence.

Most historical scholars accept as fact that the Jewish preacher Jesus of Nazareth existed, that he was born between 6BC and 4BC and that he was crucified in either 30 or 33AD. His life as a religious leader was said to have begun at the age of thirty when he was baptised, the first of five epochal events outlined in the New Testament. He preached in Galilee and recruited his first disciples, a small group that would eventually become the core of the early Church leadership. He journeyed to Jerusalem where he was proclaimed as Christ (the expected Messiah) by Peter, leading to his transfiguration. When Jesus entered Jerusalem during the last week of his life, he clashed with the money changers in the temple and was questioned by religious elders about the source of his authority. After being betrayed by Judas Iscariot for thirty pieces of silver, Jesus took part in the Last Supper with his disciples and delivered to them his Farewell Discourse. He was arrested and brought before the Sanhedrin where he stood accused of breaking the Sabbath law, practising sorcery, falsely claiming to be the Messiah and threatening to destroy the Temple. Gospel accounts say that Jewish elders then asked Pilate's Court to judge and condemn Jesus, arguing that his claim to be King of the Jews amounted to an act of treason against the Roman Empire. After some initial questioning, Pilate, acting as chief advocate, declared that he found Jesus innocent but the gathering crowd were incensed, insisting that this Jewish renegade be found guilty and executed. Pilate then ordered Jesus's crucifixion and the prisoner was taken to Calgary where he was put to death.

It did not take long for the antisemitic foundational myth to take root. In Paul's First Epistle to the Thessalonians, there was mention of the Jews 'who killed both the Lord, Jesus and the prophets.' The Gospel of Matthew offered an account of the trial of Jesus and talked of the high priest who found him guilty of blasphemy. When the Jewish Council was asked what the penalty should be, 'They answered. 'He deserves death.'' Following this, 'they spat in his face and struck him.'[1] Matthew's accounts of the Passion were perhaps the most influential of all the Gospel narratives and laid the blame for Christ's death squarely on the Jews. As the Jews entreated Pilate to kill Christ, he attributed to them words that resound down the ages and which went on to form the basis for the deicide charge: 'His blood be on us and on our children.'[2]

It was an incredibly significant line because it asserted that guilt for the crime of killing Jesus rested not just with the Jewish leaders present at the time of his trial but with Jews in any part of the world. It also implicated future generations of Jews, future inheritors of the Jewish traditions, implying that they possessed a form of inherited guilt for an act committed by their ancestors. It suggested that the moral stain of deicide would attach to Jews regardless of the country they lived in or the time that they were born. Guilt was perpetual.

The Church Fathers continued this diatribe against Jews with one example being Justin Martyr, a second century preacher, who explained to the Jews that their exile from the Holy Land had come about because they had 'murdered the Just One.' One finds the toxic accusation in the writings of Melito of Sardis, a second century bishop and major contemporary authority on early Christianity. In his volume *Peri Pascha* (On the Passover), Jews were blamed for the death of Christ. He wrote: 'God has been murdered, the king of Israel has been put to death by an Israelite right hand.' This one phrase has led Eric Werner to describe the author as the 'first poet of Deicide.'[3]

But while there remains some doubt as to whether Melito is guilty as

---

[1] Matthew 26:57-68.

[2] Matthew 27:25.

[3] Lynn H. Cohick, *The Peri Pascha Attributed to Melito of Sardis: Setting, Purpose, Sources*. Brown Judaic Studies, 2020. https://doi.org/10.2307/j.ctvzgb90c, accessed 1 April 2025.

charged, there can be few doubts about the views held by the early Church Father Saint John Chrysostom. Chrysostom, the Bishop of Constantinople, accused Jews of being 'Christ killers' and wrote a number of venomous tirades against them. He also coined the term deicide.[1] The notion was born that Jews were demoniacal, a devil in human form, and that there was no wickedness of which they were not capable. The Nicene Creed, laid down in 325, helped establish the charge of deicide and that Jews were 'parricides and the murderers of our Lord.' It led to the banning of Passover and its replacement by the Easter festival, with Constantine making it clear that it was 'unbecoming beyond measure that on this, the most sacred of festivals, we should follow the custom of the Jews.' The early Church writer Origen welcomed these changes before he clarified the notion of eternal Jewish guilt: 'Guilt for the blood of Jesus fell not only on those who lived then, but also on all subsequent generations of Jews, until the end of the world.'[2] For St Jerome, the synagogue was likened to 'a den of vice' and 'the Devil's refuge.'[3] The charge of deicide was to thunder through the Middle Ages with increasing ferocity, blackening and demonising Jewish communities across Europe and leading to acts of murderous violence and terror.

Of course, it should be pointed out that after so many centuries of clerically mandated hatred, Christian doctrine changed to absolve the Jews of responsibility for Jesus' death. Under the leadership of Pope Paul VI, the Catholic Church disavowed the charge of deicide with the publication in 1965 of the "Declaration on the Relation of the Church to Non-Christian Religions" (Nostra Aetate). It stated that the crucifixion of Jesus "cannot be charged against all the Jews, without distinction, then alive, nor against the Jews of today."

The charge of deicide has found a new lease of life in modern anti-Zionism with the incendiary accusation that Israel is 'again' killing Christ in Palestine. Replacement theologians, who portray Jesus as the original Palestinian, imply that the same Jewish mentality that led to Christ's crucifixion is being visited upon his Palestinian 'heirs.' A cartoon published during the Second Intifada showed an Israeli soldier pointing a gun at a Palestinian baby. The infant was designed to represent the baby Jesus and it was accompanied by a caption that read 'Oh, you're doing it to me all over

---

[1] Paul Johnson, *A History of the Jews*, (New York: Harper Perennial, 1988), 165.

[2] Jeremy Cohen, *Christ Killers: The Jews and the Passion from the Bible to the Big Screen* (Oxford: Oxford University Press, 2007), 32.

[3] Robert Wistrich, *The Longest Hatred* (London: Thames Methuen, 1991), 17.

again.'[1] In April 2002, the website Arabia.com showed an Israeli soldier (wearing a green jacket with the Star of David) about to bayonet a Christ like figure wearing a keffiyeh. A female figure, perhaps modelled on Mary Magdalene, was raising her hand in protest and the words 'Do not kill him TWICE' appeared above.[2] It is Jew hate repackaged as political narrative.

Refutation

Crucifixion was firstly a typical *Roman* punishment used against criminals, religious and political agitators, slaves and enemies of the state. It was designed to be an excruciating, brutal and humiliating form of capital punishment that served to deter others from committing the very worst crimes against the Roman Empire. Nor were the Romans the only empire to use this form of punishment. The Assyrian, Babylonian and Persian governments were among a number of notable practitioners of crucifixion in ancient times. But the Romans perfected this killing technique, deploying it for several centuries until Constantine I abolished it in the fourth century BC. By contrast, there is little evidence that this was a punishment used in Jewish penal law. Had the Jews been responsible for killing Jesus, it is far more likely that he would have been stoned, not crucified.

A crucial question revolves around who had the power to kill Christ. Frank K. Flinn, Professor of Religious Studies at Washington University, writes: 'Only Roman authorities could authorize crucifixions and they often did so on a gruesome, massive scale.'[3] As proof, he cites the brutal Roman crackdown on the Spartacus revolt, which led to some 6,000 slaves being crucified on the Appian Way. The same point about power and authority applies to Pontius Pilate. Pilate held the powerful position of prefect of Judea between 26 and 36 AD and, as such, one of his jobs was to maintain law and order in his province. As one writer has put it, this meant that he 'held all power when it came to administering penalties in the regions he ruled.'[4] Films,

---

[1] Abraham Foxman, "Revisiting Anti-Zionism and Anti-Semitism," *Huffington Post,* April 11, 2012.

[2] For a fuller discussion, see Daniel Goldhagen, The Devil that Never Dies: The Rise and Threat of Global Antisemitism, (New York: Back Bay Books, 2016), 384-5.

[3] Neil Schoenherr, "Romans are to blame for death of Jesus," Washington University in St. Louis, February 18, 2004.

[4] Sarah January, "The Real Reason Pontius Pilate Ordered Jesus' Death," *Grunge*, December 21, 2021, https://www.grunge.com/714309/the-real-reason-pontius-pilate-ordered-jesus-death/, accessed March 17, 2025.

such as Mel Gibson's notorious *The Passion,* show Pontius Pilate as a man given to showing mercy to the condemned Christ. He is sensitive and caring, sickened by the excesses of the crowd that are baying for Jesus to be killed. As the New Testament expert Geza Vermes writes, Pilate comes across in the film as 'a well-intentioned weakling' who gives into the crowd and their intolerant demands.[1] In Gospel accounts, he is the man who offers to commute the death sentence handed to Jesus and kill the criminal Barabas instead, even though the 'custom' of releasing a prisoner on Passover is unsupported by the historical evidence.

But far from Pilate being soft-hearted, the record suggests that the Roman procurator was a bloodthirsty and ruthless prefect who used terror as an instrument of Roman policy. Contemporary evidence comes from the Jewish philosopher Philo of Alexandria who condemned Pilate for his 'the briberies, the insults, the robberies, the outrages, and wanton injuries, the executions without trial constantly repeated, the ceaseless and supremely grievous cruelty.'[2] Other accounts also testify to his barbarity. The Jewish historian Josephus recounted an incident in which Pilate, having used Temple funds to build an aqueduct to Jerusalem, faced a crowd of protestors who were angered by his violation of Jewish custom. Pilate used plain clothed soldiers to infiltrate the crowd and, upon his signal, these soldiers removed hidden clubs and beat many protestors to death. Perhaps for this reason Vermes says this of the Prefect: 'All the reliable first-century sources depict Pilate as a tyrant who was guilty of numerous executions without trial and unlawful massacres. He was justly dismissed from office and banished by the emperor Tiberius.'[3]

Moreover, it was really only Pilate, and the Romans in general, who had the motive to kill Christ. While a small Jewish administrative elite may have objected to Jesus' religious preaching as a form of sedition, it was the *political* threat posed by this preacher that the Romans could never tolerate. Under Roman law, anyone styling themselves 'King' was essentially committing an act of treason and was seen as a fundamental threat to Roman law and order. It was one thing to pose as a religious subversive, another to challenge the authority of the empire. More importantly, one can question the idea that Roman judges could simply find a defendant guiltless but proceed to execute

---

[1] Geza Vermes, "Celluloid brutality," *The Guardian*, February 27, 2004.

[2] Aaron David Fruh, "If the Romans killed Jesus, Should We Blame Italians?" Times of Israel, April 5, 2023.

[3] Vermes, "Celluloid brutality."

them with impunity. If Roman judges executed clearly innocent people, they could face penalties such as removal from office, exile or death. Pilate would surely have known this.

Perhaps the single most powerful way to refute the deicide charge is to point out the absurdity of condemning 'all Jews' for Christ's death. It seems clear that a small Jewish religious elite condemned Jesus for what were seen as seditious teachings. But it should not be forgotten that they did so in opposition to many of their co-religionists. Jesus had a substantial Jewish following during his life. He travelled to Jerusalem for the Passover celebrations and when he arrived, according to Matthew 8:1-13, 'great crowds followed him...' There is further evidence that he was so popular among Jews that the authorities delayed arresting him during this festival. Mark 14:1-2 tells us the following: 'It was now two days before the Passover and the Feast of Unleavened Bread. And the chief priests and the scribes were seeking how to arrest him by stealth, and kill him; for they said, 'Not during the feast, lest there be a tumult of the people.''

But even if one accepts the controversial notion that this elite was responsible for putting Jesus to death two thousand years ago, the idea that subsequent generations have inherited this guilt makes no sense. Each person is responsible for the totality of their acts and moral choices. They are fundamentally untainted by the choices of people who lived before them and have no responsibility for any prior wrongdoing. This is such a basic principle of moral reasoning that it is hard to see how it can be questioned. Yet Christian doctrine cuts across this argument. It posits a notion of original sin which contends that all humans have inherited the original Adamite sin from the moment of conception. As all humans are descended from Adam, the head of the human race, they are literally 'born in sin' and animated by a fundamentally corrupt, selfish and evil nature. The only solution for this is to achieve redemption through Christ. The notion of eternal guilt was historically applied to Jews, who were seen as having a timeless, malign essence. In their case, the notion of original sin transcends the boundaries of space and time. An alleged evil committed by a tiny gathering of Jews in one part of the world condemns all Jews in perpetuity, wherever and whenever they live. The only redemption comes from abandoning their Judaic roots, rejecting Jewish peoplehood and embracing Christian doctrine. The rational man should thus reject any notion of inherited guilt, substituting for it the concept of individual autonomy and free choice.

Doubtless, the motives for demonising the Jewish faith and its adherents were complex. Perhaps some Church leaders sought to divert blame for the death of Christ away from the Romans for fear that such allegations would lead to an upsurge in anti-Christian persecution. But for others, distancing the new Christian faith from its Jewish roots was a prime means of winning new converts. If Judaism demanded such an atrocious act as deicide, it was not just a competing religion in the marketplace of ideas; it was a source of malignity, shame and evil. Moreover, such charges were a way of reducing the perceived threat from Jewish proselytising in the merging marketplace of religious ideas. Thus, Mark shifts the blame from the Romans to the Jews because he wrote his Gospel during the failed Jewish revolt against Titus. He seeks to explain the destruction of Jerusalem on the failed decisions of the city's Jewish establishment, specifically their rejection of Jesus decades earlier.

Turning to modern political antisemitism, the simplest refutation of 'Jesus the Palestinian' is that such a monicker would have made no sense at all to the prophet. After all, Jesus was a Jew from Judea whose birth name clearly indicated his ethnic origins. He claimed to be faithful to the laws of Moses, observed the Sabbath and kashrut laws, enjoyed a final Passover meal (the Last Supper) and made it his mission to preach to his co-religionists. At this death he was referred to as 'King of the Jews.'[1] Hence, virtually all of Jesus's earliest followers were Jewish, as were the writers of three of the gospels and the founder of Christianity, Paul of Tarsus. The term Palestine was imposed on Judea by the Romans in AD135 after they put down the Bar Kochba revolt. In other words, the term Palestine was imposed on the land that Jesus inhabited roughly a century *after* this death and thus there is no lineage between Jesus and the present day Palestinian Arab population of the West Bank or Gaza. Thus, the notion that Israel is crucifying Palestinians 'all over again' is nothing less than the application of racist tropes in a modern day political context.

2. Jews crave the blood of Gentiles

The Charge

Apart from deicide, no accusation against the Jews has resonated throughout Jewish history with more destructive force than that of the blood libel or ritual murder. From the twelfth century onwards, Jews were accused

---

[1] Sam Rood, "Was Jesus Palestinian?" *Inherit Magazine*, December 23, 2024.

of murdering Christian children so that they could use their blood for religious purposes, such as making matzot (unleavened bread). Often, these accusations surfaced at Easter, a time in the calendar when Christians could be reminded about the alleged Jewish responsibility for Christ's death.

In 1144, a young boy, William of Norwich, who worked as an apprentice tanner, went missing in his home town and was later found murdered, with signs of torture on his body. According to one account, William had last been seen entering the house of a Jew. He had had his head shaved before his tormentors stabbed him many times with thorn points. These accounts depicted William as a victim of ritual re-crucifixion at the hands of his Jewish assailants, in 'mockery of the Lord's Passion.' Very soon, the Jewish community faced the accusation that they had ritually murdered this young boy for religious reasons, part of an annual sacrifice that required the killing of a Christian. Thus, the blood libel was born, one of the most pernicious charges levelled at Jews throughout the ages and a mainstay of medieval anti-Jewish demonization.[1] The incendiary accusation would re-appear many times in the proceeding centuries, often accompanied by frenzied bloodletting against innocent Jewish communities.

In the thirteenth century, Lincoln became the site of another notorious blood libel, this time with a tragic outcome. A nine-year-old child, Hugh of Lincoln or Little Sir Hugh (1246-1255), was found dead in a well roughly one month after he disappeared. According to the account written by Matthew Paris, Jewish leaders from cities across England were summoned to Lincoln where they took part in a gruesome sacrifice. One Jew, acting as a judge in place of Pilate, subjected the child to torture, beating him, placing a crown of thorns on his head and then crucifying him. A local Jew named Copin 'confessed to the crime' in return for a promise of protection from the authorities. At the time, many Jewish families were gathering in Norwich, not to take part in a sadistic killing, but to celebrate a wedding. King Henry III ordered Copin's execution and for 90 Jews to be arrested and locked in the Tower of London. When eighteen of their number refused to take part in legal proceedings, claiming understandably that they amounted to a 'show trial,' Henry III had them executed.

Such was the power of the blood libel that it was invoked by Chaucer in

---

[1] Gillian Bennett, "Towards a Revaluation of the Legend of 'Saint' William of Norwich and Its Place in the Blood Libel Legend." *Folklore* 116, no. 2 (2005): 119–39. http://www.jstor.org/stable/30035273.

his Canterbury Tales. In the Prioress' Tale, a Christian boy walks through a Jewish ghetto on the way to school, singing the hymn *Alma Redemptoris Mater* (Nurturing Mother of the Redeemer) as he walks. The Jews in the ghetto are angered by this and, in an attempt to silence the child, hire an assassin to slit his throat before deposing the corpse in a privy. When the boy is found, he is still singing the hymn and is then carried to the church, though not before Jews have been put to death. The boy continues singing until a grain is removed from his tongue and he then dies, leading to his martyrdom. In this type of devotional literature, the Jew plays the role of malevolent bogeyman in contrast to the saintly and pure Christian child.

Blood libels would appear elsewhere in Christian Europe, including at Gloucester (1168), Blois (1171), Lincoln (1255) and Munich (1268). The 1491 blood libel, where several Jews were killed in an *auto da fe* near the town of Avila after confessing under torture that they had murdered a child, galvanized the Spanish Inquisition in its hunt against heretics. From the seventeenth century onwards, blood libels were common in parts of eastern Europe. One notable example was from 1690 when, according to legend, a six-year-old boy, Gabriel of Białystok, was kidnapped from his home in Zverki in the Poland-Lithuanian Commonwealth during Passover. They also appeared in more recent centuries, notably in the 1840 Damascus Affair and the Beilis Affair of 1911. Blood libels have also become commonplace in the Islamist discourse against Jews and Israelis.

Refutation

The starting point of refuting the blood libel is to note the basic laws of kashrut, that is the dietary laws that all religious Jews are required to follow. They include laws that prevent the consumption of certain types of food (pork, seafood and so on), laws mandating that meat and dairy products may not be eaten together and laws about the preparation of certain foodstuffs. One law of kashrut states that all blood must be drained from the meat or cooked out of it before it is eaten. This can be found in Leviticus 7:26-27: 'Moreover you shall eat no blood whatever, whether of fowl or of animal, in any of your dwellings. Whoever eats any blood, that person shall be cut off from his people.' This is a law enjoined not just upon Jews but mankind as a whole and is a prohibition found nowhere else in the ancient Near East. Elsewhere, we find a similar sentiment: 'And if anyone of the house of Israel partakes of any blood, I will set My face against the person who partakes of the blood, and I will cut him off from among his kin' (Leviticus 17:10). Later, Deuteronomy states that: 'Only you shall not eat the blood. You shall pour it upon the earth like water.' [Deuteronomy 12:16 and 12:23-24] Thus, if a blood spot is found on an egg, the egg is deemed by many religious authorities to be non-kosher.

The prohibition against the drinking of blood derives from the Torah's belief that the life of the animal is contained in the blood. Blood is the life (or literally the soul – nefesh) of the creature, hence eating the blood is tantamount to eating life. We can see this as early as Genesis where Jews are told: 'But flesh with its life, which is its blood, you shall not eat.' [Gen 9:4] What applies to animals applies also to humans. While there may not be a *Biblical* prohibition against the consumption of human blood, there is a Rabbinic prohibition which is based on the principle of *marit'ayin* (that is, the appearance of impropriety), the fact that one may mistake human for animal blood.

Of course, there are other reasons cited for why Jews cannot consume blood. Maimonides, one of the great Jewish religious authorities in the Middle Ages, talks of blood being hard to digest and thus being injurious as a foodstuff. [Maimonides, Guide 3:48] The great sage also talks of the psychological harm that can result from eating blood, especially the notion that humans would become like beasts and acquire animalistic traits. But the religious reasons, accompanied by the view that blood consumption is akin to idolatry, are fundamental. It was arguments like these that were recognized by some Christian authorities as a refutation of the blood libel. In 1247, following attacks on Jews in two French towns, Pope Innocent IV issued the papal bull *Sicut Judaeis*, forbidding Christians from accusing Jews of using human blood in their rituals. The Pope stated that 'in the Old Testament they are instructed not to use blood of any kind, let alone human blood.'[1] The Pope might have added that the Torah expressly prohibits murder and also condemns the type of blood sacrifices that were routinely practiced by pagan religions.

It is because of this Papal injunction that we can begin to see why the charge of the blood libel is such an egregious fraud. It accuses Jews of engaging in a practice that fundamentally contradicts Jewish law. It suggests that, despite the seriousness of the prohibition against consuming blood, Jews are told that it is a religious *obligation* to contravene this law and to do so for a *religious* ritual. It pictures religious Jews, and religious Jewish leaders, as either ignorant of their own faith or as willing to transgress Jewish law in order

---

[1] David Nirenberg, "The Impresarios of Trent," *The Nation*, November 16, 2020.

to satiate their lust. Yet no convincing explanation is ever given as to why Jews would wish to act this way. It is equally absurd to posit that Jews require the blood of gentiles in order to bake matzahs (unleavened flatbread). Matzah is made from wheat flour, mixed with water, salt and, sometimes, olive oil or egg. Blood is not one of its ingredients.

Moreover, if Jews really did need the blood of a Christian boy to satiate either their lust for revenge or for their own rituals, why is there no mention of the blood libel in the 1,200 years since the death of Christ? It seems strange that in country after country where Jewish life was overseen by their (often hostile) neighbours, there is no record of such Jewish ritual killings. The accusation of ritual murder falls down, not only on the lack of evidence that the specific victims were killed by Jews, but on the grounds that such acts contradict the basis on which Jews live.

Why did the blood libel have such force? In medieval times, Jews were frequently likened to the devil and depicted as the anti-Christ, owing to their supposedly willing rejection of Christ and their willingness to kill their God.[1] A people animated by such dark, primitive and barbaric impulses could easily be depicted as child killers, willing to pray on the most vulnerable members of society to satisfy their immoral lusts. Thus, we are given a stark reminder that there is no limit to the evil that can be visited upon a people when it is seen through a destructive prism of fear, ignorance and superstition.

3. Jews were responsible for the Black Death

Charge

The medieval demonization of Jews led to outbreaks of intense violence and bloodletting, with massacres and expulsions recorded in numerous cities. The Black Death of 1348-52 would usher in a new and more intense wave of violence against Europe's Jews, demonstrating the undeniable potency of antisemitic tropes and myths.

The bubonic plague had already ravaged parts of Asia in the fourteenth century, killing perhaps 20 million people before it struck Europe. Between 1348 and 1350, an estimated 40% of Europe's population (25 million people) was wiped out by the plague. It was a demographic disaster quite unparalleled

---

[1] For a full analysis, see Joshua Trachtenberg's *The Devil and the Jews: The Medieval Conception of the Jew and its Relation to Modern Antisemitism* (Pennsylvania: Jewish Publication Society, 2002).

in the continent's history and one from which it would take Europe more than a century to recover. It was compounded by a failure to understand its cause.

For some, this pestilence represented the wrath of God, brought down on the sinners of mankind for straying from the path of righteousness. Some people (flagellants) took this idea so seriously that they whipped themselves in order to repent for the sins of others. Others pointed to astrology and the alignment of planets as an explanation for the catastrophe. They claimed that in 1345, there had been a conjunction of three planets which caused 'great pestilence in the air' and led to mass death on earth. Still others embraced the miasma theory, which held that epidemics were caused by foul odours, ones which emanated from rotting organic matter.

It was inevitable that during a time of such profound social crisis, people would turn on the Jews, blaming them for the unfolding carnage. The main charge against the Jews was that they had poured poison down wells in a bid to decimate the water supply and kill their gentile neighbours. As further 'proof' of Jewish malignity, it was alleged that Jews had largely survived the plague, with their death rates far below those of their neighbours. The explanation was that the instigators of the plague, knowing what was to come, naturally insulated themselves from the unfolding apocalypse.

Violent attacks soon followed. In April 1348 on Palm Sunday, 40 Jews were murdered in Toulon when the Jewish quarter was sacked. In 1349, following accusations of well poisoning, Jews were massacred in Zurich after the city council ordered the community to be burned to death while in the Strasbourg massacre of February 1349, thousands of Jews in that community met the same fate. Months later, the community in Frankfurt was wiped out, followed by the annihilation of the Jewish populations of Mainz and Cologne. The pogroms that took place in these years destroyed dozens of Jewish communities and represented one of the greatest disasters for European Jewry before the Holocaust. It should be stressed that this violence took place despite pleas by various Popes for it to stop. Boniface the Innocent issued a proclamation in vain that the Jews were blameless for the catastrophe and should continue to receive protection. Pope Clement VI wrote: 'Throughout many parts of the world the same plague, by the hidden judgment of God, has afflicted and afflicts the Jews themselves and many other races who have never lived alongside them.'[1]

Refutation

Refuting the notion that Jews spread the plague is relatively easy in light of modern science. Due to advances in medicine, especially the study of transmissible diseases, we can now be fairly certain that the plague was caused by a bacterium (Yersinia pestis) that lived within fleas that in turn lived on rats. Traders inadvertently brought these rats and the fleas that lived on them on ships from Asia to Europe. The plague was spread by both human contact and inhalation and what abetted the ease of transmission was Europe's relatively primitive sewage disposal system (an open pit channelled through the middle of the street). Once infected, a person would suffer from fever, seizures and a swelling of lymph glands (buboes), with death following in a significant percentage of cases.

The assumption that Jews did not share equally in the decimation of the Plague remains contentious. It was sometimes assumed that the reason why Jews may have suffered a lower death rate than their gentile neighbours was due to a series of cultural factors that related to their health and cleanliness. Thus, medieval historian Norman Cantor said that the higher survival rate of Jews was down to a matter of 'personal cleanliness, good housekeeping, and highly selective diets.'[2]

It is indeed part of Jewish ritual to wash one's hands throughout the day: after getting up in the morning; before praying; after cutting nails or hair; before eating bread; before sexual intercourse and after intimate contact; after leaving a cemetery, and on many other occasions. A Jew bathed at least once a week before Sabbath. Furthermore, Jewish law prohibits the recitation of blessings and prayers by an open pit at latrines and at places with noxious smells. Finally, Jewish law prevents a community from leaving a corpse unburied, a factor that in medieval times would have decreased the spread of plague, typhus and other diseases. It is speculated that this may have provided Jews some protection from the plague. But while Jewish sanitary practice provided for a level of cleanliness that was far superior to the medieval norm, it is unlikely that this alone gave Jews protection from the worst ravages of

---

[1] Dan Freedman, 'Why were Jews blamed for the Black Death,' *Moment Mag*, March 31, 2020.

[2] Kathryn A. Glatter and Paul Finkelma, 'Jews, Genes and the Black Death,' *Jewish Review of Books*, February 9, 2021.

the Black Death. Hand washing and ritual cleanliness in the home would not have been enough to ward off the bacterium that caused plague.

Instead, it is speculated that genetic factors may be the reason why the Jewish death rate was lower than the gentile one, if indeed Jews suffered relatively less deaths than others. In the fourteenth century, Jews were major carriers of a genetic mutation called Familial Mediterranean Fever (FMF), which caused a variety of painful symptoms that included fever and inflammation of the abdomen and lungs. A study by the National Institute of Health points out that FMF 'mostly affects Turkish, Jewish, Armenian and Arab populations.' Moreover, it quotes research carried out by the National Human Genome Research Institute (NHGRI), which has found that genomic variants that cause FMF may also confer increased resilience to the plague.[1] Specifically, FMF patients produce abnormal levels of pyrin, a protein which plays a key role in the inflammatory response of the body during an infection. In other words, allegedly relatively lower Jewish survival rates had nothing to do with being forewarned about a pandemic they had planned, but nor were they necessarily altered by cultural practice. Instead, they were more likely to be a function of genetic biology.

4. Jews have big noses, horns and red hair

For many centuries, Jews were believed to have identifiable physical characteristics that marked them off from the rest of gentile society. Often, these were deemed to be wholly negative traits, ones which signified a corrupt and poisonous nature that was meant to inspire revulsion and dread among non-Jews. Those physical markers appear in medieval Christian art, are alluded to in various works of literature and thunder with intensity in the racially antisemitic iconography of nineteenth and twentieth century culture. The notion of a Jewish racial physiognomy, a means by which one could identify character from facial features alone, centres around three core notions: that Jews had enlarged noses, that they had horns and finally, that they had red hair.

[1] "NIH study shows genomic variation causing common autoinflammatory disease may increase resilience to bubonic plague," *National Institutes of Health*, June 29, 2020.

The Jewish Nose

Charge

If there is one physical characteristic that is believed to typify the Jews, it is their purportedly large, protruding noses. The stereotype of the aquiline (eagle-like) nose, so called because the large bridge gives it the appearance of being curved or bent, appears in medieval literature, especially from the 13th century onwards, when there was a move towards more realistic art and an increased interest in physiognomy. It came within a theological context that depicted Jews in wholly sinister terms, indeed which rejected them as the antithesis of humanity. As the great scholar of medieval Judaism, Professor Sara Lipton, explains: 'Long or large, downward-curved, snout-like or beak like noses, especially when combined with brutish expressions and shaggy beards, had long served as visual indicators of bestiality, brutality, irrationality, and evil.'[1]

The hooked 'Jewish nose' can be found in a work by Francisco de Quevedo called *un hombre de gran nariz* (To a man with a big nose), written to denigrate a literary rival by picturing him as a descendant of conversos, as opposed to a full blooded Spaniard. Images of big Jewish noses also appear in the 13th century picture Bible, commissioned by Blanche of Castile, as well as artwork two centuries later by Hieronymus Bosch. The hooknose reflected a prevailing religious belief that Jews were grounded in the material, secular world of 'here and now,' as opposed to the realm of the eternal in Christianity. In some contexts, it symbolized a state of ignorance or error, as in a fourteenth century illustration of Psalm 52 ('The Fool says in his heart: "There is no God."') In that image, the wine drinking character on the left is identifiably Jewish, with his hook nose the key facial feature.[2] This was art purportedly proving that Jews were different, a species to be shunned by civilized society.

Nineteenth century literature was no stranger to such tropes. The most infamous example of literary antisemitism from this period was the character of Fagin from *Oliver Twist*. He is initially introduced to readers as 'a very old shrivelled Jew, whose villainous-looking and repulsive face was obscured by a quantity of matted red hair.' When the character was subsequently portrayed, most famously in the film starring Alec Guinness in 1946, the

---

[1] Sara Lipton, *Dark Mirror: The Medieval Origins of Anti-Jewish Iconography*, 107.

[2] Sara Lipton, "The invention of the Jewish nose," *The New York Review of Books*, November 14, 2014.

grotesque facial features, including the hook nose, were all present, causing much reason for acrimony among sections of the Jewish community, as well as in the postwar German government.

Another less well-known example of literary racial antisemitism was the satirical book *The Operated Jew*, written in 1893 by the German psychiatrist and novelist Oskar Panizza (1853-1921). Influenced by the zeitgeist of contemporary biological racism, which argued that Jews had an irredeemable physical and moral essence which could not be altered, Panizza told the story of a Jewish doctor, a fictional Itzig Faitel Stern, who used plastic surgery to eradicate his Jewish identity. The hook nosed, thick lipped Jew underwent a series of disfiguring operations, including having his bones straightened and his larynx altered, in order to become a true bourgeois German and marry a gentile woman. But as he delivers a speech at his wedding, the man discovers all his old Yiddish traits returning, suggesting that the 'curse' of his racial Jewishness has returned.[1]

Some contemporary scientific figures also bought into this idea. In 1850, anthropologist Robert Knox wrote a description of a Jew's physical features that included these words: 'A large, massive, club-shaped, hooked-nose, three or four times larger than suits the face…Thus it is that the Jewish face never can (be), and never is, perfectly beautiful.'[2]

But as racialist thinking developed and took on ever cruder forms, so too did depictions of Jews in the minds of rabid antisemites. Thus, in the writings of the French fantasist Édouard Drumont, Jews appear in crude, racist caricature, complete with hook noses and sinister appearance. He edited the antisemitic political newspaper *La Libre Parole*, one of whose most famous front covers shows a repulsive looking Jewish man, whose grinning and devious face is adorned by a large, hook nose, holding onto the globe as a sign of his lust for domination.

By the turn of the twentieth century, such was the prevalence of myths about Jewish noses, that a German doctor Jacques Joseph, now known as a pioneer of rhinoplasty, found ample work in adjusting the noses of a largely Jewish clientele in the years before 1933. Jews believed that removing such a visible sign of their 'ethnicity' was a ticket to entering respectable society. As

[1] Oskar Panizza, and Jack Zipes, "The Operated Jew," *New German Critique*, no. 21 (1980): 63–79. https://doi.org/10.2307/487997.
[2] Beth Preminger, "The 'Jewish Nose' and Plastic Surgery: Origins and Implications." *JAMA,* Vol. 286, No. 17, November 7, 2001.

Sander L Gilman observed, 'racial identity shaped Jewish self-perception in the Diaspora.'[1] Of course, the Nazis put enormous energy into maligning Jewish physicality. They depicted the Jews as a terrifying swarm of subhuman creatures replete with swarthy features, reminiscent of the devil, protruding hook-noses and beady eyes. In a story called *The Poisonous Mushroom*, Nazi propagandist Julius Streicher wrote: 'One can most easily tell a Jew by his nose. The Jewish nose is bent at its point. It looks like the number 6. We call it 'the Jewish six."[2]

This Nazi iconography has come to influence extremists of both far left and far right in the internet age. Today, one of the main antisemitic memes found on white supremacist websites is that of *The Happy Merchant*, also known as Jew Face. It shows a hunched Jewish man, with hooked nose, bulging eyes and beard, rubbing his hands in glee to signify his depraved greed. It has been described as 'unquestionably the most popular anti-Semitic image on the internet,' suggesting that it has a reach and a pull which should not be underestimated. It has since mutated to appear in dozens of contexts, including those memes that blame Jews for creating and spreading Covid or which blame Jews for the global economic crisis.[3] Stereotypical images of 'fat bankers' controlling the Federal Reserve incorporate the visual element of the hook-nosed Jew, often rubbing his hands in glee at the latest iteration of financial disaster caused by his unstoppable greed. One classic British example was the mural by *Mear One* which showed a group of white bankers, some with hook noses, counting their fortune on a board, below which was a mass of suffering humanity.

The image has appeared in modern art too. As recently as 2020, the Italian painter Giovanni Gasparro, in his work *The Martyrdom of St Simon of Trent in Accordance with Jewish Ritual Murder,* includes hook nosed Jews with bloody fingers in his literal artistic depiction of the famous blood libel.[4] Similarly, the annual Aalst carnival in Belgium has featured a parade of floats

---

[1] Don Harrán, "The Jewish nose in early modern art and music," *Renaissance Studies, 28*(1), 50–70. http://www.jstor.org/stable/24423865

[2] "Pages from the Antisemitic Children's Book The Poisonous Mushroom," United States Holocaust Memorial Museum, https://perspectives.ushmm.org/item/pages-from-the-antisemitic-childrens-book-the-poisonous-mushroom, accessed 1st August 2024.

[3] Joseph Bernstein, "The Surprisingly Mainstream History of The Internet's Favorite Anti-Semitic Image," buzzfeednews.com, February 5, 2015.

[4] Jacob Willer, "Unwelcome rise of a truly awful artist," *The Critic Magazine*, July/August 2020.

which contain antisemitic imagery. In 2019, one float showed a group of ultra-orthodox Jews with hook noses standing on top of a bag of gold coins.

Refutation

The notion that Jews have particularly big noses is the stuff of cultural mythology. In 1911, anthropologist Maurice Fishberg provided definitive proof when he actually measured 4,000 Jewish noses in New York. What he discovered was that there was no significant difference in size with the general population. The specific figures he cited were relevant:

2,836 adult male Jews in New York City:

Straight or Greek nose: 57.26%
Retrouse or snub: 22.07%
Aquiline or hooked: 14.25%
Flat and broad: 6.42%

1,284 adult female Jews in New York City.

Straight, or Greek: 59.42%
Retrousse, or snub: 13.86%
Aquiline, or hooked: 12.70%
Flat and broad: 14.02%

As Fishberg concludes: 'The predominant type of the Jewish nose is the straight' while 'The proportion of aquiline, hooked, convex, or so-called "Jewish" or "Semitic" noses is thus rather small among the Jews of today.'[1]

He was supported in his view by Harry L. Shapiro in an entry on anthropology for Encyclopaedia Judaica. He wrote that while 'the convex profile with a depressed nasal tip is not infrequent among Jews, this is not surprising since the same nasal character is common enough in the general region from which they originate, not to mention that it also occurs in non-Jewish European people.'[2]

A more recent study at Penn University has shown that the appearance of the nose is an evolutionary adaptation. Due to the air of a cold and dry climate,

---

[1] Maurice Fishberg, *The Jews: A Study of Race and Environment* (New York: Walter Scott Publishing Co., 1911), 79,82.

[2]Ophir Yarden, "Anti-Semitic Stereotypes of the Jewish Body," myjewishlearning.com, https://www.myjewishlearning.com/article/anti-semitic-stereotypes-of-the-jewish-body, accessed 3rd April 2024.

Europeans tend to have narrower noses while Africans have broader ones to adapt to a warmer environment. Jews have come from different regions and so have different kinds of noses, alongside other religious groups.[1] Put simply, there is no such thing as a 'Jewish nose' and the matter should rest there.

Horns

Charge

Another negative image from medieval times was that of the horned Jew. For Christians, horned beasts were associated with the Final Judgement, and thus were seen as satanic in nature. In Chapter 13 of the Book of Revelation, the coming of the Antichrist references beasts with horns, creatures 'having seven heads and ten horns, and upon his horns ten crowns.' (13:1). As a result, medieval iconography began to incorporate this meme, with manuscripts from the 12th and 13th centuries representing Moses with a horned head-dress. It found its place in early modern artwork, which depicted Moses with horns, most famously in the great sculpture by Michaelangelo, and it cemented the widespread view that all Jews had the devil's horns. It may not be plausible to argue that Michaelangelo merely stumbled upon an innocent mistranslation of the Bible when he depicted the Jewish lawgiver with horns.[2] The great sculptor included the Jewish badge of shame on a painting of Aminadab, Aaron's father-in-law, a detail that some have taken as a deliberate 'othering' of the Jewish figure.[3]

What made such an association all the more plausible for Christian observers was a medieval zeitgeist which associated Jews, the Christ killers, as the devil incarnate. A great deal of medieval poetry, drama and art portrayed Jews with horns, tails, goat beards and bad odours, demonstrating that they were akin to the devil on earth.

Refutation

While no study is needed to disprove the idea that Jews have horns, it is worth pointing out the origins of this irrational belief. The Hebrew text of Exodus 34:29-30 speaks of Moses descending from Mount Sinai with his face

---

[1] A'ndrea Elyse Messer. "Nose form was shaped by climate," Penn State University, https://www.psu.edu/news/research/story/nose-form-was-shaped-climate, accessed September 4, 2025., March 16, 2017

[2] Bertman, S. (2009). The Antisemitic Origin of Michelangelo's Horned Moses. *Shofar*, *27*(4), 95–106. http://www.jstor.org/stable/42944790, , accessed April 11, 2024.

[3] Benjamin Ivry, "Are Michaelangelo's Drawings Anti-Semitic?," *Forward*, July 28, 2014.

radiant [*karan*] after conversing with God. The Hebrew word had alternative translations, such as 'glorified' or 'rays of light,' meaning that, for the Jews, it connotated an image of power and status for their revered prophet. But the popular and respected Douay-Rheims Challoner Bible wrongly translated the word *karan* as 'horned,' spawning the idea that Moses had protruding horns from his head. Those who peddle this myth today should realize that they are being influenced by an original mistranslation of a Hebrew text which has had destructive consequences for Jews.

Red Hair

Charge

It may seem amazing today to think that Jews, a population often imagined as dark haired and swarthy in appearance, were once depicted as red haired. For many centuries, the red haired Jew cropped up in various texts and images which featured unsavoury Jewish characters. In Anthony van Dyck's *The Taking of Christ*, Judas Iscariot, the betrayer of Christ, appears as a redhead. Some evidence suggests that in early productions of *The Merchant of Venice*, Shylock appears as a redhead while Fagin, the criminal mastermind in Oliver Twist, has flaming red locks. Medieval German sources also attest to a widespread belief in the Red Jews (die Rote Juden), a Jewish nation shown as a threat to Christian civilization. The association of Jews with red hair suggested to many that these people were 'dangerous outsiders working with the Devil to sabotage Christian society from within.'[1] It also suggested a clear link with villainy, which was the reason that some Biblical wrongdoers, such as Cain and Salome, were depicted as having red hair.

Refutation

Of course, having red hair is a matter of genetics and usually requires both an individual's parents to carry an MC1R gene.[2] This gene then operates on two pigments, eumelanin and pheomelanin, and the more there is of the latter, the more one's hair will be red. So how prevalent is red hair among more

---

[1] By Irene Katz Connelly, "On National Redhead Day, Explore the History of Ginger Jews," *The Forward*, November 5, 2019.

[2] Zorina-Lichtenwalter, K., Lichtenwalter, R. N., Zaykin, D. V., Parisien, M., Gravel, S., Bortsov, A., & Diatchenko, L. (2019). A study in scarlet: MC1R as the main predictor of red hair and exemplar of the flip-flop effect. *Human molecular genetics*, *28*(12), 2093–2106. https://doi.org/10.1093/hmg/ddz018

modern Jewish populations? An article in the 1906 Jewish encyclopaedia gives specific figures for the hair colour among 145,380 Jewish School Children in a number of European countries. While the majority are black or brown, only about 1% have red hair. In a separate table examining the hair colour of 7,505 Jews, the overwhelming majority of Jews in European countries had dark hair and only a small minority, varying from 0.7 to 4.36%, had red hair. Similar results were found in Maurice Fishberg's paper *Physical Anthropology of the Jews* (1903). With a sample size of 2,300 Jews, it was found that 82% of Jews studied had various shades of dark hair, about 15% had fair hair, and approximately 3% had red hair. None of this is surprising, considering that redheads are themselves a small minority in the world, though greater numbers can be found in European countries.[1] Understanding the historic context for this negative iconography is essential in refuting harmful myths about the Jews.

5. Jewish-Muslim relations were uniformly marked by a Golden Age

Thus far, all the canards and tropes identified focus on the position of Jews within Christendom. However, from the 7th century onwards, Jews interacted with the new faith of Islam and came to settle in the empires into which it expanded. Much modern historiography has come to picture Muslim-Jewish relations in somewhat idyllic terms. Many nineteenth century historians spoke longingly of a 'Golden Age' of interfaith rapprochement, tolerance and co-operation, modelling their view on the 'utopia' of Muslim Spain. They viewed this 'paradise' of integration as a riposte to a Christian Europe that persecuted its Jews and slung them into ghettos.

Foremost among those who promoted the notion of a Golden Age was Heinrich Graetz, the popular author of the monumental, multi volumed *History of the Jews*. The theme of the Arab-Jewish Golden Age was taken up by Arab nationalist writers, one of the most important of whom was George Antonius. In his book *The Arab Awakening* (1939), Antonius declared that Arab history was 'remarkably free from instances of deliberate persecution' and that 'some of the greatest achievements of the Jewish race were accomplished in the days of Arab power, under the aegis of Arab rulers, and

[1] Emil G. Hirsch, Immanuel Benzinger, Solomon Schechter, Isaac Broydé, Joseph Jacobs, Maurice Fishberg, "Hair," *Jewish Encyclopedia*, volume 6 (1906), 157-160.

with the help of their enlightened patronage.'[1] His views would be echoed by many later scholars of the Arab world who would cite the alleged harmony between Jews and Arabs before 1948 to buttress a partisan case against Zionism. It is also a key component of the anti-Zionist case made by ultra-orthodox sects such as Neturei Karta.[2]

But as scholar Mark R Cohen has argued, there is equally a neo-lachrymose conception of Arab-Jewish relations that exists among partisans in the Arab-Israeli conflict, which posits a uniformly darker picture of Jewish-Muslim existence in the Middle Ages. Bat Ye'or, the pen name of Egyptian born writer Gisèle Littman, has popularized the concept of Jewish dhimmitude, the notion that under Muslim rule, Jews were a permanently persecuted, ill-treated and downtrodden class. Her polemical writings are a clear attempt to suggest that Islamic states have mistreated minorities as a matter of religious principle and that the faith-based states have little merit to their rule. Bat Ye'or has won a number of admiring reviews for her Eurabia thesis, the notion that there is a French led, European conspiracy theory to Islamize and Arabize Europe, largely through policies of mass immigration, in such a way that it will undermine the continent's support for the US and Israel. Among those who have lauded her work are British journalist Melanie Phillips, the American political scientist Daniel Pipes, Harvard historian Niall Ferguson and far right politician Geert Wilders.

Refutation

The truth about how Jews fared under Muslim rule is not sufficiently captured by either the idyllic or lachrymose conceptions. In many ways, the Jewish experience was less fraught under Muslim rule than in Christian Europe, with less restrictions and theologically based persecution, but it was not a halcyon period of equality and integration either. As Bernard Lewis writes, Islam did not introduce an 'interfaith, interracial utopia' where people 'lived side by side in a golden age of unbroken harmony'[3] but nor was it a scene of constant, fanatical persecution.

In general, it could be said that Jews fared better under Muslim rule than

---

[1] Mark R Cohen, *Under Crescent and Cross: The Jews in the Middle Ages*, (Princeton: Princeton University Press, 2008), 6.

[2] The author remembers being harangued by a member of this anti-Zionist sect in 2015 where he was told that Jews and Arabs had always lived in peace before 1948.

[3] Bernard Lewis, *The Jews of Islam*, (Princeton University Press, 1992), 1.

the rule of Christian Europe. Despite a number of limitations and restrictions, Jews were largely not confined to ghettos as they were in Christian Europe and they could engage in a large number of professional trades. They had a defined political status in the developing Islamic societies, enjoying rights and protections that were absent in Christian Europe. They were largely free to practice their faith and enjoyed formal representation before the authorities of the states they lived in. They generally had a degree of local autonomy too, with their own chiefs, judges and courts that dealt with their respective communities' religious, family and personal matters. While a certain level of theological antisemitism could be described as indigenous to the Islamic faith, it lacked the special intensity of Christian hatred, meaning that the demonization of Jews was largely absent until the modern era. This was a reflection of the Islamic view that Jews, like Christians, were monotheists who had received a legitimate form of divine revelation but who had refused to accept Islam's supremacy. They also failed to kill the Muslim prophet, unlike in Christianity where they supposedly murdered the son of God. As long as they showed the necessary subservience, they could largely enjoy their 'protected' status. They were treated better than the polytheists and idolators who generally suffered more harshly under Muslim rule.

There were certainly periods of early Muslim rule in which Jewish communities fared well and experienced various forms of beneficence. In the seventh century, Caliph Umar I (634-644) led the conquest of Jerusalem, which had previously been under Byzantine rule. The Caliph made some concessions to Jews, allowing seventy families to live in the city and build a synagogue and religious college.[1] It was in Palestine, in the early years of Muslim rule, that Hebrew vocalization and punctuation were created and the scientific text of the Hebrew Bible was formulated.[2] Jewish poets, writers, astronomers, mathematicians and philosophers thrived during periods of the so-called Golden Age in medieval Spain (al-Andalus), many of them flocking to Cordoba, the capital of the Umayyad caliphate. Among the many famous names from this period of Judaeo-Spanish history are philosopher Solomon ibn Gabirol, the linguist and poet Rabbi Moses ben Jacob ibn Ezra, the physician and philosopher Judah ha Levi, the scholar and physician

---

[1] It was, however, under his direction that the shrine known as 'the Dome of the Rock' was built after his death on the Temple Mount.

[2] Martin Gilbert, *In Ishamel's House: A History of Jews in Muslim Lands*, (New Haven: Yale University Press, 2011), 41.

Maimonides and the astronomer and historian Abraham ibn Daud. As scholar Jocelyn Hellig notes: 'Many Jews became wealthy and influential. Several gained high positions in the administrative field, while others reached great heights in scientific, medical, literary, linguistic and philosophic achievement.' She added that the Jews 'contributed much to the welfare of Spain' and 'played an indispensable role in spreading Arabic learning to the rest of Europe.'[1] The golden period was interrupted by the intolerant rule of the Almohads and the Almoravids, but was restored in the twelfth century.

Another golden age was experienced by the Jews of Baghdad during this same period of history. The medieval rabbi, Benjamin of Tudela, recounted his visit to the city in the twelfth century, noting the freedom enjoyed by the Jewish community. He spoke of the city's many richly decorated synagogues and the respect shown to Jewish officials by the Muslim caliph. The Exilarch, the head of the Jewish community, was respected by the Muslim community and many came to pay homage to him. The period was not immune to outbreaks of violence, which occurred in the thirteenth century, but Baghdad was a great centre of Jewish religious and cultural life for long periods. Under the rule of the Ibadis, a moderate sect of Islam founded by Abdullah ibn Ibad at-Tamim, Jews took advantage of the greater tolerance shown towards non-Muslims. The Ibadis offered extensive protection to Jews and other minorities and eschewed violence for religious reasons. Modern day Oman, with its Ibadi majority, continues these peaceful and tolerant traditions. It was under Ottoman rule from the sixteenth century onwards that Jews enjoyed a considerable level of prosperity, thriving in certain professions and dominating the world of trade and commerce. Jews also achieved high diplomatic positions, including the rank of governor.

But at the same time, Muslim rule could be deeply harmful to its Jewish (and Christian) minority during many periods of its history. At times, they were subject to appalling outbreaks of murderous violence which engulfed entire communities. One such example took place in 1066 during the period of Berber rule in Spain (al Andalus). Jews had thrived in Granada, the kingdom's capital, and even had a Jewish vizier, Samuel ha Nagid. The vizier was the city's most powerful figure and the first Jew to command Muslim

[1] Jocelyn Hellig, "The Jewish Golden Age of Spain Revisited," *Religion in Southern Africa*, *3*(2), 23–33 (1982), http://www.jstor.org/stable/24763674

armies on the battlefield.[1] But some resented his power, believing that under Islamic law, Jews had to be forever subservient to their Muslim overlords. When Samuel died and his son, Joseph, became vizier, there were stirrings of discontent on display, none more so than from the poet Ibrahim ibn Masud ibn Saad al-Tujibi. He wrote a series of verses which included these lines, a clear incitement to murder:

> *Do not consider it a breach of faith to kill them, the breach of faith would be to let them carry on. They have violated our covenant with them, so how can you be held guilty against the violators?*

On December 30, 1066, a rampaging mob stormed the palace, brutally executed the vizier and murdered thousands of Jews. It was one of the bloodiest pogroms of the medieval period. Jews faced many other pogroms under Muslim rule over the centuries, and, in recent centuries, this included Safed (1834), Damascus (1848), Aleppo (1853), Marrakech and Fez (1864), Alexandria (1870) and the Farhud (1941). Decrees were issued that led to the destruction of synagogues in Egypt (1014), Iraq (1344) and Yemen (1676), razing to the ground these venerated centres of Jewish life and learning.

In general, Jews who lived under Muslim rule were scarcely treated as equals. While they were tolerated and given various freedoms to work and practice their faith, there was a price to pay in the form of being dhimmis. Dhimmitude, a form of state protection in exchange for legal subordination and second-class citizenship, had been codified under Caliph Omar Abd al-Azziz. The so-called Covenant of Umar[2], which categorized non-Muslims as ahl al-dhimma (the People of the Pact), promised to offer Jews (and Christians) security of life and property, freedom of religion and communal autonomy in return for the payment of the jizya tax. The jizya was imposed on non-Muslim subjects, arguably as 'badge of humiliation for their unbelief.'[3]

In addition, Jews were subjected to a series of prohibitions: they were prevented from owning arms and building synagogues and churches; they

[1] Aaron Reich, "On This Day: On This Day: 955 years since the murder of Jews in Granada massacre," *The Jerusalem Post*, December 30, 2021.

[2] These regulations were ascribed to Umar I but it is likely that they reflect later developments.

[3] Ziauddin Ahmed and Ziauddin Ahmad, "The Concept of Jiyza in Early Islam," *Islamic Studies*, vol. 14, no. 4, 1975, pp. 293–305. *JSTOR*, http://www.jstor.org/stable/20846971, accessed 10 Aug. 2023.

could not raise their voices at prayer times; their houses could not be taller in elevation than those of Muslims; they had to walk on one side of the road; they could not ride horses; they could not use saddles; they could not employ a Muslim and they were subject to unequal inheritance laws. Under some regimes, the discriminatory regulations were designed to demean and humiliate their victims. Thus, the Iranian Jews of Hamadan were told they could not overtake a Muslim in a public street or talk loudly to a Muslim and, worse, they had to remain silent if insulted by a Muslim.[1] In light of Muhammed's marriage to a Jewish woman (Rayhana), a Muslim man could marry a non-Muslim woman but a non-Muslim man could not marry a Muslim woman. In an unambiguous attempt to mark the dhimmis off from Muslims, they also had to wear special signs on their clothing and avoid any clothing (green colours) which would indicate an association with Islam.[2] These emblems were the origin of the yellow badges, which later spread to European societies. In later centuries, a new prohibition was added that prevented a dhimmi from serving as a witness in a Muslim court in a case that involved a Muslim.

Professor Mark Cohen argues that these laws were designed to reinforce Islamic hierarchy rather than necessarily humiliate the dhimmis. Nonetheless, these were discriminatory laws which conflict with the notion that Jews lived lives of perfect equality with their Muslim neighbours. Such equality would have been alien to the Muslim overlords who believed with great passion that one could not 'accord the same treatment to those who follow the true faith and those who willfully reject it.'[3]

Moreover, some Muslim Caliphs could be far more severe in their interpretation of dhimmitude than others. Thus, Caliph Ja'far al-Mutawakkil ordered Jews and Christians to affix images of devils to their houses, an exacting form of social humiliation designed to demean these people in the eyes of their neighbours.[4] In Yemen, in the late eighteenth and early nineteenth centuries, rulers issued a series of decrees which forced Jews to remove human waste and filth from Muslim areas. Around the same time in

---

[1] David Littman, *Jews under Muslim rule: The case of Persia* (1979), *The Institute of Contemporary History*, 7.

[2] Flora Cassen, "The Long History of Forcing Jews to Wear Anti-Semitic Badges," *The Smithsonian Magazine*, March 20, 2023.

[3] Lewis, *The Jews of Islam,* 4.

[4] Gilbert, *In Ishmael's House*, 36.

Morocco, Jews in major cities such as Fez were forced to salt the heads of decapitated rebels as a deterrent to others, a humiliation forced upon them even on the Sabbath.[1] There was also a difference between life under Sunni and Shi'ite rule, with life generally better for non-Muslims in Egypt, Syria or Iraq, as opposed to Iran.

Despite the fact that the worst manifestations of theological antisemitism were largely absent from the Muslim world, they did infiltrate parts of the Middle East in the middle of the nineteenth century. This included the accusation of the blood libel, the mainstay of Christian hatred against Jews for so many centuries. Its worst manifestations could be seen in 1840 when thirteen members of the Damascus Jewish community were arrested after being accused of murdering a monk for ritual purposes. The local consul Ratti-Menton, together with the Governor-General Sharif Pasha, conducted a brutal investigation whereby they tortured a Jewish man until he 'confessed' to the crime. Others among the accused died from torture while 63 Jewish children were also seized to put pressure on the community. The resulting international outcry led to the release of the prisoners. Such blood libels, which spread around the Arab world with some rapidity, would come to gain increasing acceptance in the twentieth century and lead to a wave of pogroms. In the Iranian city of Shiraz in 1910, the Jewish community faced an accusation of ritual murder when it was alleged that a young girl had disappeared in the Jewish quarter. A body was subsequently found, that of a young Jewish boy who had died a week earlier. Nonetheless, a mob gathered to exact revenge for this 'murder' and, with the aid of local soldiers, stormed the Jewish quarter. They killed 12 Jews and ransacked their houses, stealing whatever they could get their hands on and destroying the rest. These were not the only cases of such mob violence in the modern age.

In sum, the medieval treatment of Jews under Islamic rule is more nuanced than either the optimists or the detractors like to believe. There was no uniform golden age, nor an unbroken history of endless persecution. An impartial survey of the historical evidence reveals a more complex reality that is lost on partisans of various political causes.

---

[1] Andrew G Bostom and Ibn Warraq (eds.), *The Legacy of Islamic Antisemitism: From Sacred Texts to Solemn History*, (New York: Prometheus Books, 2008) 46.

Chapter 2

Attacks on Jewish Character and Faith

1. Judaism teaches that Jews are superior to Gentiles: the chosen people myth

Charge

The notion that Jews considered themselves a superior people who were chosen by God to rule over non-Jews has been a mainstay of anti-Judaic and antisemitic narratives for many centuries. Judaism was said to promote the belief that Jews were God's 'chosen people,' a people specially selected to receive divine blessing at the expense of their 'inferior' gentile counterparts. The Jewish faith was alleged to look down upon non-Jews as worthless and weak, justifying their ill treatment and degradation.

A contemptuous attitude towards Jews can be found in the writings of a number of Roman authors. They derided the perceived sense of Jewish exclusiveness as arrogant and disrespectful. Certain Jewish customs, such as circumcision and the Sabbath day of rest, caused considerable resentment and helped to fuel the idea that Jews were undermining the values and lifestyle in the Roman world. Roman writers such as Seneca, Petronius and Juvenal mocked Jewish customs and were bemused by such institutions as the Sabbath and the refusal to eat pork. The historian Tacitus was far more openly contemptuous of the Jews. In his *Histories*, he accused them of profaning everything that the Romans held sacred, branding their religious practices sordid and depraved, condemning them for scorning the gods and lambasting them as the basest of nations. He spoke of how the Jews had 'a stubborn attachment to one another, an active commiseration, which contrasts with their implacable hatred for the rest of mankind.'

The antisemitic tract *The Talmud Unmasked*, written by the Lithuanian priest Justinas Bonaventure Pranaitis in 1892, attempted to prove that Jewish religious texts encouraged Jews to hate and kill Christians and to see themselves as a chosen elect which could rule the world. In Protocol 1, he wrote this about the Jews: 'By the fact that he belongs to the chosen people, (he) possesses so great a dignity that no one, not even an angel, can share equality with him.' Being chosen meant that he was 'considered almost the equal of God' and that the 'whole world is his and all things should serve him.'[1] That chosenness portended some great evil for mankind was also alluded to in other 'revelations' in the book. The prophets were quoted as saying that Jews were chosen by God to rule the earth and that God had endowed Jews with genius to be equal to the task. When this rule was complete, the Chosen would sweep away all other religions from the globe and slay all those who opposed Jewish rule.

The English novelist G.K. Chesterton, a man who made a point of opposing theories of racial supremacy, assailed the Jews for their purported belief in superiority and chosenness. In his book *The Crank*, he attacked Hitler's belief in Aryan supremacy but regarded it as Jewish in origin. He wrote that if there was 'one outstanding quality in Hitlerism' it was 'its Hebraism' and added that 'the new Nordic Man (had) all the worst faults of the worst Jews: jealousy, greed, the mania of conspiracy, and above all, the belief in a Chosen Race.'[2] For Chesterton, there appeared to be a supreme irony here in that Hitler, the most depraved enemy of the Jews, had been goaded by a Jewish ideology, by Jewish ideas and by Jewish flaws. By failing to recognize this, the Jews, in effect, were at fault for their own persecution.

In his play *Geneva: A Fancied Page of History in Three Acts* (1938), the Irish playwright George Bernard Shaw drew a contrast between the particularism of the Jewish nation and the universality of Catholicism, assailing the Jewish spirit of parochialism as a form of rabid nationalism which conflicted with the spirit of brotherhood and universalism that he believed was necessary for building a better and more peaceful world. Like Chesterton, Shaw seemed to regard the Jewish concept of a chosen people as a template for Nazi ideology, condemning Hitler for the irony of 'Hebraising' his nation. Shaw did not cease to issue incendiary remarks about Jews and Zionists, calling the notion of a chosen nation a 'monstrous presumption'

---

[1] Rev I. B. Pranaitis, *The Secret Rabbinical Teaching Concerning Christians*' (Facsimile Publisher, Delhi), 39.

[2] Michael Curtis, "Considering Honor for G.K. Chesterton," *New English Review*, June 12, 2018.

which constitutes 'a dangerous paranoiac delusion.'[1] He was also well known for admiring the interwar dictators in Germany and Italy.[2]

The notion that Jews use their 'chosen' status as a stick with which to denigrate gentiles comes across in anti-Zionist attacks on the Jewish state too. In other words, it is an integral part of political antisemitism. One of the most vitriolic and notorious such attacks came from the pen of Nobel Prize winning novelist Jose Saramago in 2002. In an article for *El Pais*, he accused Jews of being 'intoxicated mentally by the messianic dream of a Greater Israel which (would) finally achieve the expansionist dreams of the most radical Zionism.' He said they had been 'contaminated by the monstrous and rooted "certitude" that in this catastrophic and absurd world there exists a people chosen by God and that, consequently, all the actions of an obsessive, psychological, and pathological exclusivist racism are justified.'[3] For Saramago, the original sin was contained in 'racist' Judaism, which was animated by a vengeful and destructive God who had conferred chosenness on one people. That too became Israel's original sin, the factor that turned it into a leper among the nations and a malign force in the international order. As a result of the Jews failing to enter modernity by shedding their ancient biblical traditions, he argued that Israel's struggles with its neighbours had a 'unique and even metaphysical quality of genuine evil,' one that distinguished its conflict from that of any other in the world.

Another celebrated writer who thought it necessary to demean Jews was Jostein Gaarder, the Norwegian author of *Sophie's World*. In his article, *God's Chosen People*, published in *Aftenposten*, Gaardner denied the legitimacy of a Jewish state that had failed to shed its biblical belief in chosenness:

> We don't believe in the idea of God's chosen people....To present oneself as God's chosen people is not just stupid and arrogant, but a crime against humanity. We call it racism.[4]

For the Greek composer and self-declared antisemite, Mikis Theodorakis, the Jews were animated by 'the belief that God loves you and you are the

[1] Saul Jay Singer, "The Anti-Semitism Of George Bernard Shaw," JewishPress.com, May 6, 2015.
[2] Nathan, David. "FAILURE OF AN ELDERLY GENTLEMAN: SHAW AND THE JEWS." *Shaw* 11 (1991): 219–38. http://www.jstor.org/stable/40681334.
[3] Giulio Meotti, "The new-old Jew hatred," *Ynet News*, October 22, 2011.
[4] Jostein Gaardner, "God's chosen people," *Aftenposten*, August 5, 2006.

chosen people.' It was a belief that enabled them to 'survive against all odds; but also something that 'gave birth to racism.'[1]

A final example came from the pen of *Independent* journalist Deborah Orr after Israel decided to release more than one thousand Palestinians in exchange for one of their own soldiers who had been captured in 2006. The price Israel was forced to pay by Hamas was painful but represented the type of compromises the country was prepared to make in order to retrieve its soldiers from harm. Yet for Orr, this lack of proportion was 'abject' because it acknowledged 'that the lives of the chosen (author's emphasis) were of hugely greater consequence than those of their unfortunate neighbours.'[2] In other words, it reflected Israel's beliefs that the Arabs, not being chosen, were somehow inferior to Jews and could thus be traded with impunity.

Refutation

There is certainly a notion of chosenness at the heart of Judaism and which is embedded in Jewish cultural identity. Deuteronomy 7:6 states, 'For you are a people consecrated to Adonai your God: of all the peoples on earth Adonai your God chose you to be God's treasured people.' In the Book of Deuteronomy 14:2, it says: 'For you are a holy people to Hashem your God, and God has chosen you to be his treasured people from all the nations that are on the face of the earth.'

The blessing for studying the Torah includes these words: 'Praised are You, Lord our God, King of the Universe, who has chosen us out of all the nations and bestowed upon us His Torah.' The basis upon which God is said to have chosen the Jews, providing them with a covenant of protection, is that they have agreed to abide by the Torah, the book of divine law that contains a series of prohibitions against murder, adultery, robbery and other immoral acts. In fact, there is some suggestion that the Jews were the last people to be offered the covenant of protection. It is believed that God first offered the Torah to the children of Esau, Ammon, Moab and Ishmael, but they declined it when they realized the prohibitions contained within it. It is only when those peoples declined God's offer that he turned to the Jews.[3]

---

[1] "Mikis Theodorakis thinks that the Palestinians should learn from the experience of the Greeks," *eKathimerini.com*, August 31, 2004.

[2] Deborah Orr, "Is an Israeli life really more important than a Palestinian's?" *The Guardian*, October 19, 2011.

[3] Alter Yisrael Shimon Feuerman, "The Myth of Chosenness," *Tablet Magazine*, January 27, 2020.

For most Jews, being chosen is not seen as a badge of racial, ethnic or religious superiority. It does not connote that Jews are better or more worthy than non-Jews and it does not signify that they, and they alone, will receive a reward in the afterlife. These Jews hold that being the 'Chosen People' means that they have a special burden of responsibility to impart a message to mankind. They must be a light unto the nations, with a mission to improve the world and fight for justice. Jews, according to the Torah, are to be 'a kingdom of priests and a holy nation' (Exodus 19:6). Being chosen is far less about privileges and far more about an obligation to ensure that mankind follows monotheism and the set of moral obligations laid down in the Torah. That chosenness does not confer special rights or membership of a special race is connoted by a verse in Amos which states: 'You alone have I singled out of all the families of the earth. That is why I call you to account for all your iniquities' (Amos 3:2). The Jews were chosen for this task, so orthodox members believe, because they were small in number. Had God selected a mighty and powerful nation, then any success they had in imparting God's word to mankind would have resulted from their power rather than the moral authority of their message. It is said in Deuteronomy: 'It is not because you are numerous that God chose you, indeed you are the smallest of people' (Deuteronomy 7:7).

That a belief in chosenness does not equate to a belief in superiority stems also from Judaism's attitude towards non-Jews. Judaism continually stresses the brotherhood of man and the need for kindness and generosity towards 'the stranger.' Jesus quoted Leviticus when he issued the famous (and much honoured) injunction to 'love thy neighbour as thyself' (19:18). Indeed, when Rabbi Hillel was asked by a non-Jew to summarize the whole of the Torah while standing on one foot, he replied: 'What is hateful to yourself, do not do to your fellow man. That is the whole Torah; the rest is just commentary. Go and study it.' Jews are enjoined to give tzedakah to the poor and not to defame others by speaking harshly of them. They are told they must save lives, any lives, even if this involves overturning important ritual observances. They are not allowed to cheat in business or take advantage of others. These verses, and the edicts associated with them, would not make sense if Jews regarded non-Jews as lesser beings

According to modern Jewish law, non-Jews must observe the Seven Laws of Noah in order to guarantee a place in the World to Come (*olam haba*). If a non-Jew follows the seven laws of Noah, then they are regarded as 'Righteous

Gentiles.' As outlined in the Babylonian Talmud and the Tosefta Avodah Zarah, those laws are not to worship any idols, not to curse God, not to commit murder, not to commit adultery or sexual immorality, not to steal, not to eat flesh torn from a living animal and to establish courts of justice. Such laws, which were first given to Noah, apply to all of humanity. Judaism does not proclaim that only Jews have a share in the world to come or that only Jews can receive divine favour. Instead, true righteousness can be attained by any individual who follows the laws set out for all mankind.

2. Jews are unpatriotic and disloyal

For centuries, Jews have been accused of disloyalty, of being unpatriotic citizens who show more attachment to their own people than to the 'host' societies in which they happen to reside. Their loyalties, concerns and values are viewed as parochial and selfish, rendering them an untrustworthy, unpatriotic and deceitful people. Indeed, any sense of Jewish patriotism is viewed by antisemites as a clever charade designed to hide Jewry's fundamental goal, which is to undermine the interests of whichever country they live in. It is also a trope with ancient roots.

In the Biblical book of Esther, Haman the Agagite, the chief minister of King Ahasuerus, conspired to exterminate the Jews of Persia after Mordechai, his arch nemesis, refused to bow down to him. The words chosen by Mordechai in refusing this demand ('I am a Jew') sum up Judaism's abhorrence of idolatry and the willingness of Jews to prefer death to false worship. The words of Haman to Ahasuerus have a chilling resonance today: 'There is a certain nation scattered abroad and dispersed among the peoples in all the provinces of thy kingdom; and their laws are diverse from all people; neither keep they the King's laws; therefore, it is not for the king's profit to suffer them.' (Esther 3:8) In the end, Haman's murderous request was thwarted by the actions of Esther and instead, it was Haman who was hanged on the gallows.

Haman took Mordechai's refusal as a sign that the Jews themselves would deny him fealty. From this, he derived a genocidal decree that the Jews had to be put to death, removing the 'stain' of disloyalty from the Persian empire. For this Persian genocidaire, the Jews were an alien force within their society because they refused to bow down to a pagan entity, cleaving instead to a monotheistic ideology. A Jewish refusal to abandon their own customs and laws was seen as unpatriotic and disloyal. In the Roman world, the perceived sense of Jewish exclusiveness, as already noted, was seen as a sign of superiority and it was condemned for being disrespectful to Roman custom. Thus, Roman writers such as Seneca and Juvenal dismissed Jewish cultural customs, such as the refusal to eat pork, while Roman historian Tacitus branded Jewish practices as sordid and depraved.

The charge of dual loyalty would become a ubiquitous line of attack against Jewish minorities in more modern times. In post-revolutionary France, Napoleon posed a fundamental question to the country's Jewish citizens: 'Do Jews born in France, and treated by the law as French citizens, consider France as their country? Are they bound to defend it? Are they bound to obey (its) laws?'[1] He came up with his own answer. 'Once part of (the Jewish youth) will take its place in our armies, they will cease to have Jewish interests and sentiments.' The notion that Jewish interests and French interests could not co-exist suggested that cleaving to a parochial identity was contrary to national interests and would represent a lack of patriotism.

Yet a post-revolutionary nation whose founding principles were tied up with liberty, equality and fraternity, was happy to turn on its Jews when the occasion demanded it.[2] That came in the form of the notorious Dreyfus affair which convulsed France in the 1890s. If the infamous affair showed anything, it was that the trope of the disloyal and unpatriotic Jew could be dredged up no matter how baseless the evidence against him. Captain Alfred Dreyfus was accused of selling military secrets to Germany in 1894. After being court martialled and found guilty of treason, Dreyfus was publicly humiliated and sentenced to life imprisonment on Devil's Island. Among those celebrating his fate was the French journalist Edouard Drumont whose newspaper *La Libre Parole* contained a number of vicious cartoons and caricatures. When it was clear that Dreyfus was innocent, he was eventually freed and pardoned but the charge of dual loyalty was openly celebrated by reactionary conservatives in France and beyond.

Similar attacks were launched against Disraeli, the Anglo-Jewish Prime Minister who embroiled his country in the Eastern Crisis. He gave British support to Ottoman Turkey, which was seen as a counterweight to Russia, despite the fact that the Turks had carried out a massacre of Bulgarian Christians who had risen against Turkish rule. For one eminent professor, this

---

[1] "Napoleon, the Jews and French Muslims," *The New York Times*, March 18, 2007.

[2] Douglas Johnson, "The Dreyfus Affair," *History Today*, Volume 35 Issue 7 July 1985.

had little to do with upholding imperial interests or balance of power politics. He argued that if England was drawn into this conflict, it would be a 'Jewish war, waged with British blood to uphold the objects of Jewish sympathy or to avenge Jewish wrongs.' Disraeli was perceived to be a disloyal politician because he favoured Jewish (read anti-Christian) interests, not British ones. Others attacked Disraeli for his 'foreign mentality,' his 'Hebrew policy' and for being an 'Oriental dictator.'[1]

Germany's defeat in the First World War caused intense bewilderment among the country's elites and the accusation that conspirators had robbed the country of victory. It would give rise to the most notorious and damaging accusation of dual loyalty in the twentieth century, namely the Stab in the back myth (*Dollschosslegende*). It stated that the reason Germany lost the war was because of plotting by defeatist and pacifist civilians who had stirred up unrest in a bid to end the war. Among the chief culprits were Jews (see separate section).

Charles Lindbergh, by contrast, accused Jews of conspiring to embroil the United States in the next global war. In his Des Moines speech of September 1941, he assailed 'a minority of our own people' (Jews and their British allies) who were purportedly forcing the US into a needless and destructive war. Rather chillingly, he added that their reasons for wanting to go to war were 'not American.'[2] The notion that a country's Jews were involved in treasonous disloyalty to their nation was also a theme in the postwar Soviet campaign against 'rootless cosmopolitans,' a campaign which targeted actors, critics and doctors. The majority of those identified were Jews and the paper attacked these people for their 'clannishness' and 'tribelike solidarity.'[3]

Before and after the creation of Israel in 1948, charges of dual loyalty would play a role in the ethnic cleansing of close to one million Jews from Arab countries. Arab Jews were accused of being agents or collaborators with the 'Zionist regime' and subjected to a wave of pogroms and murderous assaults in the years leading up to Israel's creation. After 1967, Egypt round up hundreds of Jewish men and labelled them 'Israeli prisoners of war.' They

---

[1] Colin Holmes, *Anti-Semitism in British Society*, 1876-1939, (London: Hodder & Stoughton, 1979). 11-12.

[2] This was from his Des Moines Speech, September 11, 1941.

[3] Konstantin Azadovskii and Boris Egorov, 'From Anti-Westernism to Anti-Semitism: Stalin and the Impact of the Anti-Cosmopolitan Campaigns on Soviet Culture,' January 2002, *Journal of Cold War Studies* 4(1):66-80.

were no longer Egyptian Jews. Similarly, in 1969, nine Iraqi Jews were executed for 'spying' for Israel, a charge that made sense only by viewing them as disloyal collaborators for a foreign regime. Even in modern America, a bastion of western, liberal values, President Nixon railed against Jews in his administration whom he suspected to be spies, traitors and subversives.[1]

It is also a common theme with modern anti-Zionists who charge Jews with prioritising the interests of the Jewish state over their respective countries. In one recent notable example, Democrat Representative Ilhan Omar, criticising the influence of the pro-Israel group AIPAC, said that she wanted to 'talk about the political influence in this country that says it is okay to push for allegiance to a foreign country.'[2] The clear insinuation was that those engaged in pro-Israel lobbying were deeply disloyal to their own country because their 'allegiance' was being drawn towards another. This charge has been one of the consistent themes of today's anti-Israel movement.

Refutation

Law of the land: There are many angles from which to refute the generic charge of Jewish disloyalty and lack of patriotism. The notion that Judaism encourages Jews to detach themselves from the countries they live in is refuted by a principle in Jewish law called *dina d'malkhuta dina.* This is roughly translated as 'the law of the land is the law' and states that Jews are bound by the civil law of their respective nations. Moreover, it is a religious requirement to follow this principle, providing that such civil law is applied to all citizens, Jews and non-Jews alike, that the government is seen as having legitimacy and that the nation's law does not contravene the spirit of laws in the Torah. For Jews living under a dictatorship, the principle would clearly not apply. The principle derives from a letter written by the Biblical prophet Jeremiah to the Babylonian exiles: 'Seek the peace of the city to which I have exiled you and pray to the Lord on its behalf; for in the peace thereof you shall have peace' (Jeremiah 29:7).

The reason why Jews had to cleave to the principle of *dina d'malkhuta dina* was the high cost of treason and disloyalty. Reflecting an age-old condition of powerlessness, Jews simply could not afford to betray whichever

---

[1] Stephen J. Whitfield, "Nixon and the Jews," *Patterns of Prejudice* 44, no. 5 (2010): 445, 447.

[2] "Ilhan Omar attacks pro-Israel lobby and critics again call remarks antisemitic," *The Guardian*, March 2, 2019.

king, vizier or sultan ruled over them. Instead, they had to follow a survival strategy of pragmatism and accommodation, demonstrating their loyalty to a regime in order to receive its protection. As Ruth Wisse points out in her book *Jews and Power*, Jews played vital roles in many gentile societies. They were highly able court physicians, financially astute court bankers, skilled minters and creative craftsmen. Jews could hardly use these skills to overthrow a regime but they were used as leverage to prove their indispensability to the government, thus enabling their long term survival.[1] Thus, the real story of Purim was not one of treacherous (and subversive) Jews scheming to overthrow a regime but of how one determined Jew used loyalty to protect her people.

Modern patriotism: In the era of the modern nation state, the Jews' desire for social acceptance saw extraordinary levels of assimilation and acculturation, as well as a desire to win acceptance through the expression of patriotism. The spur was the American Revolution of 1776 and then the French Revolution of 1789, with these seismic events fostering the principles of religious toleration and civic equality. In the latter case, Jews were liberated and de-ghettotized across Europe in a process that led, within two generations, to gaining a raft of civic rights.

In France, Jews were caught up in the revolutionary elan and embraced the ideals of assimilation and acculturation with a profound fervour. Despite the perils of exclusionary nationalism and antisemitism, there was a belief that a rich symbiosis of Jewish and French culture was possible.[2] By the mid-nineteenth century, Jews were experiencing emancipation in Britain too and though there were outbreaks of prejudice against Jews, life was generally tolerable. Emancipation also came to Austria-Hungary and the new states of Italy and Germany, though full social acceptance and equality was still some way off. The Italian Jews had every reason to embrace their new nation, given that it promised liberal equality and tolerance in contrast to the old Catholic states where antisemitism was more common. So too did Jews in the new Austro-Hungarian empire, a multinational, multi-dynastic state headed by Emperor Franz Joseph, a unifying figure to whom Jewish citizens showed loyalty and affection. The patriotism of the German Jews has been well noted, despite the fact that there were significant barriers to entry in advanced

[1] Ruth Wisse, *Jews and Power*, (New York: Schocken Books, 2007).

[2] Lisa Leff (2006), *Sacred bonds of solidarity: The Rise of Jewish Internationalism in Nineteenth Century France*, (Stanford, California: Stanford University Press, 2006.

professions such as the civil service, academia and the military, and the German state was not a haven of multiculturalism. Yet such was the growing devotion of Jews to their nation that Walter Rathenau, later the Foreign Minister of the postwar Weimar Republic, was led to say: 'My people are the Germans and no one else. The Jews are for me a branch of the German nation like the Saxons, Bavarians or Wends.'[1]

Of course, not all of Europe's nations awoke to the tumultuous sound of emancipation and liberal values. Tsarist Russia was a noticeable absentee whose regime persecuted its Jews and subjected them to discrimination, internal exile and murderous pogroms. It is true that some Jews joined revolutionary groups that sought to overthrow the Tsar in the late nineteenth century. But officially, the Jewish community prayed for the Tsar's survival and did its best to seek favour with a hostile imperial overlord. Moreover, many Jews fought for the motherland in its battles against Turkey and Japan and even the revolutionary Jewish ideologues could argue that they were battling for a stronger and more humane Russia.

In general, nineteenth century Jews had every incentive to express their patriotism in European states that promoted secular education, religious freedom, equality and modernity. Jews could now be free and equal citizens of their country, identifying as Jewish citizens of their nations. Such patriotic pride could be expressed in many ways, whether through military accomplishment, a contribution to the arts or sciences or some other form of devoted service to the ruling regime. Secular citizenship also offered a refreshing means of escaping the Jewish past, with the promise of a new civic identity replacing the perceived defects of traditional Jewish identity. In the words of David Aberbach, patriotism was 'a natural expression of thanks for the revolutionary changes brought by emancipation.' There was often a heavy price to pay for this because, as Aberbach observes, the eagerness 'to embrace a variety of patriotisms and national cultures' often meant the 'renunciation of Judaism and conversion to Christianity.'[2] To gain acceptance into the intellectual elite, such renunciation was often essential rather than just desirable, as such illustrious figures as Mahler, Heine and Mendelssohn discovered.

---

[1] Walther Rathenau, *An Deutschlands Jugend* [*To Germany's Youth*], (Berlin: S. Fischer Verlag, 1918), 9.

[2] David Aberbach, "The Patriotism of Gentlemen with Red Hair: European Jews and the Liberal State, 1789–1939," *International Journal of Politics, Culture and Society* 30, 129–146 (2017), 131.

The expression of civic pride and patriotic attachment was also expressed in prayers for the respective ruling elite. This itself derived from the rabbinic era where Jews were enjoined, in the Ethics of the Sages, to 'pray for the welfare of the monarchy [shelomo shel malchut], given that the alternative was that 'people would swallow each other alive' (Ethics of the Sages 3:2). Then there is this verse from Jeremiah: 'And find the protection in the city where you have been exiled to, and pray to God on its behalf; for in its prosperity you shall succeed' (29:7).

Traditional prayers for local government, called Hanoten Teshuah (He who grants deliverance), became part of Jewish liturgy by the early 17th century, predating the creation of modern, liberal states. The first English version of the prayer appears in the 'History of the Rites, Customs and Manner of Life of the Present Jews throughout the World' (1650), with this wording: 'They pray to God that He would preserve him in peace and quietness, and that He would prosper him and make him great and powerful and that He would also make him favourable and kind to their nation.'[1] The patriotism embodied by the Jewish faith was part of the pitch made by Menasseh ben Israel in his 1655 Humble Addresses to Cromwell. He stated clearly that the Jews gather together in synagogues and that, before the minister blesses the Jews, 'he blesses the prince of the country under who they live.'

In 1663, Samuel Pepys noted in his diary that he had visited a synagogue in London on Simchat Torah and that, amid the cacophony of the service, there was a prayer for the King.[2] Yet the prayer was not so much for an individual as a system of government of which the monarch was an indispensable part, a government that was capable of maintaining order, creating a system of just laws and regulating the social affairs of men. The fate of the Jews was tied up with the fate of governments. After 1688 and the Glorious Revolution, Britain gradually developed a model of constitutional monarchy in which power shifted to the elected Commons with the monarch becoming an increasingly titular figure.[3]

But in some respects, the ultimate proof of Jewish patriotism came in the

[1] Nic Abery, "The History Behind the Prayer for the Royals," eJewish Philanthropy, June 5, 2012, https://ejewishphilanthropy.com/the-history-behind-the-prayer-for-the-royals.
[2] Mencahem Butler, "A Simchat Torah Story from 1663 London," *Tablet*, September 25, 2013.
[3] Raphael Zarum, "Why do Jews pray for the royal family?," *The Jewish Chronicle*, May 5, 2023.

modern era of mass warfare when Jews, living in different nations, were pitted against each other in defence of their respective countries. It is not true that Jews only started to fight against each other in the twentieth century. In fact, Jewish soldiers found themselves on opposing sides in a number of wars in the nineteenth century, including the Franco-Prussian War and the American Civil War. But it was in the global wars of the twentieth century that Jews volunteered or were conscripted *en masse*, indeed out of proportion to their numbers. It is estimated that approximately 1,500,000 Jews fought during the First World War, with more a third of that number fighting for Russia, nearly a quarter of a million in combat for the United States and the rest divided between the Allied powers of Britain and France and the Central Powers of Germany and Austria-Hungary. Sir Martin Gilbert put it well when he said: 'German Jews fought and died as German patriots, shooting at British Jews who served and fell as British patriots.'[1] He could just as easily have been talking about the Jews of Austria-Hungary and those of Russia during the same period.

In the Second World War, approximately 500,000 Jews fought for the Soviet Union with up to 40% dying in combat. Some 550,000 Jews were represented among the US armed forces while over 60,000 Jews fought for Britain. 100,000 Jews fought in the Polish armed forces, making up 10% of the numbers, a figure commensurate with their percentage in the population as a whole. In addition, they played a major role in the French Resistance and made up some 10% of the Free French fighting forces. The story of Finnish Jews who fought alongside the Germans during the Second World War remains one of the most incredible stories from the war.[2] In all these cases, Jews fought for their respective nations with the same sense of patriotic duty as their gentile counterparts and won many medals for bravery.

But what of the Jewish attachment to Israel? Does this not prove that since 1948, there has been a divided loyalty among Jews, forcing them to choose between supporting the country of their birth and a Middle Eastern state that claims to represent them?

It is a misnomer to believe that loyalty to one's own country precludes a strong attachment to another. It is perfectly possible to believe that there

---

[1] Martin Gilbert, *The Holocaust: The Jewish Tragedy* (Harper Collins, 1986), 21.

[2] Mark Bernheim, "How Finland's Jews Fought Alongside the Nazis," *jewthink.org*, January 7, 2021, https://www.jewthink.org/2021/01/07/how-finlands-jews-fought-alongside-the-nazis, accessed March 7, 2025.

should be strong and growing relations between one's home country and any other country with which one has a strong connection. Thus, many commentators laud the special relations between the UK and the US and, post Brexit, the UK and many other European countries. They want those ties to be cemented at an economic, social, cultural, educational and diplomatic level and argue that such bonds serve patriotic interests. As one journalist puts it: 'The fundamental fallacy…is that national loyalty is a zero-sum game.'[1]

The fact that most Jews have some attachment to Israel is not proof of treason at any level. Jews are patriotic citizens of the countries they live in while also possessing a deep emotional, spiritual and personal attachment to the land and people of Israel. They believe at a wider level that the core values and principles embedded in their home society are replicated by the Israeli nation, with no conflict between the two. The Supreme Court justice Louis Brandeis expressed his support in this way:

> 'My approach to Zionism was through Americanism. In time, practical experience and observation convinced me that Jews were by reason of their traditions and their character peculiarly fitted for the attainment of American ideals. Gradually, it became clear to me that to be good Americans, we must be better Jews, and to be better Jews, we must become Zionists.'[2]

An attachment to Israel and Zionism makes Jews no different to any other people. Many nations have diaspora communities around the world with whom there is an intense and emotional bond. Greece, to take just one example, offers citizenship to those who can show Greek ancestry. There are many Greek people living around the world who would consider themselves Greek and might even consider moving to the country, but that hardly means that they are guilty of dual loyalty. It simply means that national and ethnic identity is a complex matter, with many forces acting on an individual's sense of belonging.

The accusation of dual loyalty is a toxic and dangerous one, justifying discrimination, ethnic cleansing and mass murder. During the First World War, the Ottoman Turks under Enver Pasha accused the country's Armenian

---

[1] Gregory Wallance, "Ilhan Omar's dual loyalty charge was about more than anti-Semitism," *The Hill*, March 7, 2019.

[2] Rick Richman. "Three Jews, Two Links, One Lesson," *jewishjournal.org*, October 23, 2019.

Christians of colluding with the Russians. This led to the mass deportation of the community, effectively a death sentence, while others were simply massacred or Islamized. About 120,000 Japanese-Americans, two thirds of whom were American citizens, were interned during the Second World War as they were deemed to be a threat to national security following the attack on Pearl Harbour. This policy of incarceration and exclusion, fanned by decades of racist policies, came about despite reports showing that Japanese-Americans were largely loyal to the United States.[1] One should similarly view the accusation against Jews as a form of hostile racism with equally dire consequences.

Conclusion: Of course, this is not to deny that there are some Jews in certain places and at certain times who display extreme levels of disloyalty to their respective nations. The cases of Julius and Ethel Rosenberg, two American Jewish civilians who passed vital information to the Soviet Union about America's nuclear programme[2], and Fanny Kaplan, Lenin's would be assassin in 1918, show that Jews have not been immune to betraying their nation or its leaders, regardless of the perceived rightness of their cause. But they are hardly unique in that respect. Every national group produces a set of miscreants who stray far from the moral guidelines set by their society. In general, Jews, like their gentile counterparts, embrace their nations with a sense of patriotism and belonging.

3. Jews are cowardly and physically weak

Charge

As well as being accused of disloyalty and treachery, Jews have been depicted as cowards, shirkers and weaklings. Jews have been caricatured and imagined as selfish individualists who care more about prolonging their own existence than risking their lives for others. In turn, antisemites have long bought into the canard that Jews are physically weak and lack courage, making them unsuitable recruits for the army. The stereotype has stuck that 'Jews are not a people known for physical strength.'[3]

There may be a number of sources for this view. For one thing, brute force

---

[1] Patricia Miye Wakida, "How a Public Media Campaign Led to Japanese Incarceration during WWII," *PBS*, September 23, 2021.

[2] Oliver Kamm, "The Rosenbergs were both Jewish and traitors," The *Jewish Chronicle*, July 19, 2021.

[3] Curt Schleier, "'The Mighty Atom,'" *The Jewish Standard*, November 23 ,2017.

and military prowess have not been traditionally celebrated by Jewish culture, at least outside of Biblical narratives. A small and permanently beleaguered minority, forced to live at the whims of their (often cruel) rulers, has preferred strategies of negotiation, compromise and accommodation, as well as living on their wits, in order to survive in hostile environments. In later centuries, Jews could not become officers in the pre-modern national armies of central and eastern Europe and could not thus be associated with the martial qualities that such professions demanded. Worse, their conscription into the Russian army was highly unpopular and proved a major reason for emigration.

There are a number of moments at which such accusations have been made with particular intensity, especially in the twentieth century. One of the most notable examples was the so called Judenzählung or Jew census that was initiated in October 1916 by Prussian War Minister, Adolf Wild von Hohenborn (1860-1925). The charge against the Jews was that 'large numbers of men of the Israelite faith who are fit for military service are either exempt from military duties or evading their obligation to serve under every conceivable pretext.' As a result, Jews were said to have 'obtained assignments in administrative or clerical posts far away from the front lines, either with the rear echelon or in the homeland.' The census was designed to investigate these complaints, requiring the commanding officer of each regiment to complete a questionnaire that showed the exact number of Jewish officers, medical personnel and enlisted men stationed at the front. It also asked for a tally of the number of Jews killed in action, how many had been decorated for bravery and how many were serving behind the front lines despite being fit for service. In other words, it was designed to prove whether or not German Jews were shirking their military obligations during a time of existential crisis.

The notion of 'Jewish cowardice' has fed into one of the most persistent myths of the modern age, namely that the Jews went 'like lambs to the slaughter' during the Holocaust, conniving in their own suffering by refusing to resist their murderous Nazi tormentors. It was the Polish partisan leader Abba Kovner who urged his fellow Jews not to be 'led like sheep to slaughter' and added that it was 'better to die fighting like free men than to live at the mercy of the murderers.' His words were actually a call to arms yet after the war, they were twisted to suggest he had condemned his co-religionists for passivity. The same phrase was used in a more accusatory tone by the archivist Emanuel Ringelblum who asked of his fellow Jews: 'Why have we allowed ourselves to be led like sheep to the slaughter?'[1] The psychologist Bruno Bettelheim claimed that, millions of Jews, 'like lemmings, marched themselves to their own death,'[2] cementing a view of Jews as passive and complicit in their own destruction. A number of postwar Holocaust films only augmented this perception, among them *Schindler's List* (1993) and *The Debt* (2010). In the latter film, the Nazi war criminal, Dr. Vogel, utters these lines: 'Why do you think it took only four soldiers to lead thousands to the gas chambers? Because not one of out of thousands had the courage to resist.' He does not receive a riposte.

Refutation

The notion that Jews moved through the medieval or premodern period in complete docility is belied by the facts. For one thing, Judaism does not preach passivity in the face of aggression and there is no equivalent to the Christian doctrine of 'turning one's cheek' or giving free rein to an assailant. Jewish law is clear that in confronting imminent aggression, one may use force in self-defence, even if it is pre-emptive. While there is no glorification of violence in Judaism and while war is seen as a necessary but avoidable evil, the faith has never been an inherently pacifist one. The right and obligation of self-defence is embodied in the famous directive from the Babylonian Talmud: 'If someone comes to kill you, rise up and kill him first.'[3]

As further proof, one can also look at the cavalcade of Jewish warriors from the Old Testament who have done battle in the defence of their people, with the most notable figures including the prophet Joshua, King David and Samson. So often, their heroic exploits celebrate the victory of the underdog, and feature an embattled hero elevated by an enduring faith in God. Thus, we see Joshua tasked with guiding the Children of Israel across the River Jordan into Canaan following the death of Moses, another great warrior. Without heavy slings, battering rams or tunnelling equipment, he had to lead his people against the Canaanites and enter their walled cities, which were heavily

---

[1] Tom Lawson, *Debates on the Holocaust*, (Oxford: Oxford University Press, 2010), 235-6.

[2] Michiko Kakutani, "Books of The Times, "Bettelheim's Beliefs and the Ways They Evolved,"" *The New York Times*, December 27, 1989.

[3] There are several principles upon which his directive rests: the defender must not be an aggressor; the threat faced by the defender must be imminent; the force used in self-defence must be proportionate; it is best to try avoiding harm by de-escalating the situation faced by the defender; the defender's beliefs about the threat must be reasonable.

fortified. In the end, he triumphed against the town of Jericho, breaching its walls after the Israelites had marched around the city blowing trumpets of ram's horns. Thanks to his skills as a military commander, administrator and man of faith, Joshua took a tribe of homeless wanderers and turned them into a nation.

King David, who ruled the United Kingdom of Israel for 40 years, is perhaps best remembered for his encounter with Goliath. This mighty Philistine giant, clad in armour and measuring six cubits and a span (about 10 feet), issued a daily challenge to the Jewish people to engage in combat. He promised that if he was killed, his people would live in servitude to the Jews but the same would apply if the Jewish fighter died. Such was his imposing physique that the Israelites were cowed into terror but David, a young shepherd imbued with courage, took up the challenge. Armed with a staff, a slingshot and five stones, David felled Goliath with one shot and proceeded to cut off his head.[1] In modern culture, this is the classic victory of the underdog and a masterful example of raw courage. But it is also a prototype for the lightly armed warrior defeating a superior opponent using tactical nous and ingenuity.

The story of Samson, the Nazarite judge, is also well known, especially his suicidal death. According to the Biblical account, Samson possessed superhuman strength in order to defeat his enemies. He slew a lion with his bare hands and killed 1,000 soldiers using the jawbone of an ass (Judges 15:16). But Samson was also foolish and indiscreet, revealing to Delilah that the secret to his strength was that his hair has never been cut. After wooing him to sleep, she arranged to have his hair cut and he was then captured by the Philistines who gouged out his eyes. When he was brought to a temple for a sacrifice to Dagon, Samson, whose hair has begun growing again, asked his captors if he could lean on the temple pillars so he could rest. Praying to God for strength, Samson broke the pillars, collapsed the temple and killed all those inside, including himself.

Of course, there are also times when Jews exhibit a reluctance to act. In the Book of Numbers, the Israelites express fear upon hearing about spies in the land of Canaan: "We seemed like grasshoppers in our own sight, and we must have seemed the same to them" (Numbers 13:33). But the examples

[1] Some Biblical scholars believe that Goliath was felled by Elhanan, the son of Jair.

above provide ample evidence that Jewish courage is seared into the religious culture of the Jews.

Jews also had a military history for centuries prior to the creation of Israel in 1948, with many renowned warrior heroes. Perhaps the most famous group of ancient Jewish rebels were the Maccabees, a name that is associated with the Jewish priest Judah Maccabee, often nicknamed 'the hammer.' It was Judah who led the Maccabean revolt against the Seleucid empire between 167–160 BCE, resorting to guerilla warfare due to the qualitative edge of his enemy. The conflict lasted several years and led to the retaking of Jerusalem and the purification of the Temple, which had been defiled under Seleucid rule. Today, the victory of the Maccabees is celebrated in the annual festival of Chanukah with Judah Maccabee feted as a national liberator and courageous hero.

Another of Jewish history's great martial heroes was Simon bar Kokhba, a warrior regarded by some contemporaries as the long-awaited Messiah. He led a revolt against Roman rule between the years 132 and 135 CE, following the Romans' decision to establish a new city, Aelia Capitolina, over the ruins of Jerusalem, as well as a Temple to Jupiter on the Temple Mount. Early victories among the rebels led to the establishment of the House of Israel but this independent state was soon crushed when the Emperor Hadrian sent an army to invade Judea. The final fortress to fall was that of Betar, captured by the Romans in 135 C.E. The rebels were defeated and the results were catastrophic for the Jewish population, with an estimated 985 villages razed to the ground and 580,000 Jews killed. Yet it took a sizeable Roman force to defeat the Bar Kokhba revolt, something that would have been unnecessary if the rebels had not fought bravely and with tenacity. The revolt was not the last final Roman-Jewish clash in ancient times. The middle of the fourth century saw the Jewish revolt against Constantius Gallus, a ruler of the eastern provinces, though this was crushed by the Romans with the death of thousands.

The Middle Ages are often remembered as a time of terrible persecution for Jewish communities, especially across Europe. Yet Jews fought with Muslim soldiers to defend Haifa from the Crusaders, as well as Jerusalem. The Visigothic Kings used Jewish warriors to defend the Pyrenean passes, many Jewish warriors fought in Toledo against the Moors and a Jew, Yehuda Ibn Ezra, commanded the fortress of Calatrava in the twelfth century. In Poland and Lithuania, the Jews of Khazar were noted for their 'physical vigor and warlike traditions.'[1] Jews were fighters as well as victims, showing reserves of martial prowess when needed.

In more modern times, Jews were heavily involved in their nation's battles and hundreds of them became generals and admirals. But the notion that Jews deliberately avoided exposure to areas of danger, that they were weak and cowardly shirkers, was belied by the statistics of modern warfare. The results of the Judenzählung showed that nearly 80% of Jews served on the front lines,[2] a figure which disproved the idea that they were unwilling to put their lives in danger. Furthermore, 12,000 died and some 18,000 received the Iron Cross for bravery. Russian Jewry produced a number of military commanders of great prowess, among them Iona Yakir, Boris Feldman, Grigory Shtern and Yan Gamarnik, the contributions of whom were overseen by the towering presence of Leon Trotsky.

During the Second World War, more than 160,000 Jewish fighters at all levels of command received citations and there were more than 150 Jewish 'Heroes of the Soviet Union,' the highest honour that a soldier in the Red Army could obtain. American Jews received over 50,000 awards for their war service, with three posthumously honoured with the Congressional Medal of Honour. In addition, it is estimated that they received 66 Distinguished Service Crosses, 41 Distinguished Service Medals and 244 Legions of Merit. This does not mean, of course, that Jews were braver and more courageous than their gentile counterparts. But it does disprove the idea that Jews were shirkers, seeking to avoid the most dangerous parts of the fighting. Indeed, the Second World War produced many stories of Jewish fighting courage. Among the most famous stories is that of *X Troop*, perhaps the model soldiers for the film *Inglorious Basterds*, who 'carried out some of the most daring missions of the war.' These were European Jewish emigres who were desperate to join the war effort and bring down the Nazi regime. The training for X Troop was said to be brutal, involving hiking over mountains with weapons, training with live ammunition, parachuting and scaling cliffs. One member of *X Troop*, George Lane (born Lanyi Gyorgi) gathered vital intelligence that ensured the Allied landings in 1944 could take place. Another

---

[1] Reuben, Ainsztein, "The War Record of Soviet Jewry." *Jewish Social Studies*, vol. 28, no. 1, 1966, 3–24. *JSTOR*, http://www.jstor.org/stable/4466227, accessed December 24, 2023.

[2] Amos Elon, *The Pity of It All: A Portrait of the Jews in Germany 1743-1933*, (Penguin, 2004), 338.

member, Ian Harris (born Hans Ludwig Hajos), singlehandedly captured a German regiment with a Tommy gun. Doubtless, there would be many more such stories of individual valour were it not for the fact that, after the war, many members of this group chose to maintain silence about their identities and their wartime roles.[1]

Early Zionists such as Jabotinsky, had lambasted the shtetl Jews for their alleged cowardice, passivity and sickliness. He had called on Jews to turn into the polar opposite of their perceived negative caricature – to be proud, independent, beautiful and commanding people. The dream was called *shlilat hagolah*, meaning the negation of exile.

Today, the Israel Defence Forces are living proof of the fighting spirit of the Jew under arms. Indeed, the formidable exploits of this army and the courageous actions of its soldiers, sailors and airmen provide, perhaps, the most telling riposte to the age-old stereotype of the meek Jew. In the war of independence, the nascent Israeli forces beat back an attempt by five neighbouring countries to exterminate Israel at birth. 19 years later in the Six Day War, Israeli forces achieved a seemingly miraculous victory against the combined forces of Egypt, Syria and Jordan when much of the outside world might have expected the Jewish state to crumble. In 1973, Israeli armoured brigades crossed the Suez Canal and encircled the Egyptian third army, one of the great military victories of a war that had started so badly for Israel. Other acts of incredible heroism and bravery by Israeli forces include Operation Entebbe in 1976, Operation Opera in 1981, where Israeli pilots destroyed Saddam Hussein's nuclear facilities, and many of the intelligence led operations carried out by Mossad. The names of some hardened Israeli warriors are renowned the world over and their victories taught at military colleges: Yitzhak Rabin, Ariel Sharon, Moshe Dayan and Israel Tal to name just four. Israel, it should not be forgotten, has compulsory military service for both men and women, one of the very few countries in the world where this is the case. If this really was a nation of timid Jews who were too afraid to defend their homeland, one might expect that it would have outsourced its military activity to other, more courageous powers. Yet while it is true that Israel receives substantial amounts of US military aid each year, it is still the case that Israelis, the majority of whom are Jewish, do the fighting, training and, ultimately, the dying.

[1] "X Troop - The Secret Jewish Commandos of WWII," *History Guild*, June 21, 2022.

What then of the accusation that Jewish victims of the Holocaust went like lambs to the slaughter? The notion that Jews marched to their deaths at the Nazis' behest derives, at least in part, from the ease with which Nazis massacred their victims. Images of emaciated bodies piled high, of crowds waiting to be herded into gas chambers and of young victims clinging to barbed wire or being taunted by Nazi guards give credence to the idea of Jewish passivity. In addition, the Jewish Councils (Judenrate) did co-operate with the Nazis, albeit under heavy compulsion. They were designed to help facilitate anti-Jewish regulations and laws in occupied territory, to report numbers of Jews in their administrative areas, turn over residences to the Nazis, confiscate valuables and present workers for labour and deportation. They administered the Jewish ghettos and co-operated with the German forces.[1]

Yet, this picture is distorted in so many ways. The Jewish Councils knew that opposing Nazi orders would lead to collective reprisals and almost certain death for many. Facing a bewildering moral dilemma, the Councils often chose to co-operate with Nazi demands in the hope that it would allow some of the community to survive rather than see it face a draconian form of collective punishment. Sometimes, this meant betraying underground resistance fighters, such as the decision of Vilna's council chairman, Jacob Gens, to bring underground leader Yitzhak Wittenberg to the Nazis. In Kovno by contrast, there was co-operation with the underground while in Diatlovo, council members played a role in the partisan underground. Blaming the Jewish Councils for the mass murder of Jews wrongly assumes that they acted uniformly but also ignores the consequences of resistance.

In fact, Jewish resistance to the Nazis was one of the most ubiquitous features of the war. The most famous act of defiance was the uprising that took place in the Warsaw Ghetto in April 1943. The Nazis had come to liquidate the ghetto, having suspended an earlier action in January 1943 due to a ferocious Jewish response from the Jewish Combat Organization, or ZOB. Approximately 700 poorly trained and inadequately armed Jewish fighters tied down German troops in the Warsaw ghetto for close to one month. They waged guerilla warfare against a superior enemy, using hand grenades, knives and Molotov cocktails, while the general ghetto population refused orders to

[1] Maurice Friedberg, "The Question of the Judenrate," *Commentary Magazine*, July 1, 1973.

assemble and burrowed in bunkers. In the end, the Nazis razed the ghetto to the ground and deported most of its survivors to camps where they were later murdered. But this action was significant because it was the first urban uprising anywhere in occupied Europe.[1]

But it was not the only act of Jewish resistance. In the Vilna ghetto, the United Partisan Organization (FPO), formed in 1942, carried out armed resistance by joining Soviet partisan units. Jews also rose up against German guards at a number of extermination camps: at Treblinka in August 1943, at Sobibor in October 1943 and at Auschwitz in October 1944. That there were not more camp revolts was doubtless due to the lack of weapons available as well as the general powerlessness of most victims.[2]

Jews also resisted as members of the various partisan units that operated in many countries across occupied Europe, including France, Ukraine, Belorussia, Poland and Belgium. Jews were certainly crucial to the story of the French resistance during WWII. Forming up to one fifth of the active resistance fighters, Jews were heavily overrepresented in the movement, both in France itself and in its overseas African colonies. The anthem of the resistance, the Chant de Partisans, was written by two Jews: the novelists Joseph Kessel and Maurice Druon. Jews also played key roles in founding the resistance literature of the movement, including *Libération*, *Défense de la France* and *Franc-Tireur.*[3] But they also contributed to the military operations of the movement. Jews were heavily represented among sections of the FTP ("*Franc-Tireurs Partisans*") while Joseph Epstein (Col. Gilles) was responsible for all military actions led by the communists at Paris. Jews were among some of its most prominent members: José Aboulker (1920-2009) led the anti-Nazi resistance in Algeria; Romanian chemical engineer Joseph Boczov (1905-1944), who took part in military operations in the Spanish Civil War, founded and led the *derailleurs*, a detachment that specialized in derailing SS and Wehrmacht trains and Austrian born Irma Schwager (1920-2015) convinced German soldiers to turn against the Nazis. These are but a

---

[1] Joseph L Lichten, "The Uprising of the Warsaw Ghetto: The Legend of Yesterday and the Reality of Today," *The Polish Review*, vol. 13, no. 2, 1968, 47–57. *JSTOR*, http://www.jstor.org/stable/25776773, accessed 3 Aug. 2025.

[2] For more reading: Gottlieb, Roger S. "The Concept of Resistance: Jewish Resistance During the Holocaust." *Social Theory and Practice*, vol. 9, no. 1, 1983, pp. 31–49. *JSTOR*, http://www.jstor.org/stable/23556575, accessed August 3, 2025.

[3] Renée Poznanski, "Was the French Resistance Jewish?" *Tablet Magazine*, accessed May 3, 2016.

tiny number of the thousands of Jews who were active in the French resistance.

Resistance movements could be found in other European countries too. Jews were well represented among the officers and leaders of the Greek People's Liberation Army (ELAS), with many Jewish fighters, including women, contributing their linguistic skills to the organization.[1] Several thousand Jews also fought in the Yugoslav partisan movement that was led by Tito, among them General Voja Todorovic, head of the land forces after the war, and Dr. Rosa Papo, who was the first woman to become a general in the Balkans.

In addition, up to 30,000 Jews are believed to have fought with the Soviet partisans between 1941 and 1944. They fought in terrible conditions, being forced to confront not just the inevitability of cruel Nazi reprisals but also being informed upon by local peasants. As Ginsburg says: 'The life of the partisan was harsh and often short.'[2] Nonetheless, despite these risks, Jews were the third-largest nationality group among the Soviet partisans, behind the Russians and the Ukrainians. Among the most famous such fighters were the Bielski partisans, led by four Jewish brothers (Tuvia, Asael, Zusya and Aron) who were born in Poland. The primary goal of this unit was to rescue Jews and provide them with shelter in their forest hideout. Nonetheless, the Bielski group became an official participant in the Soviet war machine, taking part in guerilla raids against German supply convoys and other targets, though without compromising their own identity. By the end of the war, the Bielski partisans claimed to have killed 381 enemy fighters.[3]

Of course, millions of Jews did perish within the ghastly apparatus of Nazi murder and most did not actively resist in the ways already described. But this did not reflect Jewish individuality so much as Jewish powerlessness. Millions of unarmed, weakened and emaciated Jews found themselves at the mercy of a depraved regime which, together with its vast army of collaborators, was intent on annihilating them. These Jews did not resist, not because they were inherently weak, cowardly or indifferent, but because they

---

[1] "Partisans and Countries," Jewish Partisan Educational Foundation, https://www.jewishpartisans.org/countries/greece, accessed September 23, 2025.

[2] Benjamin Ginsburg, *How the Jews defeated Hitler: Exploding the Myth of Jewish Passivity in the Face of Nazism,* (Lanham: Rowman & Littlefield Publishers, 2013), 115.

[3] For more, read: Nechama Tec, *Defiance: The Bielski Partisans*, (Oxford :Oxford University Press, 1993).

could not. Yet the survival of even these powerless Jews was testament to their enduring spirit of resistance to tyranny.

Perhaps it is comforting for the gentile world to lapse into the myth of Jewish passivity. For one thing, it provides comfort to divert attention from the west's own moral failure to rescue (many) Jews, instead blaming the victims for not fighting back. On this view, if the duty to resist trumped the duty to intervene, blame for the destruction lies, at least partly, with the Jews. On the other hand, the notion of Jewish passivity may be a form of projection, revealing far more about the role of bystander apathy among the world's major powers. Whatever the real explanation, the myth of Jewish passivity during the Holocaust has been exploded, and should never again be resurrected.

4. Jews are avaricious

If one stereotype has become attached to the Jews more than any other, it is their allegedly unhealthy relationship with money. Antisemitic superstition has it that Jews are obsessed with wealth. Not only do they have it in abundance but they are accused of cheating, deceiving and manipulating others in order to get their unfair share of it. On this view, Jewish wealth is not hard earned but the result of gross dishonesty and malice. That Jews are so often depicted being surrounded by money emphasizes, for antisemites, that the acquisition of wealth, by fair means or foul, is part of their unchanging essence. The Jewish primal sin is avarice, and one with dire repercussions for the rest of mankind.

The charge of Jewish greed was prefigured in the New Testament with the charges laid against Jewish moneylenders in the Temple and the traitorous greed of Judas Iscariot, who sold out his master for 30 silver coins.[1] The trope was reinforced in the minds of many during the Middle Ages when charges were laid against Jews for avarice because they had become moneylenders. A number of Jews, knowing that Christians were barred from lending money by the Church, entered this business and, in some cases, charged high rates of interest to their clients. For many, this cemented the image of the Jew as a 'bloodsucking profiteer' who lived at the expense of poorer gentiles.

Images of Jewish avarice are found throughout the canon of English and European literature. They are manifested in the character of Barabas from

---

[1] Torrey, Charles C. (1943). "The Name "Iscariot."" *The Harvard Theological Review*. 36 (1): 51–62.

Christopher Marlowe's *The Jew of Malta*, a figure who is presented to his audience as somewhat devilish and usurious and who is motivated by avarice. In William Shakespeare's *The Merchant of Venice*, a Jewish moneylender, Shylock, lends money to a merchant, Antonio, on condition that he can have a pound of Antonio's flesh if the merchant cannot repay the loan. Antonio does indeed default on the loan and is taken to court by Shylock but his case is undermined by his own daughter, Portia. She argues that 'the quality of mercy is not strained' and that her father had set an impossible condition for the merchant as the bond did not entitle him to obtain the merchant's blood, only his flesh. Shylock's vengeful nature builds upon tropes of antisemitism, as does his avarice. Despite some passages that attempt to humanize him, Shylock is a figure of archetypal greed who intends harm to Christians and who is unbending in his unjust demands. The nineteenth century literary embodiment of 'Jewish greed' is Fagin from Dickens' *Oliver Twist*. Fagin is a vicious, miserly criminal who takes advantage of desperately poor children and forces them to serve his needs. He is an inhuman icon of greed and exploitation with physical features as repulsive as his character.

European and Russian thinkers were more than happy to demonize the Jew as a creature of untrammelled greed. One can find crude antisemitic stereotyping of Jews as avaricious and miserly in the writings of Baudelaire, Gustav Freytang and the Brothers Grimm. Voltaire, a philosopher and writer noted for his progressive attacks on 'ignorant' religion, wrote these words: 'The Jew does not belong to any place except that place in which he makes money: would he not just as easily betray the king on behalf of the emperor as he would the emperor the king.' Elsewhere he wrote: 'The only thing that properly belongs to the Jews is their stubbornness, their superstitions and their hallowed usury.'[1] For German philosopher Immanuel Kant, one of the most influential thinkers of the eighteenth century, the Jews owed 'their not undeserved reputation for cheating (at least the majority of them) to their spirit of usury…'[2] Pierre Joseph Proudhon believed that the Jew was 'always fraudulent and parasitical,' operating in business through 'sharp practices.'[3] The English political philosopher Edmund Burke described Jews as an

---

[1] Arthur Hertzberg, *The French Enlightenment and the Jews*, (New York: Columbia University Press, 1968), 303.

[2] Goldhagen, *The Devil that Never Dies*, 66.

[3] ibid. p. 67.

'economic and religious threat to English society,' believing that their influence was inextricably tied up with their 'moneyed-interest.'[1]

In the nineteenth century, the unholy connection between Jews and money reached its apotheosis in the writings of Karl Marx. In his essay, *On the Jewish Question*, Karl Marx wrote: 'What is the secular basis of Judaism? Practical need, self-interest. What is the worldly religion of the Jew? Huckstering. What is his worldly God? Money.' 'Money,' he goes on to say, 'is the jealous god of Israel, in face of which no other god may exist.'[2] For Marx, the evils of modern capitalism were embodied in a Jewish character that was irredeemably crude, greedy and materialistic. That was why Marx argued that the 'emancipation of the Jews is the emancipation of mankind from Judaism.' There was no place in civilized society for assimilated Jews, living as Jews with a separate ethnic identity. But it was also necessary to liberate humanity from the clutches of Jews. In an article from 1856 called *The Russian Loan*, Marx wrote that 'we find every tyrant backed by a Jew, as is every Pope by a Jesuit' and that 'the cravings of oppressors would be hopeless' were it not for 'a handful of Jews to ransack pockets.'[3] This is deranged conspiracy theory dressed up as economic justice.

A somewhat less crude characterization of Jewish workers can be found in the writings of other Victorian economic thinkers, among them J.A. Hobson. He wrote that while the Jewish worker was 'admirable in domestic morality and an orderly citizen' he was also 'almost devoid of social morality.' This was because his 'superior calculating intellect' was 'used unsparingly to enable him to take advantage of every weakness, folly and vice of the society in which he lives.'[4] Similar sentiments can be found among contemporary American critics. Thus, we find American sociologist and eugenicist Edward A Ross essentialising the Jews as a people with 'inborn love of money-making,'[5] author Burton Henrick offering a portrait of

---

[1] Rachel Schulkins, 'Burke, His Liberal Rivals and the Jewish Question' Otherness: Essays and Studies 3:2.

[2] Daniel B Schwartz, "Marx and the Jewish Fingerprint Question," *The Jewish Review of Books*, Spring 2020.

[3] Michael Ezra, "Karl Marx's Radical Antisemitism," *The Philosophers' Magazine*, https://philosophersmag.com/karl-marx-s-radical-antisemitism, accessed March 10, 2024.

[4] David Robson, "So were we 'void of social morals?'" *The Jewish Chronicle*, January 7, 2016.

[5] Talia Lavin, *Culture Warlords: My Journey into the Dark Web of White Supremacy* (New York: Hachette Books, 2020), 28.

American Jews as relentlessly and aggressively acquisitional and Henry Ford depicting them as avaricious, controlling and obsessed with profit.

Refutation

The medieval association of Jews with money and greed cannot be understood without reference, both to prevailing religious restrictions imposed on Jews in Christian Europe, the attraction of commerce and also the cultural skills that the Jewish tradition imparted to its followers. It is indeed true that Jews were heavily represented among the commercial classes of medieval European societies. Jews in medieval Christian Europe could not legally own land or be members of guilds, something which excluded them from many trades. This restricted them to practising only certain professions, such as trading goods across countries, and others which directly involved money, such as tax collecting. It is true that a number of Jews did become money lenders but many others became peddlers, artisans, tradesmen and household servants. Thus, the myth that medieval European Jews were *all* moneylenders should be laid to rest. For those who did lend money, it is true that some did charge high rates of interest. In part, this reflected the risks of the profession for it was hardly guaranteed that a creditor could repay a loan and there was the added risk of a debtor turning on his Jewish business partner, a feature of many pogroms and expulsions in Europe. Perhaps, only a small percentage of Jews who entered this profession were incredibly rich. Nonetheless, there was a real association of Jews with commerce. As historian Howard Sachar has written of Jews in the eighteenth century:

> Perhaps as many as three-fourths of the Jews in Central and Western Europe were limited to the precarious occupations of retail peddling, hawking, and 'street banking,' that is, moneylending.[1]

However, it is equally a myth that Christians did not practice usury. Many chose to break with Christendom's religious restrictions in the Middle Ages until, by the 18th century, religious bans were largely redundant. As Rowan Dorin explains, 'From the beginning of the thirteenth century to the middle of the fourteenth, every major European polity that ordered the expulsion of its

---

[1] Howard Sachar, "A History of the Jews in the Modern World," *The New York Times*, September 4, 2005.

Jewish community also ordered the expulsion of foreign Christian usurers.'[1] Dorin points to the 'stubborn (and often pernicious) narrative according to which medieval Jews held a near-monopoly over medieval moneylending.'[2]

Another plausible explanation for Jewish commercial representation lies in understanding how the religious requirements of Judaism imparted to Jews a unique set of cultural and intellectual skills. In their book *The Chosen Few*, authors Maristella Botticini and Zvi Eckstein argue that the reason why Jews came to specialize in 'the most skilled and economically profitable occupations' came about due to the historic transformation of Judaism following the destruction of the Temple in 70 AD. In that fateful year, the Romans destroyed the Temple and upended the Jewish community in Palestine. But at the same time, it led to a shift in the religious leadership from an elite group of high priests in Jerusalem to a more dispersed rabbinical and scholarly community. Without the pivotal centre of Judaism in place, it was now incumbent upon every Jewish male, wherever he was, to learn the tenets of the written Torah. Judaism now required adults to not only read and study the Torah but to send their children to schools and synagogues for the same reason. Such a membership requirement represented a transformational moment for Jews growing up in a world governed by illiteracy.[3]

Naturally, not all Jews followed this costly requirement and, preferring short term economic benefits to any sense of religious obligation, left the faith. Thus, as Jewish literacy increased, the Jewish population shrank. In the Abbasid empire, Jews left farming and entered skilled and well-paid professions requiring literacy. Crucially, this was despite the *lack* of restrictions on land ownership. Jews left farming because their enhanced literacy enabled them to seek out commercial opportunities and skilled professions. When they later migrated to Europe, they came in search of the same opportunities and the same professions. The door was open to Jews and they became traders, financiers, bankers, physicians and moneylenders. They had the advantage of being great networkers with extended family members in many nations and capital accumulated as traders.

---

[1] Rowan Dorin. *No Return: Jews, Christian Usurers, and the Spread of Mass Expulsion in Medieval Europe* (Princeton: Princeton University Press, 2023), 4.
[2] ibid. 10.
[3] For a fuller discussion, read: Maristella Botticini and Zvi Eckstein, *The Chosen Few: How Education Shaped Jewish History, 70-1492*, (Princeton University Press, 2014).

Explanations for Jewish commercial success lie far more, even today, with the cultural and religious emphasis on education, literacy and learning, all of which are seen as pillars of achievement and social advancement. Alternative explanations that posit a Jewish 'love of money,' engage in lazy, essentialist explanations that are based on racist tropes.

A number of other myths need to be slain here. The first is that Judaism encourages all its adherents to become rich for their own sake; that it is a religion of pure wealth creation. It is true that the great rabbis saw little merit or nobility in poverty. Jews are enjoined to seek legitimate employment rather than be a burden to others. They view material wealth as a form of security which enables them to make an impact on the world. But there are important religious obligations too for the less fortunate. The word *tzedakah* literally means justice or righteousness and obliges Jews to act fairly towards others. One element of this involves protecting the poor from exploitation and establishing means by which to create a minimum standard of living. The demand for social justice goes hand in hand with social prohibitions against merely accumulating vast amounts of wealth. Thus, philanthropy has been actively encouraged within the Jewish community and there are innumerable examples of beneficent contributions from Jews to the worlds of art, science and medicine.

Among Jewish philanthropists one can cite:

- The department store magnate, Nathan Straus, whose concern with high infant mortality led him to invest money in milk stations in poorer areas of New York so that babies could drink pasteurized milk. It is estimated that his efforts saved the lives of some 445,000 children. He wrote in his will: 'What you give for the cause of charity in health is gold.'[1]
- Business leader Herbert Herff (1891-1969) raised funds to establish southern America's first blood bank (in 1938) and, years later, his foundation was the first in Memphis to provide funding for sickle cell anaemia.
- The Victorian financier Sir Isaac Lyon Goldsmid (1778-1859) helped found University College in London in 1825.
- The financier Daniel Iffla-Osiris (1825-1907) left the majority of his

[1] Lina Gutherz Straus, *Disease in Milk: The Remedy, Pasteurization—The Life Work of Nathan Straus* (E. P. Dutton, 1917).

fortune to the Pasteur Institute in Paris. He wrote in his will: 'I have always had a keen desire to promote scientific discoveries that might help alleviate the suffering of others…'[1]

- The business magnate Julius Rosenwald (1862-1932) helped to advance African-American education in the twentieth century. The Rosenwald fund created a rural school building program which helped construct 5,000 schools (Rosenwald schools), shops and teachers' homes, using matching funds. By 1932, over one third of all black children in the American South were receiving an education in a Rosenwald school.
- The Institute for Advanced Study in Princeton, which has hosted some of the world's most pre-eminent thinkers, among them Kurt Godel, Albert Einstein and John von Neumann, was founded by Abraham Flexner with a $5 million endowment from two Jewish philanthropists, the businessmen Louis Bamberger (1855-1944) and his sister, businesswoman Caroline Bamberger Fuld (1864-1944).
- Henri James Simon (1851-1932), Germany's sixth richest man in 1911, was described as 'the most generous benefactor Berlin ever had.'[2] He funded a number of archaeological digs in Egypt and Iraq and gave away over 20,000 objects to the museums of Berlin, including its famous Nefertiti bust.
- Solomon Guggenheim (1861-1949) established the Solomon Guggenheim Museum in New York in 1939 via a foundation bearing the same name. He was keen to foster an appreciation for modern art.
- The Hungarian born businessman Sir Sigmund Sternberg (1921-2016) was one of the founders of the Three Faiths Forum, an interfaith organization providing space for people to discuss issues of belief and identity.

These cases are but the tip of the iceberg. Jews are not enjoined to make fortunes and keep all their money for themselves and their loved ones. Those who pour money into charitable projects and who become benefactors and philanthropists are highly regarded in the community.

---

[1]https://www.pasteur.fr/en/research-journal/news/daniel-iffla-osiris-great-19th-century-philanthropist-and-institut-pasteur-s-most-generous-donor, accessed September 24, 2025.
[2] Tony Paterson, "Jewish philanthropist lost in the sands of time thanks to the Nazis," *The Independent*, December 4, 2012.

It is important to bust other myths regarding Jews and money. One is the popular notion that all Jews today are wealthy. It is a myth with destructive consequences, as one recent example will show. In 2006, a young Jewish mobile phone salesman, Ilan Halimi, was lured to an apartment bloc in the Parisian banlieues where he was ambushed and then held captive by the so called 'Gang of Barbarians.' They threatened to kill him unless his family handed over 450,000 Euros, a demand that was impossible to meet. When it was clear that the money would not be forthcoming, Halimi was brutally tortured, burned and left for dead. He later succumbed to his injuries. While initially denying that the crime had a racist motive, the Parisian chief prosecutor released a statement saying that 'certain people interviewed let it be known, in an indirect way, that the choice of a Jew guaranteed the payment of a ransom.'[1]

Another starting point for addressing this trope might be a 2016 Pew Research study of income by religious groups in America. While it did show that on average, Jews had the highest percentage of household incomes above $100,000 of any religious group (44% of Jewish households), it also pointed to the 16% of households with less than $30,000 in income.[2] That is the figure given for the US poverty line for a family size of four. In a later Pew study from 2020, it was reported that U.S. Jews were generally 'a relatively high-income group, with roughly half saying their annual household income is at least $100,000.' This figure was 'much higher than the percentage of all U.S. households at that level.' But at the same time, the 2020 study found that more than a quarter of American Jews, including over half of those who earn less than $50,000 per year, said that, in the prior year, 'they had difficulty paying for medical care, their rent or mortgage, food, or other bills or debts.'[3] So, while Jews may be overrepresented among the better off economic classes in American society, including on the Forbes rich list, they are also represented among the poorer classes too.

In the UK, an Office for National Statistics report from 2020 showed that 'median hourly pay was highest among those who identified as Jewish,' with

---

[1] Kim Willsher, "Brutal murder was anti-Semitic crime, says Sarkozy," *The Guardian*, February 22, 2006.
[2] David Masci, "How income varies among U.S. religious groups," Pew Research Center, October 11, 2016.
[3] "Economics and well-being among U.S. Jews," Pew Research Center, May 11, 2021.

Hindus a close second.[1] But there are also sections of Anglo-Jewry that face a cost-of-living crisis and deprivation. A report from 2022 highlighted the growing costs of kosher food in the UK, leading to 'surging' demands on local charities.[2] In Israel, the IMF has estimated GDP per capita to be the 14th highest in the world. Yet despite this, nearly 2 million Israelis were reported to be living below the poverty line, with the ultra-orthodox well represented in this figure.[3]

The final myth is that where Jews have achieved financial success and prosperity they have done so dishonestly. Antisemitic iconography about Jewish bankers, financiers and wealth creators tends to depict them as ruthless exploiters of their society, and as dishonest and cunning brokers who will stop at nothing to accumulate their ill begotten gains. Jewish wealth is seen as something automatically suspect and tainted, whereas few doubts are raised about the finances of other ethnic and religious groups. This too reflects age old tropes that are designed to demonize Jews and present them as an outcast group that threatens the integrity of wider society. While there are Jewish white-collar criminals and dishonest Jewish businessmen, they are themselves outliers in a community that is overwhelmingly law abiding.

---

[1] "Religion, education and work in England and Wales: February 2020," Office for National Statistics, February 26, 2020.

[2] Rosa Doherty, "Jewish children going to bed hungry in kosher cost of living crisis," *The Jewish Chronicle*, May 26, 2022.

[3] "Nearly 2 million Israelis below poverty line in 2023; 1 in 4 children are poor," *The Times of Israel*, December 18, 2024.

Chapter 3

Modern Conspiratorial Antisemitism

1. Jews played a major role in the slave trade

Charge

The transatlantic slave trade involved the purchase and transportation of between twelve and fourteen million people from African countries to the Americas between the sixteenth and the nineteenth centuries. Millions more died in slave raids and wars, as well as from sickness during the passage across the Atlantic, leading some to term this practice 'the Black Holocaust.' European merchants used slave labour to help develop the plantations that existed in the Caribbean and in parts of what became the USA, enriching themselves enormously in the process.[1]

Transatlantic slavery was marked by the commodification of people and by the excessively cruel treatment of slaves by their owners. But it also led to demands for abolitionism which, in Britain, led to the outlawing of slavery in the early nineteenth century. The slave trade was 'an integral and indispensable part of European expansion and settlement of the New World'[2], as one historian puts it. Today, it remains one of the gravest blots against the western conscience because of its wilful exploitation and inhuman treatment of the innocent. The slave trade had many participants. They included the major European colonial powers, primarily Britain, France, Portugal, Spain, the Netherlands, as well as merchants from the Italian and German states. They included tribal chieftains in West Africa who sold black people in exchange for beads, cloth and alcohol.

In recent years, a claim has been made that alleges Jewish control of this

---

[1] Steven Mintz, "Historical Context: Facts about the Slave Trade and Slavery," Gilder Lehrman Institute of American History, https://www.gilderlehrman.org/history-resources/ teacher-resources/historical-context-facts-about-slave-trade-and-slavery, accessed April 11, 2024.

[2] David Brion Davis, "The Slave Trade and the Jews," *The New York Review of Books*, December 22, 1994.

nefarious industry. It largely stems from a book called *The Secret Relationship Between Blacks and Jews* (1991). The book, published by the Nation of Islam, tries to show that Jews dominated the transatlantic slave trade and were its principal beneficiaries. In its words, there was 'irrefutable evidence that the most prominent of the Jewish pilgrim fathers (sic) used kidnapped Black Africans disproportionately more than any other ethnic or religious group in New World history.' Jews are described as 'key operatives' in the crime of slavery, having played an 'inordinate' and 'disproportionate' role in its history and acquired 'a monumental culpability in slavery.'[1] The book is full of attempts to appropriate Jewish Holocaust memory and use it to hurl spiteful and venomous tirades against Jews. Slave vessels were called 'Holocaust ships' and their traders likened to 'the Nazis at the concentration camps of Auschwitz, Treblinka or Buchenwald.'[2]

Support for the Nation of Islam thesis was not slow to come. A leading member of the Afrocentric movement, Leonard Jeffries, a lecturer at the City College of New York, gave a speech in Albany where he declared: 'Everyone knows rich Jews helped finance the slave trade.'[3] Professor Tony Martin of Wellesley College said that a group of Jewish rabbis had produced centuries of black suffering and that their degradation via the curse of Ham was 'the pretext upon which the slave trade was built.'[4] He would go on to publish *The Jewish Onslaught: Dispatches from the Wellesley Battlefront*. In the UK, the Labour activist Jackie Walker argued that 'many Jews (my ancestors too) were the chief financiers of the sugar and slave trade, which is of course why there were so many early synagogues in the Caribbean.[5]

Refutation

At the outset, it is not true that *no* Jews were involved in the transatlantic slave trade. In general, Jews are recorded as having participated in the slave trade in a number of places, including Curacao, where Jews owned slaves until

[1] Henry Louis Gates Jr. "Opinion | Black Demagogues and Pseudo-Scholars," *The New York Times,* July 20, 1992.
[2] The Nation of Islam, *The Secret Relationship Between Blacks and Jews* (Chicago: The Final Call, 1991), 207.
[3] David Mills, "Half Truths and history: The Debate over Jews and Slavery," *The Washington Post,* October 17, 1993.
[4] "Rally at Elite Black School Brings Together Leading Black Anti-semites," *Jewish Telegraphic Agency*, April 26, 1994.
[5] Caroline Mortimer, "Anti-Semitism row: Momentum organiser Jackie Walker readmitted to Labour party following racism allegations," *The Independent*, May 28. 2016.

emancipation freed them in 1863; in colonial New York City where evidence from wills that were published in 1915 by the American Jewish Historical Society showed some Jews owning slaves; in Barbados, where slave owning and trading among Jews was not unknown and in the American South where Jews functioned as merchants, owners and commission agents for slaves. Some Jews in England were also prominent in this practice, that is once they had been re-admitted to the country by Cromwell.

There were some Jewish slave traders and slave owners and Jews therefore counted among the many peoples that took part in this nefarious human trafficking. One of the most famous was Judah Benjamin, one of the most prominent politicians of his era. He was the Jewish Secretary of State for the Confederacy, the breakaway republic of 11 states that seceded from the Union because they believed the institution of slavery was under threat from Abraham Lincoln. Benjamin used the American constitution to justify slavery, arguing that it guaranteed citizens the right to their 'property.' He also believed that African Americans were not ready for emancipation and that any such slave liberation could lead to an outbreak of mass violence against former slave owners.[1]

He was not the only prominent Jewish slave owner. The American educator Emma Mordecai was another prominent supporter of the Confederacy. An observant Jew throughout her life, Mordecai bemoaned the fact that her black slaves wanted freedom at the end of the Civil War, believing that they would find slave life easier than liberation.[2] Solomon Cohen Jr., a senator, banker and lawyer, owned eight slaves and hired out others while the German born banker and businessman Mayer Lehman owned seven as of 1860. There were even Jewish slaveowners who supported the North in the Civil War, perhaps the most famous of whom was the political philosopher Francis Lieber (1798-1872), who wrote the code of military law for the Union armies.[3] Some British Jewish merchants were also involved in the eighteenth-century slave trade, though their overall influence was negligible.

---

[1] Rich Tenorio, "The Jewish Politician and Slave Owner Who Was the Brains of the Confederacy," *Haaretz.com*, October 19, 2021.
[2] Rich Tenorio, "Slave-owning Jewish Confederate woman documents wartime Passover in newly published diary," *The Times of Israel*, April 11, 2025.
[3] Matthew J Mancini, "Francis Lieber, Slavery, and the 'Genesis' of the Laws of War," *The Journal of Southern History* 77, no. 2 (2011): 325–48. http://www.jstor.org/stable/41306198.

Finally, it can be argued that both the Old Testament and the New Testament were widely used to justify slavery and imperialism.'[1] Taking the former, Leviticus allows Hebrews to buy bondmen and bondwomen (25. 44-46) from surrounding nations, or from strangers dwelling in their land, stipulating that they are treated as possessions, meaning that they can be inherited as such. Jewish law, however, limits the power of a slave master, stipulating that if slaves lost an eye or a tooth from being struck, they could go free.[2]

However, the NOI's thesis is fundamentally flawed. The book singles out Jews who were involved in the slave trade as if to suggest that they and they alone were responsible for this evil. As Faber points out, there was 'no mention of the many thousands of Portuguese, Spanish, Dutch, French and British merchants, shippers, and colonists who were slave traders and slaveowners.'[3] The inescapable truth is that the vast majority of those who took part in the slave trade, whether as ship owners, slave owners, investors or agents, were non-Jewish.

The figures that are available show that Jewish involvement in the slave industry was extremely small and relatively insignificant. Jews were not dominant as investors in companies that relied on slavery. When the Dutch West India Company chartered in 1621, just 18 Jews participated and their share of the total invested (36,000 florins) constituted just 1.2%. Within a few decades, the number of Jewish stockholders increased, rising to 11 out of 169 (6.5%) by 1658. At most, they formed 10% of the company's shareholders, still a small minority. Interestingly, they were outweighed by the far larger number of Jews who held deposits in the country's Exchange Bank, indicating that these people had financial acumen but preferred not to invest in the Company. Jews also largely shunned the Royal African Company, representing just under 7% of its shareholders by 1699.[4]

Yet another company that gave investors the opportunity to benefit from the slave trade was the English South Sea Company. Established in 1711, the company was granted a monopoly to deliver slaves to South America and the

---

[1] David Aberbach, "Jews and slavery: the myths and the truth," *The Jewish Chronicle*, July17, 2020.

[2] Wilhelm Bacher, Lewis N. Dembitz, Gotthard Deutsch, Samuel Krauss, "Slaves and Slavery," *Jewish Encyclopaedia* (1906), Volume 11, 403-408.

[3] Eli Faber, *Jews, Slaves and the Slave Trade* (2000), 7.

[4] ibid. p. 21-6.

South Seas. By 1714, Jews made up only 1.6% of all shareholders.[1] At the same time, almost all those English businessmen who engaged in private trade with Africa were gentile and the export cargoes of Jewish merchants from the period 1702-1712 amounted to less than one percent of the total.[2] In addition, Jews formed only about 1% of the Londoners who belonged to the Company of Merchants Trading to Africa, the company founded in 1750 that replaced the Royal Africa Company. Overall, this suggests only miniscule involvement from English Jews in the slave trade.

Among the great English centres of slave trading in the eighteenth century were London, Bristol and Liverpool. None of the owners of London's slave fleet were Jewish, as of 1726, and the Lloyd's compilation of ship registers from the 1760s onwards indicates the ships remained in non-Jewish hands. The same pattern is repeated in Bristol, a town in which Jewish settlement started only in the 1750s and in Liverpool too, a city where by 1790, Jews numbered a small fraction of 1% of the total population.[3] The story of transatlantic trade would scarcely be changed if Britain had not re-admitted its Jews in the middle of the seventeenth century.

When it comes to British colonies, the same pattern of minority ownership or involvement in the slave trade can be observed. A census from 1679-80 of slaves in the Bahamas found that Jews owned 0.8% of the total (300 out of 37,495). A 1680 survey of slave ownership in Port Royal, Jamaica, indicated that Jews owned some 48 slaves out of a total of 21,500, indicating a Jewish share of 0.22%. In Jamaica, few Jews made a living from plantation agriculture and though far more Jews participated in this trade in the 1780s, their overall share was small.[4] By 1817, Jamaica's Jews still owned a tiny fraction (less than 2%) of all slaves in the colony. The Jewish merchants of Barbados similarly 'played practically no part as slave factors,' taking consignment of less than one percent of the approximately 80,000 slaves delivered to that island between 1698 and 1739.[5] Jews in eighteenth century Barbados were largely shopkeepers and town dwelling merchants. In addition, of the 12,460 slaves that arrived in Barbados from Africa between 1781 and

---

[1] ibid. p. 31.
[2] Ibid. p. 34.
[3] ibid p. 41-2.
[4] ibid. p. 64, 116.
[5] ibid. p. 94.

1806, nearly 99% arrived on vessels that were owned by non-Jews while the vast majority of slaves exported from the island were also owned by non-Jews.

Overall, as Eli Faber concludes in his magisterial study *Jews, Slaves and the Slave Trade*, the Jewish involvement in slavery 'was one that had little impact' as their participation in it was 'quite small.'[1] When it came to mainland America, some Jews owned slaves, in common with their gentile neighbours, but the proportion was relatively insignificant. In Newport, as of 1774, most of the 13 Jewish families owned slaves but in total, only 2.9% of the total. Jews owned approximately 1% of the slaves in Philadelphia while in South Carolina, only one half of one percent of the slaves that were imported were carried on vessels owned by Jews.[2] Another historian writes that Jews accounted for just 1.25% of all southern slave owners, a tiny fraction.[3] In effect, contrary to the views of the Nation of Islam, if no Jews had been present in the Continental United States, the institution of slavery would scarcely have been diminished.

It is also worth noting that many Jews lent their voices to the abolitionist movement in the nineteenth century. They included figures like August Bondi (1833-1907), a refugee from Austria who embraced the cause of abolition with zeal and determination. He fought with the famous abolitionist John Brown at the Battle of Black Jack (together with other Jewish fighters), ensuring that Kansas would join the Union. During the Civil War, he fought for three years for the Kansas Cavalry, attaining the rank of first sergeant. Another was Ernestine Rose (1810-1892), a woman described as a 'dazzling orator, utopian and freethinker.' She cited her Biblical heritage to argue the case for why women should join the cause of abolishing slavery: 'I am an example of the universality of our claims: for not American women only, but a daughter of poor crushed Poland, and the downtrodden and persecuted people called Jews...I go for emancipation of all kind - white and black, man and woman. Humanity's children are, in my estimation, all one and the same family.'[4] She argued that the Constitutional clause which stated that 'all men are born equal' applied to black people too. The Bavarian born rabbi and

---

[1] ibid., 1.

[2] ibid p. 140.

[3] J Rodriguez *The Historical encyclopaedia of world slavery, Volume 1*, ABC-CLIO, 1997 p. 375.

[4] Norman H. Finkelstein, *Heeding the Call: Jewish Voices in America's Civil Rights Struggle,* (Philadelphia: Jewish Publication Society, 1997), 28.

scholar David Einhorn condemned slavery as antithetical to the spirit of the Mosaic laws, and in the German language periodical he founded, *Sinai*, denounced the institution as 'this cancer of the Union.'[1] Support for ending slavery in America came from European voices too, including the poets Berthold Auerbach and Heinrich Heine and the Prussian born reform rabbi Gustav Gottheil. There were many more Jewish advocates of abolition, in America and beyond its shores, and influential Jewish opponents of the segregation and discrimination that followed the end of the American Civil War.

Many of these people were spurred on by those aspects of Jewish religious culture which supported the notion of abolition. After all, one of Judaism's core religious narratives is the liberation of Jews from Egyptian bondage, an event which is celebrated in the Jewish calendar in a number of ways: through the festival of Pesach; on the Sabbath; in the fourth commandment, which mandates resting on the Sabbath in memory of the liberation from Pharoah, and in the Hebrew siddur (prayer book). The liberation from Egypt is about a people being freed from bondage and tyranny and has served as the template for many modern liberation struggles.

Thus, at the height of the Civil War between King Charles I and the forces of Parliament, the puritan Oliver Cromwell would describe the Exodus as 'the only parallel of God's dealing with us that I know in the world,' casting the King as an embodiment of tyranny.[2] At a eulogy delivered for George Washington in 1799, Thaddeus Fiske described the late President as 'the deliverer and political saviour of our nation' and added that he had 'been the same to us, as Moses was to the Children of Israel.'[3] A century later, when Martin Luther King was asked what era he would like to live in, he replied as follows:

> *I would take my mental flight by Egypt and I would watch God's children in their magnificent trek from the dark dungeons of Egypt through, or rather across the Red Sea, through the wilderness on toward the promised land. And in spite of its magnificence, I wouldn't stop there.*[4]

Decades after King's death, another political genius, in a message to the Jewish community of South Africa on the eve of Passover, issued his own

[1] Naim Peress, "The Jewish Slaveholders," *The Jerusalem Post*, April 11, 2019.
[2] Zaki Cooper, "Why the Exodus is the greatest story ever told," *The Jewish Chronicle*, March 26, 2021.
[3] Robert P. Hay, "George Washington: American Moses," *American Quarterly* 21, no. 4 (1969): 780–91. https://doi.org/10.2307/2711609.
[4] This was from the final speech given by Martin Luther King on April 3, 1968.

stirring tribute to the liberation story in Exodus. Lauding the 'immortal words' of Moses, 'Let my People go!,' Nelson Mandela, Chairman of the ANC, said that the story would 'continue to inspire us in our quest for democracy and justice in South Africa today.'[1] The main story of Judaism then is not the capture and enslavement of other peoples but, in the words of David Aberbach, that 'of an enslaved people who break free, accept their own laws, and create their own independent state.'[2] As the political scientist Michael Walzer has so eloquently put it, 'Whenever people know the Bible, and experience oppression, the Exodus has sustained their spirits and (sometimes) inspired their resistance.'[3]

Slavery remains a terrible blot against those who traded in and owned human chattel. There is no defence against the many people of different religious and ethnic backgrounds, among whom one counts Catholics, Huguenots, Quakers, Muslims and black African chieftains, who engaged in this insidious and destructive practice for several centuries. Undoubtedly, Jews did participate in the slave trade as investors, importers and exporters and owners. However, at no point can one say that they dominated or controlled the slave industry. The number of slaves carried on Jewish vessels was a miniscule fraction of the millions who were transported. The number of slaves owned by Jews was a tiny percentage of the total in the United States, reflecting, at least in part, the fact that Jews gravitated to urban environments rather than engage in plantation agriculture.

2. Jews were responsible for the global wars of the twentieth century

The twentieth century spawned numerous theories about the alleged power of Jews in world affairs. The notorious forgery *The Protocols of the Learned Elders of Zion* purported to uncover the minutes of a secret meeting between a group of world Jewish leaders who were conspiring to take over the world. These 'Elders' had plans to soften up the non-Jewish world by controlling land supply, the press, politics, the banking system, as well as

---

[1] "Message to the Jewish Community on the Occasion of Passover from Nelson R. Mandela President of the African National Congress," https://archive.nelsonmandela.org/index.php/za-com-mr-s-1098, accessed 28 March 2024.

[2] "David Aberbach, "Jews and Slavery: the myths and the truth," *The Jewish Chronicle*, July 17, 2020.

[3] Cooper, "Why the Exodus is the greatest story ever told," *The Jewish Chronicle*.

subverting the elements of modern religion and culture. Such claims have been made by numerous antisemites in modern history and a few choice examples will suffice to make the point.

In a camping trip in 1919, Henry Ford was quoted as attributing all evil to Jews and Jewish capitalists and adding: 'The Jews caused the war.'[1] He would go on to publish *The Dearborn Independent*, a newspaper that claimed a vast Jewish conspiracy to attack America in the postwar years. It was around this time that the so called 'stab in the back myth' was promulgated. On this theory, the German army did not lose the First World War and Germany did not suffer a military defeat. Instead, it was the German Jews, together with their communist allies, who were responsible for losing the war after they stabbed their countrymen in the back in an act of unconscionable treason. This conspiracy theory was reinforced in a number of ways in 1918 and 1919: by leaflets in Berlin which blamed Jews for the strikes that broke out across Germany in January 1918; by Friedrich Ebert welcoming home German troops in December 1918 by telling them: 'No enemy has vanquished you'; in the German White Paper on the Responsibility of the Instigators of the War, published in 1919 with the permission of the Ministry of Foreign Affairs, and in the memoirs of General Hindenburg, who later became Weimar President.[2]

The so called *Dollschosslegende* would become a key plank of Nazi propaganda in the 1920s and 1930s, helping to fuel resentment and hatred towards the country's Jewish population. It persuaded millions that 'an undefeated army had voluntarily laid down its arms in the hope of a just peace' at the behest of 'sinister elements of German society,' principally Jews.[3]

The notion that Jews had helped to instigate the Second World War found resonance among the far right, as well as other groups. It came naturally to the Nazis to blame the Jews, conceived as a single global entity, for their own suffering. In March 1933, a boycott of German goods was inaugurated by Jews in the US and Europe, leading the UK Daily Express to declare in one headline: 'Judea Declares War on Germany.' A month later, the Nazis introduced a one-day boycott of German goods, which followed a wave of violence and thuggish behaviour directed towards Jewish businesses and

---

[1] "Ford's "Anti-Semitism," PBS.

[2] Alan Kramer, "The poisonous myth: Democratic Germany's 'stab in the back' legend," *The Irish Times*, January 21, 2019.

[3] David Mikics, "The Jews Who Stabbed Germany in the Back," *Tablet Magazine*, November 9, 2017.

individuals. Members of the SA stood outside Jewish shops and retail outlets while the Star of David was painted across thousands of doors and windows. It set the tone for the hysterical claim that Jews were responsible for 'goading' Germany into war in 1939. That was the year in which Hitler gave a speech in the Reichstag in which he made this chilling prediction:

> *If the international Jewish financiers in and outside Europe should succeed in plunging the nations once more into a world war, then the result will not be the Bolshevization of the earth, and thus the victory of Jewry, but the annihilation of the Jewish race in Europe.*[1]

This was a clear attempt to allege a nefarious plot by a global entity against Germany and world civilization, forcing Hitler to undertake an act of 'self-defence.' It provided a pseudo-justification, not only for the barbarism of World War II, but the most criminal act of mass murder in history. Later, some came to believe the 'Jewish war conspiracy theory' when they came across a letter sent by Chaim Weizmann, president of the World Zionist Organization, which stated:

> *I wish to confirm in the most explicit manner the declarations which I and my colleagues have made during the last month and especially in the last week: that the Jews stand by Great Britain and will fight on the side of the democracies.*[2]

For antisemites, an innocent but powerful declaration of patriotism by a prominent leader within Anglo-Jewry was an act of provocation designed to stir Germany into 'revenge.'

For the Nazis then and for Holocaust deniers today, malevolent Jewish conspirators were fundamental to German designs on Europe. They were also critical as to why the US would declare war on Germany, according to other contemporary Nazi sympathizers. At an America First rally in September 1941, the famous aviator Charles Lindbergh decried the groups that were pushing the government to declare war on Germany. These groups were 'the British, the Jewish, and the Roosevelt Administration.' He went on:

> *But I am saying that the leaders of both the British and the Jewish races, for reasons which are as understandable from their viewpoint as they*

---

[1] Adolf Hitler, Speech to the Reichstag, January 30, 1939.

[2] "Chamberlain Welcomes Agency's War Aid; Says It Will Be 'kept in Mind,'" *Jewish Telegraph Agency*, September 6, 1939.

are inadvisable from ours, for reasons which are not American, wish to involve us in the war.[1]

His speech combined the idea that Jewish aims and values were 'un-American,' that Jews were pursuing interests fundamentally opposed to those of their 'host' country, with the notion that they were seeking to usurp the policies of their 'host' government. He was invoking the notion of dual loyalty as well as the idea that Jews were, with others, driving their country's foreign policy.

In the twenty first century, you continue to find examples of people and organizations ready to blame the Jews for the world's conflicts. In 2006, the actor Mel Gibson, who had long been accused of making antisemitic comments, was pulled over while driving on the Pacific Coast Highway. In a drunken tirade at the police officer, Gibson declared: 'The Jews are responsible for all the wars in the world,' before asking the officer if he was a Jew (he was).[2]

Islamist antisemites are certainly ready to blame Jews whenever a war occurs. Article 22 of the Hamas Charter contains the following conspiratorial tirade against world Jewry:

> [Their involvement in] local and world wars can be spoken of without fear of embarrassment. In fact, they were behind the First World War, through which achieved the abolishment of the Islamic Caliphate, made a profit and took over many of the sources of wealth…They were also behind the Second World War, in which they made immense profits by buying and selling military equipment, and also prepared the ground for the founding of their [own] state…No war takes place anywhere in the world without [the Jews] behind the scenes having a hand in it.[3]

Refutation

For this accusation to make sense, we have to treat the Jews as if they were a single global entity, pursuing the same narrow interest at all times, and one which is at odds with that of their respective nations. It is to conceive of Jews, not as if they were a group of communities in dozens of countries spread

---

[1] Charles Lindbergh, "Who are the War Agitators?," September 11, 1941.
[2] Audrey Gillan, "Mel Gibson apologises for anti-semitic abuse," *The Guardian*, July 31, 2006.
[3] The Hamas Charter 1988, Intelligence and Terrorism information Center at the Center for Special Studies.

across the world, but a singular group guided by an interconnected purpose where geographical differences are irrelevant. Yet a glance at the First World War disproves this. Jews fought on multiple sides of the conflict, both as loyal soldiers within the Central Powers (Germany, Austria-Hungary, the Ottoman Empire and Bulgaria) and the Allied forces (Britain, France, Russia and, much later, the United States). As has already been noted, patriotism was instilled in Jewish soldiers by their communal leaders, with fountains of praise offered to whichever 'fatherland' the Jews were fighting for.

Nor is it remotely plausible to suggest that Jews started the First World War. In analysing the causes of this war, it is pertinent to start with Imperial Germany and the machinations of its autocratic leader, Kaiser Wilhelm. Germany's emperor pursued a *Weltpolitik* (world policy) which was designed to enhance his country's overseas possessions and its range of deterrent power.[1] Famously, he engaged in a naval arms race with Britain, then the world's leading naval power, and caused geo-political crises in places such as Agadir and Tangier. It was the Kaiser who spurred on Germany's ally, Austria-Hungary, to take an aggressive stance towards Serbia in 1914 following the assassination of Franz Ferdinand, as well as Germany that declared war on Russia in September 1914. The other set of conflicts were localized in the Balkans and involved a range of territorial, ethnic, religious and geo-strategic issues. The catalyst for war was the assassination of the Archduke Frank Ferdinand, the heir to the Austro-Hungarian throne, by a group of Serb nationalist assassins. The greater Serb movement sought independence for those nations that were under the control of Austria-Hungary, including Bosnia, where the Archduke was killed. As Serbia was allied to Russia and Austria-Hungary to Germany, it was natural that the failure to negotiate a reasonable outcome between Austria-Hungary and Serbia would suck in the belligerent powers on both sides and cause a major European conflagration. It seems almost redundant to point out that the key political and military figures in all of Europe's major nations were non-Jewish.

Some claim that the Second World War has its seeds in resentment caused by Germany's loss in the First World War. Again, antisemites believe that Jews played a central role. Yet the *Dollschosslegende* is another egregious myth designed to exonerate those who were really responsible for Germany's

---

[1] Press, Steven. "Buying Sovereignty: German "Weltpolitik" and Private Enterprise, 1884–1914." *Central European History* 55 no. 1 (2022): 15–33.

defeat in World War 1. For three years, the war on the Western Front was an indecisive affair, with both sides merely exchanging parcels of land on either side at a horrendous cost in human life and material. Towards the end of 1917, a new factor emerged in the shape of the impending US entry into the war. A huge American army was designed to buttress the forces of Britain, France and their allies on the western front and provide the final spur to the land defeat of Germany. But events also seemed to be moving in the Germans' favour with the wave of revolutionary unrest that swept away the Provisional Government in Russia. Suddenly, a new Bolshevik government signalled that it did not intend to honour its commitments to the Allied powers and sought a negotiated peace with Germany, the end result of which was the Treaty of Brest-Litovsk. Combined with the defeat of the Italian army, this signalled a new phase of the war in which Berlin would regain the initiative in Europe and finally triumph over her enemies.

But Germany's 'final push' in June 1918 failed to land the decisive blow and the French army, led by Marshal Foch, prepared for a decisive counter offensive, one which commenced in July 1918. In August, the British expeditionary forces counter attacked while some days later, the Emperor of Austria made it clear that his country could not continue the war. General Erich Ludendorff would trace Germany's military collapse from this point in time. By the end of September, the German general staff realized that the war could not be won and Ludendorff dispatched an ultimatum to Berlin demanding an armistice from the Allies. It was at this point that the civilian government started to negotiate pursuing peace with their enemies and the military saw this as a convenient cover for their own military failure to defeat the Allies. It is also true that some Jewish leaders were members of the new civilian government that negotiated an unpopular peace deal with the Allies, as well as the treaty that followed. But none of this obscures the fundamental point about why Germany lost the war in 1918.

It is equally mendacious to declare that German aggression in 1939 was a defensive response to Jewish aggression in the years before. From the moment that he became leader of the National Socialist party in 1919, Hitler had declared his belligerent intent to destroy the rules-based order and re-assert German dominance in Europe. He sought to tear up the financial, territorial and military restrictions imposed by the Treaty of Versailles by refusing to pay reparations, retaking lands such as the Rhineland and Danzig and rebuilding a powerful German army and air force. He carried out these measures in unilateral fashion, gambling that western powers would fail to respond. Hitler announced conscription in 1933 as the first part of an attempt to restore the once mighty German army. He built the Luftwaffe, the German air force, in direct violation of the Versailles treaty and marched his troops into the Rhineland in 1936 and Austria in 1938.

Had the Western powers responded forcefully to each of these violations, war might have been averted, or significantly delayed. But these powers came to believe that the peace dictated in 1919 was a Carthaginian one which needlessly humiliated a great power and wrongly maintained its 'pariah' status. What followed was a Western policy of appeasement that was fundamentally ill suited to satiating the needs of the German dictator. For Hitler was no mere nationalist. He was instead a revolutionary statesman whose vision of a racially pure Aryan empire in Europe required the acquisition of 'living space' in neighbouring countries, as well as the enslavement of their populations. Appeasing Hitler only fed an appetite for further demands. To argue that the protests of various Jewish organizations against the Hitlerite regime 'caused' the regime to go to war is to believe that a fanatical dictator like Hitler would have been restrained in their absence.

It equally makes no sense to argue that American Jews 'dragged' their government into war in 1941. The United States fully entered the war in December 1941 following the Japanese attack on Pearl Harbour. Even then, the US only declared war against Japan, and it took the German declaration of war against America to bring the US into the European theatre of conflict. It was these events that catalysed Washington to enter the fray, not a propaganda campaign by the Jews or anyone else. Indeed, at a time when Jews were campaigning for a tougher stance to be taken against Nazi Germany, America was in the firm grip of isolationism that held back any commitment to international security.

In the previous two decades, various American administrations had refused to join the League of Nations, restricted immigration, decreased the size of their military and committed the country to neutrality pacts, according to which they would not intervene in European or Asian conflicts. As the 1930s dragged on and the Depression took its toll, the voices of groups like the America First Committee urged their government to pursue an 'independent American destiny' and non-entanglement in international politics. Perhaps their most charismatic and popular spokesman was Charles Lindbergh, a galvanising figure who urged the US not to arm Britain in 1940 because this would lead to the defeat of Germany. The antisemitic Catholic priest, Father Coughlin, also asserted that intervention against Germany and Italy would be a disaster, wholly contrary to American interests.[1]

At the start of 1940, the majority of Americans shared the view that their country ought not to intervene in the European conflict, a pressure that was shared in Congress. No matter how much the Jews demanded intervention against fascism, they could not move the dial of American public opinion or Congressional opinion on their own. What began to change in that year was the stark realization that as Nazi Germany was overrunning Europe and bulldozing democratic governments, the threat to US interests was becoming palpable. There was growing support for arming the UK as a means of protecting the 'American periphery,' a policy that led to the 'destroyers for bases' deal and, later, Lend Lease. But the ultimate decision to go to war was decided by the actions of Axis powers, not Britain or the Jews.

3. Communism is a Jewish movement

The most impactful event of the First World War was the Bolshevik revolution of October 1917. The events in Petrograd in which a small group of Bolshevik revolutionaries overthrew the Provisional Government would have seismic consequences both in Russia and around Europe. The revolution unseated a government that had maintained its commitment to Allied forces in the fight against Germany and put in place a new one that wanted to end the war altogether. The new government issued decrees that upended the social and political order and promised an economic revolution based on freedom and equality. It also introduced a form of state sanctioned terror against all those who opposed the new regime, with unprecedented powers to arrest, torture and kill 'enemies of the state.' The birth of state communism and Lenin's notion of 'permanent revolution' galvanized communist fellow travellers on the Continent, leading to a new regime in Hungary (under Bela Kun), a temporary revolt in Berlin (led by the Spartacists in 1919) and the growth of communist parties around the world.

The revolution was to spur another of the major historical canards associated with the Protocols, namely 'Judaeo-Bolshevism,' the belief that 'Communism was a Jewish conspiracy' with Jews 'responsible for its

---

[1] Albin Krebs, "Charles Coughlin, 30's 'Radio Priest,'" *The New York Times*, October 28, 1979.

crimes.'[1] Among those who believed this was the British antisemitic journalist and agitator Henry Hamilton Beamish, a man who once said that 'Bolshevism was Judaism.' In 1919, the Church-National Enlightenment Bureau, an organ of the Finnish White Guard, published 'What is Bolshevism?' in which it was proposed that Bolshevism was a Jewish plot and that its leaders were almost entirely Jewish. White emigres in Germany spread the notion that Bolshevism had been inspired and created by disaffected Jewish radicals with their propaganda taken up by the Nazi movement. In 1924, Dietrich Eckhart produced a pamphlet Der Bolschewismus von Moses bis Lenin ("Bolshevism from Moses to Lenin") in which Moses was depicted alongside Lenin as a Communist.

These viewpoints cemented the perception that communism was being foisted on western civilization by hordes of 'Asiatic' Jews with their demented scheme for world domination. It led to outbreaks of murderous violence, including the massacres of the Russian Civil War in which as many as 100,000 Jews were murdered. Lurid tales of communist atrocities, whether or not exaggerated, were seized upon by sections of the political and media class, eager to portray Judaeo Bolshevism as a subversive 'red menace' that was threatening to destroy the social and political order. Tsar Nicholas II had little doubt that Jews constituted the majority of the political radicals opposing him, saying that they formed nine-tenths of the troublemakers, while Swedish writer Alfred Jensen wrote in 1921 that 'approximately 75 per cent of the leading Bolsheviks are of Jewish origin.'[2] Though coming from a largely philosemitic perspective, Winston Churchill wrote an article in 1920 which, while it praised the efforts of patriotic and Zionist Jews, also railed against 'the international Jews,' the adherents of a 'sinister confederacy' who were part of a 'world-wide conspiracy for the overthrow of civilization.'[3] His political nemesis, Adolf Hitler, believed that Russian Bolshevism was an attempt undertaken by the modern Jewry to achieve world domination. In 1941 he wrote:

---

[1] Izabella Tabarovsky, "A Specter Haunting Europe: The Myth of Judeo-Bolshevism," *Fathom Magazine*, October 2019.

[2] K. Gerner, 'Degrees of Anti-Semitism: the Swedish Example,' in Jews and Christians, Who is Your Neighbour after the Holocaust?, ed. M. Bron Jr. (Acta Sueco-Polonica, No. 2) (Uppsala, 1997).

[3] Daniel Mandel, "Winston Churchill - A Good Friend of Jews and Zionism?," *Jerusalem Center for Security and Foreign Affairs*, May 11, 2009.

The Jewish Bolshevik rulers in Moscow have unswervingly undertaken to force their domination upon us and the other European nations and that is not merely spiritually, but also in terms of military power ... Now the time has come to confront the plot of the Anglo-Saxon Jewish war-mongers and the equally Jewish rulers of the Bolshevik centre in Moscow.[1]

Refutation

The notion that communism was, and is, a Jewish movement is an irrational fantasy based on *some elements* of reality. That is to say that, like other tropes of antisemitism, this one cites certain facts about Jews and then amplifies and twists them, according to the various pre-existing paradigms of antisemitic ideology.

Let us deal with those elements first. Clearly, a number of the leading figures within the worldwide communist movement were Jews. They include: Karl Marx, the father of modern communism; Leon Trotsky, one of the two architects of the Bolshevik revolution and the head of the Red Army during the Russian Civil War; Adolph Jaffe, Chairman of the Petrograd Military Revolutionary Committee that removed the Provisional Government; Yakov Sverdlov, the chairman of the All-Russian Central Executive Committee; Grigory Zinoviev and Lev Kamenev, two leading Soviet politicians who vied to take control of the USSR in the 1920s; Maxim Litvinov, the USSR's foreign minister until 1939 and Genrikh Yagoda, one time head of the NKVD (the Secret Police). Though Lenin was not Jewish, many of his supporters were. It is estimated that among the 29 people who accompanied Lenin on his sealed train back to Petrograd in 1917, roughly one half were Jewish.[2]

Outside of Russia, a number of communist figures were also Jewish. Among them were Bela Kun, the man who led Hungary's short lived communist republic in 1919; Rosa Luxembourg, one of the two leaders of Germany's Spartacist movement, who was murdered by the Freikorps after the revolt in Berlin failed; Werner Scholem (1895-1940), a leading member of the German Communist party; Matyas Rakosi, the communist leader of Hungary until 1956; Rudolf Slansky, General Secretary of the Czech

---

[1] Hillgruber, Andreas (1987). "War in the East and the Extermination of the Jews," *Yad Vashem Studies*, Volume XVIII, pp. 103-132.

[2] Seth Frantzman, "Was the Russian Revolution Jewish?," *The Jerusalem Post*, February 7, 2018.

Communist party and in 1948, Ana Pauker, who effectively ran Romania for Stalin before falling from grace. In the government of the Russian Socialist Federative Soviet Republic of 1917–1922, there were six Jews out of 50 people, some 12%. In addition, of the 48 People's Commissars of the Hungarian Soviet Republic that was formed in March 1919, 30 were Jews.[1] It is also the case that in postwar Poland, Jews were overrepresented in the state security services between 1944 and 1956, with 30% of the top officers being Jewish. Jews then were highly prominent as communist leaders, ideologues, writers, spokespeople and activists in many countries.

Jews were also well represented in communist party membership. To take one example, in America, it is estimated that half of the Communist party membership was Jewish in the 1930s and 1940s, and among their more famous members were Julius and Ethel Rosenberg, a couple convicted and executed for espionage against the US.[2]

But that is really where the notion of 'Jewish Bolshevism' ends. The reality is that most Jews in the twentieth century were not supporters of communism, preferring either more liberal political philosophies (in the West) or Jewish political causes such as Bundism and Zionism. Conversely, most communist leaders and ideologues were not Jewish and had little interest in religion. There was also little specifically 'Jewish' about communism in that the concerns of those on the political left were international, rather than parochial. The religion of the radical left was entirely secular. Similarly, one cannot discover in Judaism the vital causal spring that persuaded many Jews to become communists. What motivated them to become radicals was social and intellectual influences, often those opposed by their co-religionists. Finally, communist regimes frequently turned against their Jewish populations. Let us take each of these ideas in turn.

Most communists not Jews: Most of the twentieth century's communist leaders were not Jews. That is certainly true of the founder of Soviet Bolshevism, Vladimir Lenin, even if he did claim descent from a Jewish grandfather. It is equally true that all of his successors (Stalin, Khrushchev, Brezhnev, Andropov, Chernenko and Gorbachev) were non-Jews, as were all the communist leaders of other states, including China, North Korea, Laos,

---

[1] McCagg, William O. "Jews in Revolutions: The Hungarian Experience." *Journal of Social History*, vol. 6, no. 1, (1972), 78–105.

[2] Ruth Wisse, "Why Do American Jews Idealize Soviet Communism?," *Tablet Magazine*, October 23, 2017.

Cuba and Vietnam. Where communist parties still exist in 2025, they too are mostly run by non-Jews.

It is equally true that the vast majority of Jews were not communist. Voting patterns in Russian elections between 1905 and 1917 are hard to discern, given that women were excluded from the vote (until 1917) and there were additional restrictions imposed by the Tsarist regime. But what is clear is that the majority of voting Jews rejected the politics of revolutionary Bolshevism. A greater number supported the Mensheviks, who were themselves a less radical socialist party, and an even greater number supported the Jewish socialist party called the Bund. Another segment of Jews supported the liberal position of the Kadets, a party that advocated equality and universal suffrage. Then there was a liberal Jewish party called the *Folkspartei*, which claimed some support from the Jews and various Zionist and religious parties. Russian Jews largely rejected the politics of revolution, and 'the majority of Russia's Jews opposed (the) takeover' of 25 October 1917.[1]

Russian Jews also in general rejected socialism. The Constituent Assembly elections in 1918 are an interesting test case of this. In the votes cast for Jewish parties, the majority (417,215 out of 498,198) went to Zionist and religious parties, another 31,123 went to the Bund and only 29,322 went to socialist parties. There is no clear information on how Jews voted for non-Jewish parties but the 'Jewish parties' represented the majority of Jewish voters and the figures show a rejection of radical left-wing politics.[2] The revolution that Jews did support overwhelmingly was that of March 1917, which led to the overthrow of the Tsarist regime and the creation of the Provisional Government. With its promises of equality, freedom and toleration, Jews saw in this government the chance to flourish as a community, free from the shackles of persecution and violence. Support for the Bolsheviks did increase after the Civil War, in large part because the Whites had spent the Civil War carrying out massacres of the Jewish population with an almost fanatical glee. By contrast, the Reds outlawed pogroms and rejected the politics of antisemitism altogether.

In its heyday, the US Communist party attracted no more than 100,000 supporters. With a pre-war Jewish population of 5 million, that means that

[1] Michael Stanislawski, "Why Did Russian Jews Support the Bolshevik Revolution?," *Tablet Magazine*, October 25, 2017.

[2] Zvi Gitelman, "Russian Revolutions of 1917," The Yivo Encyclopedia, https://encyclopedia.yivo.org/article/245, accessed October 13, 2025.

less than 1% of American Jews were actively supporting the country's main communist movement.[1] It means that when it came to political membership and voting intentions, Jewish communists were classic outliers within their community, shunning the mainstream choices made by their co-religionists.

Communists disavowed Jewishness: At the same time, it is false to assert that those Jews who did support the communist movement, whether as ideologues, activists or leaders, did so as an authentic expression of their Jewishness. For many Jews, communism was their true religion and identity which far transcended any parochial or ethnic attachment. They believed that the utopian universalism of the Marxist society, with its proletarian revolution, would sweep away every form of nationalism and solve, at a stroke, the 'Jewish question.' The conflict between Jewish civilization and communism was all too readily apparent in the young Karl Marx, a man descended from rabbis but who was anxious to distance himself from the Jewish people. Marx viewed Judaism through the lens of economic exploitation and class warfare, believing that the true God of the Jews was money and that their values were exploitative. Trotsky too was also keen to distance himself from his origins, once declaring: 'I am not a Jew but an internationalist.'[2] In his autobiography, Trotsky wrote these lines:

> In my mental equipment, nationality never occupied an independent place, as it was felt but little in everyday life…It never played a leading part – not even a recognized one – in my list of grievances.[3]

The German leader of the Spartacists, Rosa Luxembourg, similarly disavowed paying special attention to antisemitic persecution in favour of an internationalist humanism. In a letter written to her fellow socialist, Mathilde Wurm, who had recommended she read Spinoza and who had spoken of the 'special suffering of the Jews,' Luxembourg responded:

> I am just as much concerned with the poor victims on the rubber plantations of Putumayo, the Blacks in Africa with whose corpses the

---

[1] Harvey Klehr, "Few American Jews Were Communists, and Many Fewer Were Spies," *Mosaic*, June 11, 2019.
[2] Richard Pipes, "Trotsky the Jew," *Tablet Magazine*, October 17, 2011.
[3] Frantzman, "Was the Russian Revolution Jewish?"

> Europeans play catch [...] they resound with me so strongly that I have no special place in my heart for the ghetto.[1]

Other communists did everything to discourage their ethnic connection to Jewishness. Thus, Matyas Rakosi, also known as the bald butcher, was given to antisemitic remarks and had to be reminded by the speaker of the Hungarian parliament that he had a Jewish mother and should not deny that. He was a typical example of what Isaac Deutscher called 'non-Jewish Jews.'[2]

In the paranoid imaginings of antisemites, figures like Trotsky, Marx, Bela Kun and Rosa Luxembourg were stealthily advancing Jewish interests at the expense of the interests of their 'host' countries. Yet such a view makes no sense when there was little element of 'Jewish self-consciousness' among the communist leaders. Stanislaw Krajewski is surely correct to observe: 'Among the most significant features of Jewish communists was their desire to leave the Jewish world, often to stop being Jewish, so that at least their children would have no Jewish sentiments, and no Jewish problems.'[3] Furthermore, as Rabbi Joseph B. Soloveitchik has observed, Jewish Bolsheviks 'wanted to convince Stalin that they were first and foremost communists rather than Jews.'[4] Of course, this does not apply to all Jewish communists.

Judaism does not automatically lead to communism: It is true that Judaism places a great emphasis on social justice. There is the belief in creating a perfect world (tikkun olam), supporting the underdog and challenging tyranny within society. As such, one can see why some Jews might have chosen the path of communism, all the more so in a society led by the Tsars which actively repressed Jewish communities. Many Jews were attracted to the promise of a communist utopia precisely because they saw it as the primary means by which the structures of oppression and inequality that bedevilled them would become obsolete. Some observers have discerned a strain of messianic thinking in the universal utopia of Marxism. Among those who made this link were Karl Löwith in his *Meaning in History*, where he

---

[1] Rory Castle-Jones, "Actually, Rosa Luxemburg Was Not a Self-Hating Jew," *Tablet Magazine*, August 16, 2016.

[2] Isaac Deutscher, *The Non-Jewish Jew and Other Essays* (London: Verso, 2017).

[3] Stanislaw Krajewski, "Jews, Communism and Jewish Communists," https://jewish studies.ceu.edu/sites/jewishstudies.ceu.edu/files/attachment/basicpage/8/01krajewski.pdf, accessed September 11, 2025.

[4] Krajewski, Stanislaw. "Jews, Communists and Jewish Communists, in Poland, Europe and Beyond." Covenant Volume 1, Issue 3 (October 2007).

claimed to have discovered the traces of a 'transparent messianism' that had its 'unconscious root in Marx's own being, even in his race.'[1] He drew a correspondence between the notion of the persecuted proletariat and that of the chosen people and between the transition of a society towards communism and the advent of the Kingdom of God. Other thinkers, such as Martin Buber and Arnold Toynbee, chose to see Marxist philosophy as a 'socialist secularization of Jewish eschatology.'[2]

But it is equally possible to construct a path between Judaism and non-radical political movements, such as liberalism, conservatism and nationalism. Judaism places great emphasis on the importance of contributing to one's existing society and paying homage to its rulers, provided that they allow Jews to worship freely and govern in a just fashion. This is the polar opposite of the idea that one should not only oppose but seek to destroy an existing government of which one disapproves. Furthermore, if traditional Judaism, when translated into secular politics, inevitably fed into communist politics, one must ask why the vast majority of religious Jews reject it. Radical Jews, far from imbibing the heart of the Jewish message, have often been the most alienated among their community.

<u>Communists hostile to Jews</u>: It is equally true that communist regimes were invariably hostile to their Jewish populations, either engaging in outright persecution or clamping down on their religious freedoms and practices. The examples are legion and involve both attacks on Jewish institutions as well as people. Even though Lenin rejected the persecution of Jews, he believed that Jewish assimilation into wider society would cure antisemitism. In practice, this amounted to a demand that Jewish communal life be dissolved. In 1919, as part of a campaign against religious bodies, the Bolshevik government seized Jewish communal properties, including synagogues, and dissolved a significant number. This action forced many rabbis to resign their posts and seek positions abroad. Later, the Yevsektsiya, the Jewish section of the Communist party's propaganda department, decided on a policy involving the 'systematic destruction of Zionist and bourgeois institutions.' Schools and communal institutions were shuttered as part of a drive to propagandize among the Jews.

---

[1] Karl Löwith, *Meaning in History*: *The Theological Implications of the Philosophy of History* (Chicago: University of Chicago Press, 1949), 44.

[2] Enzo Traverso, "Marx, Radical Enlightenment and the Jews," in *The Jewish Question* (Brill, 2018), 11-28, 11.

Another famous example of antisemitism was the so-called Doctors Plot of the early 1950s when Soviet dictator Joseph Stalin accused nine eminent doctors in Moscow, most of whom were Jewish, of taking part in a vast plot to poison members of the top Soviet political and military leadership. They were accused of being part of an international Jewish bourgeois organization and a media campaign whipped up a storm of abuse towards other prominent members of Soviet Jewry. Many Jews lost their academic positions and found themselves hounded from public life, with the media portraying the community as 'rootless cosmopolitans' and 'individuals devoid of nation or tribe.' As Irving Horowitz points out: 'The frequent charge of "cosmopolitanism" in the xenophobic world of Great Russian chauvinism was a virtual code word for being Jewish, or better, anti-national.'[1]

This hostility continued in later decades under Brezhnev. Following Israel's victory in the Six Day War, the Soviet Union embarked on a campaign of hostility towards Zionism that relied on existing antisemitic tropes. There was a virulent, decades long campaign of Jew hatred that involved the production of a vast literature of anti-Zionist books, articles, lectures and films, all overseen by zealots within the Communist party. The Soviets used the Novosti Press Agency, which worked in over 100 countries, to disseminate this propaganda, ensuring that every piece of anti-Israeli agitprop reached tens of millions of people around the world. Cartoons denouncing Zionism featured the kind of imagery that one would have seen in *Der Sturmer*. Some books, including those by Ukrainian author Trofim Kichko, condemned Jews as inherently racist and alleged that there was collaboration between Jews and the Nazis.[2]

The Soviet authorities made it increasingly hard for Jews to emigrate, regarding would be emigrants as a treasonous security risk. If Jews were to be tolerated in the USSR, there was a price to be paid, namely their identity and freedom. The expectation was that Jews in the USSR would be good Russians, conforming to Russian norms and practices, thereby shedding their own religious practices. That meant abandoning the speaking of Yiddish and shunning Zionism completely. This policy also resulted in Jews being relatively politically powerless. Indeed, 'of the 5,312 members elected to the

---

[1] Irving Louis Horowitz, "Cuba, Castro and anti-Semitism," Springer Science, 2007.

[2] Izabella Tabarovsky, "Soviet Anti-Zionism and Contemporary Left Antisemitism," *Fathom*, May 2019.

Supreme Soviet in the republics by 1967, only 14 were Jewish.'[1] Jews were not granted membership in the Council of Nationalities.

There are echoes of such bigotry and discrimination in other communist regimes allied to Moscow. The 1968 Polish political crisis, also known as the Students' March, was accompanied by a virulent antisemitic campaign that led to the forced emigration of some 13,000 Jewish Poles. It had been preceded by a purge of Jews from the Polish army (150 military officers were fired) and the party, including the chief editor of the party's official newspaper. Gomulka had previously said that he did not want a 'fifth column' in Poland.

In Cuba, opposition to Israeli policy has become saturated with hateful language reminiscent of *Der Sturmer*. On official organs of the Cuban media, Israel's assault on Hezbollah in 2006 was described as a war against Palestine and Lebanon by 'arrogant Jews, armed to the teeth by the United States.' The Cuban National Assembly lambasted the actions of the 'Zionist entity' as a 'horrendous and shameless action, a genocide which challenges universal public opinion, laughs at the United Nations, and threatens to invade other countries, reminiscent of the era of Nazism.'[2] It should not be forgotten that some 90% of the Jewish community fled the country in the wake of the Castro revolution, due in part to the suspicion that the 'atheistic state' being set up by the revolutionaries, together with the seizure of businesses, would make life intolerable for most Jews.

In sum, communism is not a Jewish or Judaic movement. Jewish communism is an egregious myth which is used to justify persecution and mass murder and has no rational foundation. There have been and are Jewish communists, including highly influential ones, but they remain on the fringes of Jewish society in terms of their political leanings. Most Jews have not voted for the communist parties in their countries. Historically, the communist movement has often been accompanied by deep hostility to Jews, Israel and Zionism, with regimes keen to denounce parochial Jews as fifth columnists and traitors. But it is also sadly true that influential Jewish communists, among them Rakosi, Trotsky and Yagoda, committed crimes of oppression and violence that deserve the most severe condemnation.

---

[1] Leonid Garbuzo, "Struggle to Preserve Ethnic Identity: The Suppression of Jewish Culture by the Soviet Union's Emigration," *Boston University International Law Journal, Vol. 23:159,* 161.

[2] Horowitz, "Cuba, Castro and anti-Semitism."

4. Jews control the media in their own interests

1. Media

Charge

The notion that Jews control the media is a key trope used in the Protocols. In the twelfth protocol, the 'Elders' state unequivocally that the Jews will 'absolutely control the Press' so that 'not a single announcement will ever reach the public without our control.' It went on to say that the Jews had managed to 'possess ourselves of the minds of the goy communities to such an extent that they all come near looking upon the events of the world through the coloured glasses of those spectacles we are setting astride their noses.' There is talk of imposing stamp taxes on the press, of owning the majority of journals in order to control the commanding heights of literature and journalism and of controlling the newspaper militia, ensuring complete control over the masses.

In America, there are a number of figures and organizations that propagate this trope of Jewish media dominance. The accusation of Jewish control has been made by the musician Kanye (Ye) West. During an interview on a Revolt TV programme that was posted (and later removed) on October 16, Ye could be heard blaming 'Jewish media' and 'Jewish Zionists' for various alleged social ills.[1] His words were echoed by the broadcaster Joe Rogan. In a discussion with the actor and comedian Mark Normand, Rogan responded to the glowing praise that the former had heaped on American Jews for their contributions to national life by invoking their "pulling all those strings at CNN, Hollywood..."[2]

The notion that Jews control the media has also been made more explicitly by film maker Oliver Stone. In an interview with the Sunday Times, Stone described Hitler as an 'easy scapegoat' and that he 'did far more damage to the Russians than [to] the Jewish people, 25 or 30 [million killed].' When asked to explain why more people did not know this, he replied: 'The Jewish domination of the media … There's a major lobby in the United States. They

---

[1] "Kanye West Lashes Out at 'Jewish Zionists' on 'Drink Champs,'" *Rolling Stone*, October 16, 2022.

[2] Ryan Smith, "Joe Rogan Suggests Jews Control Media in Old Clip Amid Antisemitism Furor," Newsweek, February 10, 2023.

are hard workers. They stay on top of every comment, the most powerful lobby in Washington.'[1] He later apologized for his remarks.

Similarly explicit was the racist diatribe in 2012 from Louis Farrakhan, leader of the Nation of Islam, in which he said that Jews, "Control movies, television, recording, publishing, commerce, radio, they own it all."[2] A year earlier, during the war to remove Colonel Qaddafi from Libya, he had fulminated about the powers behind the US decision. He declared:

> The stupid mistake that we make is to think that the president is the supreme power. Never was. Money is the power in America. ... All of you know what I'm talking about, Zionist control of the government of the United States of America.[3]

In the UK, the far-right British National Party published a booklet called *Who are the Mind Benders?: The people who rule Britain through control of the mass media (1997).* It alleged a Jewish conspiracy to control the media and brainwash the British people and was heavily criticized for trafficking in racist tropes.[4]

A popular twenty first century antisemitic meme among the far right shows a poster with a quote attributed (falsely) to Voltaire, which states: 'To learn who rules over you, simply find out who you are not allowed to criticize.' Next to the quote is the Nazi image of a hook-nosed Jew superimposed on an arm whose hand is trampling on the masses.

Indeed, even those who are well disposed to Israel and the Jews can fall in line with this canard. No less a figure than Rupert Murdoch issued a tweet in 2012 in which he asked: 'Why is Jewish owned press so consistently anti-Israel in every crisis?'[5]

Refutation

Contrary to the giddy imaginations of antisemites, most major media outlets are not owned or run by Jews and the vast majority of print and broadcast journalists, editors and media operators are not Jewish. Jews do

---

[1] Ben Child, "Oliver Stone apologises for 'antisemitic' remarks," *The Guardian,* July 27, 2010.

[2] "Farrakhan blasts Jews for pushing war with Iran," *The Forward*, February 28, 2012.

[3] Leah Nelson, "Black Extremists Blast Obama's Decision to Weaken Qaddafi, with One Predicting Spaceships," *Southern Poverty Law Center*, April 1, 2011.

[4] "Nick Griffin: Right-wing chameleon," *BBC News*, June 29, 2001.

[5] Michael Wolff, "Rupert Murdoch and the Jews," *The Guardian*, November 19, 2012.

feature among the richest media owners in the world but the majority of these owners are gentile. Jews have founded, managed and edited some of the world's leading publications and among the legendary names in the 'hall of fame' one can cite Carl Bernstein (who helped break the Watergate scandal), Thomas Friedman, Jeffrey Goldberg, Masha Gessen, Wolf Blitzer and Jake Tapper. But again, they are heavily outnumbered by their non-Jewish peers in nearly every field of the media. Indeed, some of the most influential voices in the media today (The Wall Street Journal, Washington Post, Fox News, BBC, NPR, Thomson Reuters, Forbes, Huffington Post, The Guardian) are not owned or run by Jews. The fact that there are many notable Jewish figures in the media, with many Pulitzer Prize winners among them, should not blind us to this fact. If the 'elders' really did outline a sinister Jewish plot to take over the global media, they have clearly failed.

But for antisemites, such facts cut no ice. To be a Jew in a position of media influence is sufficient evidence of wrongdoing, nefarious intent, plotting and conspiracy, usually on a co-ordinated scale. This suggests that the sole interest of Jewish journalists is to promote and advocate solely parochial interests, and ones which are naturally to the detriment of wider society. A common theme is that Jews promote the interests of the State of Israel, obscuring the fact that the interests of the Jewish State often align with those of western states. Another is the canard that all Jewish journalists, like all Jews, advocate for progressive causes, whether that is rights for racial minorities, mass immigration, freedom and respect for sexual minorities and asylum for refugees. These are seen by the far right as a means to degrade the 'white' nation, eviscerate its power and mongrelize its population.

It is particularly egregious to suggest that the sole preoccupation of Jewish journalists is to provide some defence of Israel or Jews more widely. It would certainly have been news to the readers of *The New York Times* (owned by a Jew) during the Second World War. The terrifying accounts of the Holocaust which were reaching Western observers from 1941 onwards did appear in the Times but were 'mostly buried inside its gray and stolid pages, never featured, analyzed or rendered truly comprehensible.'[1] For the owners and editors of this paper, the atrocities being inflicted upon the Jews were little different to those visited upon millions of other war victims. *The Times* only

[1] Max Francel, "150th Anniversary: 1851-2001; Turning Away From the Holocaust," *The New York Times*, November 14, 2001.

featured the massacre of Jews on six occasions during six years of war and only once did the fate of the Jews feature in a lead editorial. So much for prioritising the interests of Jews above all others. With good reason, one writer has described this as 'surely the century's bitterest journalistic failure.'[1] Part of the reason may have been that the papers were simply following the lead of western governments, themselves failing to prioritize the rescue of the Jews, and also the fact that, in the United States, such were the levels of antisemitism in polite society, that any emphasis on Jewish suffering would have been interpreted as unpatriotic and parochial.

The same analysis applies today to the media when it comes to reporting on Israel. Indeed, two myths need to be slayed. First, it is wrong to assert that the mainstream western media is uniformly pro-Israel in its reporting and, second, it is a fantasy to believe that all Jewish journalists are part of some orchestrated plot to promote the interests of the Israeli government and silence the country's critics.

Firstly, the notion that the western mainstream media is in the grip of a 'pro-Israel' fervour is belied by the sheer levels of disingenuous reporting, media misinformation, biased headlines, double standards and decontextualization that one finds on this subject. The term Pallywood (which combines the words Palestine and Hollywood) describes the way with which the Palestinian authorities manipulate western media audiences into believing their twisted and distorted views of the conflict and in which they stage atrocities for the media's benefit.[2] The term was particularly apposite following the killing in Gaza of a young child, Muhammad al-Durrah, in 2000. France 2, which aired the footage, blamed Israeli forces for the child's death, a charge initially accepted by the Israeli authorities. Later, it emerged that Palestinian gunfire may have cut down the boy and that the scene of his death was not all it was made out to be.[3]

In 2002, tales of an Israeli massacre in Jenin during Operation Defensive Shield appeared in numerous western media outlets. By way of background, Israeli forces had launched an operation in Jenin that was designed to

---

[1] Alison Leigh Cowan, "Mourning Max Frankel, the New York Times' unflinching Jewish journalist," *The Jerusalem Post*, April 8, 2025.

[2] The very real examples of media manipulation should not be taken to suggest that there are not real examples of Palestinian civilian suffering in both Gaza and the West Bank.

[3] James Fallows, "News on the al-Dura front: Israeli finding that it was staged," *The Atlantic*, October 2, 2007.

eliminate the city's terrorist infrastructure. In 2002, roughly 40% of the terrorist attacks inside Israel had emanated from Jenin and there was an overwhelming need to deal with the problem at source. When the IDF arrived, they encountered buildings that had been booby trapped and soldiers had to engage in hand-to-hand combat and pitched battles with gunmen. By the time that they left, 52 Palestinians lay dead, fourteen of whom were civilian, while 23 Israeli soldiers lost their lives. Yet foreign observers told a more lurid tale, a 'myth of Jeningrad.' Israel was accused of perpetrating a massacre, of behaving like the Nazis or the Taliban and of committing a war crime of terrible savagery. One columnist even said that Israel was guilty of genocide.[1]

Western journalists are also notorious for omitting the blatant war crimes perpetrated by Hamas and Fatah in the Gaza and West Bank respectively. In recent years, Hamas has made a determined effort to muzzle the foreign media in order to ensure the victory of its political narrative. A Freedom House report (2023) rates Gaza as 0 out of 4 for media freedom, stating clearly that 'the media are not free in Gaza' and that bloggers and journalists 'continue to face repression from the Hamas government's internal security apparatus.'[2] The social media accounts of those who had reported on the misfiring of Palestinian rockets or the military capabilities of Palestinian armed groups have been blocked. Hamas has also made journalists apply in advance for permission to film in certain areas, such as Gaza's fishing port. Both Israel and Hamas have been accused of harassing journalists who seek to report on peaceful protests though, in the former case, security issues were likely prevalent. In 2022, Hamas issued a set of restrictions on foreign correspondents operating in Gaza, among which were an order for those correspondents to employ Palestinian 'sponsors' (also known as fixers) who would, in turn, have to submit reports on where those correspondents had gone and what they did, a prohibition on reporting about Gazans killed by misfiring rockets and a requirement that they blame Israel for the conflict. Though those rules were rescinded, there was still the risk, according to the Press Association, that Hamas had 'signaled its expectations' and that this could

---

[1] Charles Krauthammer, "Opinion | Jenin: The Truth," *The Washington Post*, May 3, 2002.
[2] "Gaza Strip: Freedom in the World 2023 Country Report," Freedom House, https://freedomhouse.org/country/gaza-strip/freedom-world/2023, accessed September 12, 2025.

exert 'a chilling effect on critical coverage.'[1]

It is hardly surprising then that many western media outlets, including the BBC, *The Guardian*, *The New York Times* and *The Economist* have so often failed to report objectively on the complex realities of the Arab-Israeli conflict. Worse, they have, on occasions, become mouthpieces for incendiary and virulent claims of Israeli malevolence, ones which simply collapse under the simplest scrutiny.

Nor do Jewish journalists routinely operate a form of groupthink whereby they uniformly and uncritically support whichever Israeli government is in power. The western media is filled with the voices of Jewish journalists who lament for the State of Israel and what are seen to be its tragically misguided policies. From Peter Beinart and David Remnick[2] in *The New Yorker* to Noam Chomsky in *Democracy Now*, and from Antony Loewenstein in the Australian media to Jonathan Freedland in the UK, there are a plethora of powerful voices that offer harsh critiques of the Jewish state. A large number of left-wing Israeli writers are also invited to write in western publications. In recent years, anti-Israel screeds have been written by Gideon Levy, Ilan Pappe, Miko Peled, Oren Yiftachel, Mira Bar-Hillel, Gershom Gorenberg and many others. If one wishes to find critical voices that challenge the Israeli narrative, one only needs to read the foreign news section of major mainstream publications where voices such as these proliferate. While it is true that they are counterbalanced by less extreme views, it would be impossible to hear these negative voices if a 'pro-Israel' lobby was in charge of the western media.

This ignores an even more fundamental point, namely that the prime concern of many, perhaps most, Jewish journalists is not to comment much on Israel at all. News, political analysis and foreign reporting have attracted many Jewish media voices, but so too have film, radio and theatre, the arts, scientific knowledge, business and the economy, technology, sports, culture and heritage. Moreover, even for those specialising in news and politics, Israel often comes second to local and domestic politics, the conflicts with Russia and China, the future of the European Union, climate change and environmental emergencies, migration and refugees, real crime, terrorism and a host of other issues. The notion that Jews in the media use all their time and resources to pursue a single minded 'pro-Israel' agenda would be farfetched

---

[1] "Hamas issues, rescinds rules to media to skew coverage to pro-Gaza, anti-Israel line," *Times of Israel*, August 10, 2022.

[2] Remnick came out as a supporter of BDS in 2016.

even if they owned and controlled every mainstream newspaper in the world. The allegation can only be made by those with a warped mindset, according to which the Jews are the source of all malignity in the world. They believe that all Jewish voices are purely obsessed with defending Israel, reflecting a total denial of diversity within the Jewish community.

Of course, there are some Jewish journalists whose main concern is to support Israel in the international arena and to argue that positive relations between the Jewish state and its western allies are an important factor in international politics. These more conservative commentators believe that Israel is a shining beacon of liberal values and democratic norms, and that it serves as a guiding light for Middle Eastern regimes with more autocratic tendencies. They argue that Israel does not receive a fair hearing at the hands of the Western media and that it is singled out for disproportionate scrutiny in the halls of international opinion. They refuse to renounce their Zionism or their Jewishness for anybody.

For the determined antisemite, these people drip poison into the body politic and are proof positive that Jews have an insidious desire to undermine Western society by force feeding it an alien ideology. Much of that perception is driven by a host of other antisemitic tropes, some of which are related to Israel, and these will be dissected in the following chapter.

2. Banking

Charge

If the canard of Jewish control of the media is false, what about the claim that they 'own' the banking system and the financial institutions upon which we all rely? The accusation relies on pre-existing notions that Jews are greedy, money obsessed, miserly, profit driven and aggressive in their negotiation with non-Jews. As we have seen, the obsessive linkage between Jews and money has an ancient lineage but was given rocket fuel by the medieval exclusion of Jews from gentile occupations and trade associations. In the eighteenth and nineteenth centuries, a number of Jewish businessmen founded banking dynasties in Europe and America, the most famous of which was the Rothschild dynasty. The Rothschilds became synonymous with financial power and business acumen though, for antisemites, the name Rothschild was shorthand for how Jews were trying to control the global financial system. Other famous Jewish names in the financial system include the Lehman Brothers, the Salomon Brothers and Goldman Sachs.

In the twentieth century, the *Protocols of the Elders of Zion* solidified a myth that an elite group of Jews were plotting to dominate the world's financial resources in order to cement their control of the world. The idea was taken up by many contemporary antisemites, including Henry Ford, who went on to promulgate it in the pages of the Dearborn Independent. It came naturally to the Nazis to portray Jews in the most sinister terms. Cartoons depicted the Jew as a sinister octopus with malevolent tentacles, the archetype of a grasping, controlling creature with an insatiable ambition to suck up the earth's financial resources. Other animalistic representations along the same theme have seen the Jew likened to the cunning serpent or a spider trapping gentiles in its net.

They are often used to accompany the idea that the Jews control the Federal Reserve (the central banking authority of the US) and, with it, all the economic troubles that prevail at any time. To cite just one example, the antisemite Wickliffe Vennard published *The Federal Reserve Corporation*, in which he alleged that Jews dominated the Fed and that Hitler, like Jesus, had come into power 'to chase the money changers from the Temple.' The attack was continued by Sheldon Emry, leader of the Identity church movement, who wrote that 'Most of the owners of the largest banks in America are of Eastern European ancestry and connected with the Rothschild banks.' According to Bo Gritz, presidential candidate in the 1992 US elections, eight Jewish families controlled the Federal Reserve System.[1]

The Rothschild family are often singled out for opprobrium. The nineteenth century French antisemite Georges Dairnvaell wrote a pamphlet (under the pseudonym Satan) in which he claimed that Nathan Rothschild witnessed France's defeat in the Battle of Waterloo in 1815, then quickly returned to London (paying a fortune to cross the Channel during a storm) before the news broke, all in order to make 20 million francs on the stock exchange. He did this by initially spreading rumours of Britain's defeat in order to force a sale of shares, then buying them cheaply in time for news of a British victory, at which point he made a killing.[2] It spawned an industry of

---

[1] "Jewish 'Control' of the Federal Reserve: A Classic Antisemitic Myth," *The Anti-Defamation League*, January 30, 2017, https://www.adl.org/resources/backgrounder/jewish-control-federal-reserve-classic-antisemitic-myth, accessed October 14, 2025.

[2] Brian Cathcart, "The Rothschild Libel: Why has it taken 200 years for an anti-Semitic slur that emerged from the Battle of Waterloo to be dismissed?" *The Independent*, May 3, 2015.

conspiracy theories that have lasted until today. In 2015, a cartoon depicted the Rothschilds as a pig that was feeding other countries' intelligence services. The dynasty have been blamed for the COVID pandemic while, in the lurid imagination of Louis Farrakhan, the Rothschilds dominate the Federal Reserve.[1]

Refutation

Of course, there have been a multitude of Jewish bankers, among them some of the most illustrious names in the industry. It is equally true that there have been many prominent Jews in senior positions within the financial industry, including three successive chairs of the Federal Reserve, half of the people who served as US Treasury Secretary between 1995 and 2020 and one quarter of the presidents of the World Bank between 1946 and 2020. But the idea that these people collectively dominate the world's financial system is far-fetched and outlandish in the extreme.

For one thing, the majority of powerful banks are not owned by Jews. Half of the ten most powerful banks in the world today based on market capitalization are based in either India or China, including such names as HDFC Bank and the Bank of China. The most powerful bank, J P Morgan Chase, was founded by non-Jew J P Morgan while the second, Bank of America, was founded by the son of Italian non-Jewish immigrant parents. Other names on that list include Morgan Stanley (founded by a group of non-Jews) and Wells Fargo (founded by Henry Wells, the son of a Presbyterian minister). Of course, some of these banks, and others besides, will have had Jewish CEOs or CFOs from time to time. But for this to be evidence of a concerted Jewish plot to dominate the industry, these individuals would have had to be acting in concert to promote a collective 'Jewish' agenda. Jews, like any other people with drive, ambition and skill, have a determination to succeed in new industries and do so to further their individual talents, not as representatives of a collective group. It is within that context that we should understand, and celebrate, Jewish achievement, like that of any other people.

There are specific canards about Jews and banking that can be easily demolished. The accusation made against Nathan Rothschild in 1815 is patently false. He was nowhere near Waterloo during the battle and there are no contemporary reports of a storm. Nor is there any evidence that Rothschild

[1] Rainer Zitelmann, "The Corona Crisis: The Rothschilds? Bill Gates? The Search For A Scapegoat Has Begun," *Forbes*, March 23, 2020.

had employed a special informant to provide him with secret intelligence about the battle or that he was the first person in London to learn of this news.[1]

It is equally untrue that the Federal Reserve was created by Jews or has been run by them for private benefit. The Federal Reserve was created in 1913 to serve as the central banking system and fiscal agency of the US government. Far from being 'set up by Jews,' the bank was established by the Federal Reserve Act which was passed by the 63rd Congress and signed into law by President Wilson. It is true that one of the key figures in the Board's early years was Paul Warburg, an enthusiastic advocate of central banking who is considered one of the Reserve's founders. Any suggestion that this advocacy was orientated to purely Jewish interests reflects little more than the lurid imagination of antisemites who are determined to demonize Jews in any environment.

5. Jews control Hollywood to promote themselves and undermine America

Charge

In 1921, an article appeared which claimed that 'the motion picture influence of the United States…is exclusively under the control, moral and financial, of the Jewish manipulators of the public mind.'[2] The paper was *The Dearborn Independent*, the birthchild of antisemitic conspiracy theorist Henry Ford, and his unforgivable diatribe was part of a long running campaign of demonization against global Jewry. Ford was not alone in his malevolent Jew baiting. William Dudley Pelley, founder of the racist organization *The Silver Legion of America*, claimed that Jews controlled the cinema and that they should be resisted.[3] He applauded the fact that the chief censor of Hollywood and the man who applied the Hays Code to film production, the Catholic Joseph Breen, was a rapid antisemite who put pressure on studios to avoid making films that could offend Nazi Germany. He once fumed that these Hollywood Jews 'seem to think of nothing but money making and sexual

[1] Brian Cathcart, "Nathan Rothschild and the Battle of Waterloo," Rothschild Archive, https://www.rothschildarchive.org/materials/nathan_and_waterloo.pdf, accessed October 1, 2025.

[2] David Turner, "Antisemitism in America: the societal limits of 'Exceptionality,'" *The Jerusalem Post*, May 10, 2012.

[3] Jason Daley, "The Screenwriting Mystic Who Wanted to Be the American Führer," *Smithsonian Magazine*, October 3, 2018.

indulgence' and that studios were run by people 'whose daily morals would not be tolerated in the toilet of a pest house.' He called these people 'the scum of the earth.'[1]

This trope has been shared by some modern media figures. In a 1996 interview with Larry King, Marlon Brando claimed that Hollywood was 'run by Jews' and 'owned by Jews.'[2] Brando, a man with many Jewish friends and a strong respect for Jewish culture, later apologized. The comedian Dave Chappelle added that it was 'not a crazy thing to think' that Jews ran the cinema industry, given the numbers of Jews working in that industry.[3] In an interview for *Playboy*, British actor Gary Oldman issued a defence of Mel Gibson and his infamous drunken rant against the Jews. Oldman remarked: 'Mel Gibson is in a town that's run by Jews and he said the wrong thing because he's actually bitten the hand that I guess has fed him.'[4] He later apologized and said he was 'deeply remorseful' for his comments. Even the reputable *Spectator* magazine featured a piece in 1994 that claimed a 'Jewish cabal' controlled the industry. The article, in *The Spectator*, authored by William Cash, a Hollywood correspondent for *The Daily Telegraph*, contended that Jews had created an 'invidious and protective culture' that denied employment to non-Jews.[5]

Was there a co-ordinated Jewish plot to control the film industry in the past? Did Jews seek the ruination of American values through their alleged control of film? Did they use their position to prioritize the interests of Jews, for example, by showing Jews in a especially positive light? And do American Jews run Hollywood today?

Refutation

Firstly, it is no secret that nearly every single Hollywood studio was started by a Jewish businessman. The roster of moguls included: Carl Laemmle, who founded Universal; Adolph Zukor, one of the founders of

---

[1] Thomas Doherty, "Was Hollywood's famed censor an antisemite?," *Forward*, December 11, 2007.

[2] "Weeping Brando apologises to Jews," *Independent*, April 12, 1996.

[3] Andrew Lapin, "The origins of Dave Chappelle's antisemitic 'Jews control Hollywood' trope," *The Times of Israel*, November 17, 2022.

[4] Ryan Reed, "Gary Oldman Apologizes for Stereotyping Jews," *Rolling Stone*, June 25, 2014.

[5] Bernard Weinraub, "The Talk of Hollywood: A Stereotype of Jews in Hollywood Is Revived," *The New York Times*, November 7, 1994.

Paramount; William Fox, who lent his name to the eponymous studio; Louis B. Mayer at MGM and Harry, Albert, Sam and Jack Warner (the Warner Brothers). The only major studio without a Jewish founder was RKO. Jews are also disproportionately represented among its most famous producers, directors, screenwriters and cinematographers. The greatest and most bankable directors of the golden period included such luminaries as William Wyler, Billy Wilder, Fred Zimmerman, Ernst Lubitsch, Stanley Donen, Sidney Lumet, Woody Allen, Mel Brooks, Stephen Spielberg, Mike Nichols, Anthony Mann, Joe Mankiewicz and Stanley Kramer. In total, Jewish film directors have picked up roughly one third of the Oscars for best film. Their films were produced by an extraordinary array of Jewish cinematographers, screenwriters and art directors, to say nothing of actors and actresses. If Jews did not control Hollywood, they certainly dominated many areas of film production.

But the reason why Jews gravitated to Hollywood was not because of some co-ordinated, nefarious plot to achieve 'ethnic control' of the film industry and control the lives of gentiles. The reality is that at the start of the twentieth century, cinema was regarded as a fairly low form of entertainment, the kind that was suitable for immigrants and educated masses. It was not conceived as a legitimate art form. In the words of historian Neal Gabler, 'Big money, gentile money, viewed the movies suspiciously - economically as a fad, morally, as potential embarrassments.'[1] This meant that Jewish newcomers would not have to face competition from established parties or interests, reducing barriers to entry. It was also a form of entertainment that required little capital to get started and it appealed to the Jewish immigrant sense of entrepreneurialism. In the words of one historian, Jewish immigrants needed 'economic opportunities requiring a minimum initial investment, operating on a cash basis, and not containing a management structure of potentially hostile Gentiles.'[2] By choosing film, Jews were fulfilling their desire to be economically independent of a boss or a fixed wage. There is, however, a caveat if we are looking at Hollywood today, namely that in one sense it is not really owned by Jews. The studios and telecommunications empires that are identified as Jewish are owned and controlled by non-Jews: MCA by Mashushita, Columbia and Tri-Star by Sony, Fox by Murdoch,

[1] Neal Gabler, *An Empire of Their Own: How the Jews invented Hollywood*, (New York: Random House, 1998), 53.
[2] Lester Friedman, *The Jewish Image in American Film*, 1982, 7.

Time-Warner by stockholders and a corporate board. Nonetheless, pointing out that Jews have enjoyed a predominant influence in Hollywood, and continue to do so, is not antisemitic. But that is not where the debate ends.

Secondly, the notion that these Jews sought to subvert and ruin traditional American values is belied by the facts. Firstly, the studio heads agreed to a rigorous form of self-censorship of their films through the so-called Hays Code (the Motion Picture Production Code of 1930). From 1934 to 1968, the Code meant that Hollywood was a 'patrolled landscape' in which certain themes were prohibited, among them obscenity, white slavery, miscegenation, rape and profanity. Under Appendix 2 section VIII, no film could ridicule established religions and ministers of faith could not be cast as comic characters or villains. In terms of national feelings, the Code stipulated that 'the just rights, history, and feelings of any nation are entitled to most careful consideration and respectful treatment.'[1] That period of 34 years covers the majority of the period in which Jewish moguls held unparalleled sway over the industry, meaning that Jewish producers and filmmakers, far from having an untrammelled right to produce their own content, had to submit to industry codes and regulations.

Jewish studio heads realized that the content of film had to engage with the dreams, aspirations and values of the watching public. They had to promote the American dream and the idea that individuals could aspire to greatness, whatever their background. They engineered films that supported individual rights, family stability, Christian morality, heterosexuality, capitalism and democracy. They created a dream factory in which the celebration of traditional American values was of fundamental importance.

A case in point was *Casablanca* (1942), one of the most iconic films ever made. It centres on the world weary and somewhat cynical owner of Rick's Café, a man who refuses to take sides and acts as if he cares little for others. Yet the film shows glimpses of his romantic idealism, sentimentalism and willingness to help freedom fighters. He helps two Bulgarian refugees win a game in his casino so that they get passage to America. He allows the band in his café to play La Marseillaise, even as Vichy officers are in his bar. He even allows his former lover Ilsa to escape with her husband, a true leader of the anti-Nazi movement, putting his own feelings for her to one side for the greater good of the war effort. The film exudes a spirit of patriotism that has

---

[1] The Motion Picture Production Code of 1930, https://www.umsl.edu/~gradyf/theory/1930code.pdf, accessed March 15, 2024.

perhaps never been bettered. Behind the film was a huge layer of Jewish talent. The film was directed by Michael Curtiz, a Hungarian-American Jew who directed numerous classics of the sound and silent era, its two screenwriters were Julius and Philip Epstein, its producer was Hal Wallis, employed by Warner Brothers, and its music was composed by Max Steiner.

Some years later, RKO produced *The Best Years of Our Lives* (1946), a classic film about how servicemen attempted to re-adjust to civilian life following wartime traumas. The film captured a public mood of sympathy towards veterans and suggested that, despite their travails, men could still find love within their family structures. The production company was Samuel Goldwyn Productions and the director was the Jewish William Wyler.

Another film that celebrates American values is *Mr Smith Goes to Washington* (1939), a Columbia production about a naïve and idealistic youth leader who is picked to fill a vacancy in the US Senate and whose encounters with political corruption turn him into a hero. The film, produced by the Jewish Cohn brothers, is about a little man who saves democratic values by attacking a rotten establishment. It celebrates the triumph of decency over cynicism, the power of an individual to shape history and the importance of pursuing lost causes.

These films did not try to subvert American ideals. They tapped into them, embodied them and reinforced them in the minds of the public. Thinking as businessmen, the Jewish movie moguls, backed by a huge number of Jewish directors, scriptwriters and actors, tried to convey the American experience, but in such a way that it reflected prevailing values, tropes and ideals. In the words of one author, when the Jews held sway in Hollywood, their films were 'paeans to patriotism, faith and family.'[1] When Jewish filmmakers made movies that appeared to be more subversive and reactionary (*Midnight Cowboy, The Graduate*), they were simply reacting to a changing zeitgeist in which countercultural forces were in the ascendant and more traditional values under attack. Hollywood was conceived as a mirror of society, much as were other national cinemas.

Let us come to the fundamental charge against 'Jewish' Hollywood. If the conspiracy theories about Jewish control of Hollywood are correct, the moguls have sanitized and idealized the image of the Jew, placing parochial

[1] Don Feder, "Hollywood Jews aren't Jewish," AFA Journal, July 1996, https://afajournal.org/past-issues/1996/july/hollywood-jews-arent-jewish, accessed April 10, 2024.

Jewish concerns at the ideological heart of cinema, while cementing negative images of other minorities. On this analysis, Hollywood was full of films which reproduced malign and lazy stereotypical representations of non-Jewish minorities while granting Jews a hallowed status. Moreover, Hollywood, on this view, prioritized such sensitive subjects as antisemitism, the Holocaust and the struggle for a Jewish state and emphasized, positively, the Jewishness of its Jewish characters.

There is a little truth in this analysis. At different times in the classical era, Hollywood has traded in negative stereotypes of various minorities, fitting in with a contemporary zeitgeist that chose to marginalize and demonize various 'outsider' groups. Native American men were often portrayed as warriors, perpetuating the view that they were uncivilized and somewhat one-dimensional savages who needed to be tamed by white Americans, while their women were mysterious and highly alluring objects of sexual desire. Many films portrayed African American men as brutal thugs and criminals, and black women as sassy and attitude driven. Early Hollywood films, most notably *Gone with the Wind* (1939), used black domestic servants as a stock character. Female Latino characters have often been defined by reference to their allegedly fiery and seductive nature. Too often, filmmakers (Jews and non-Jews alike) have taken too long to challenge existing social prejudices and stereotypes, and conformed to outdated viewpoints.

But what about the depiction of Jews? A glance at Hollywood films from the Golden Age of the 1930s through to the modern age reveals a much more complex and nuanced picture than the antisemitic narrative suggests, one in which, for long periods, Jews were absent from the screen, that is as people who were visibly and identifiably Jewish, with their concerns as a national group sidelined or ignored altogether.

Prior to the Golden Age, when Jewish mogul influence was at its height, silent films often depicted Jews using crude and one-dimensional stereotypes such as the venal businessman, the rogue trader and the malevolent schemer. These films offered a racialized, essentialized portrait whereby Jews were a malevolent outsider whose trickery and scheming harmed gentile Americans. The Jewish moguls did alter this perception with a more sympathetic and nuanced understanding of their co-religionists.[1] This new understanding

[1] Nathan Abrams, *The New Jew in Film: Exploring Jewishness and Judaism in Contemporary Film*, (I.B. Tauris, 2011), 2.

culminated in *The Jazz Singer* (1927), the first feature length film with synchronized dialogue and music which heralded the arrival of the sound age. The film told the story of a cantor's son who pursued his dream of becoming a famous jazz singer despite the resistance of his father. The jazz singer abandons outdated family traditions in order to pursue a novel form of American music, using blackface as his means of expressing a hybrid identity. The film's guiding theme was assimilationist and would set the tone for the next generation of films about Jews.

In the golden age of the 1930s, few films are overly concerned with Jewish issues and there are few Jewish characters to speak of. Perhaps only one major film deals with antisemitism, the little-known production *The Yellow Ticket*, while *The House of Rothschild* is part of the biopic canon. *The Life of Emile Zola* (1937), one of the decade's most lauded dramas, does cover the Dreyfus trial but there is scant reference to the fact that the artillery officer is a Jew. Instead of overtly identifying Dreyfus's ethnic background, we merely see military officers pointing to his name on a sheet of paper with 'Jew' listed next to his rank. The film thus fails to provide the essential context for the injustice to which Zola responded.

Films that dealt with Nazi Germany also tended to sideline the persecution of Jews with the most famous, *Confessions of a Nazi Spy* (1939), focusing on the broad threat posed by Nazi tyranny to a democratic state. One of the few films to specifically tackle Nazi antisemitism was *Professor Mamlock* (1938), the story of a Jewish surgeon in Weimar Germany who is tortured by the new regime and realizes too late that Hitlerism must be resisted rather than met with apathy. But this is a Soviet film, not an American one, and Hollywood never produced anything at this time to match it. Indeed, the first explicitly anti-Nazi film made by a Hollywood studio, *The Mortal Storm* (1940), depicts Nazi Germany's horrifying descent into violence and its persecution of dissidents. But the film, which features an explicitly Jewish family and ostensibly deals with Nazi antisemitism, does not mention the word 'Jew' even once.

Other films transform Jewish characters into gentile ones. Thus, the governor's assistant Irving Pincus is reborn in the film *His Girl Friday* (1940) as Joe Pettibone. In *Golden Boy* (1939), fight promoter Roxie Gottlieb is renamed Roxie Lewis while a Jewish tailor in the play *The Gentle People* becomes an Irish one in the film *Out of the Fog* (1941). There are many more examples where the Jewish ethnicity of a character is replaced by a gentile one.

Studio heads generally did not cast a Jew in a Jewish role and, as a result, encouraged Jewish actors to Americanize their names. Thus, actors tended to shed their identifiable ethnic ancestry, among them Emmanuel Goldenberg (later Edward G Robinson), Leo Jacobi (later Lee J Cobb), Muni Wisenfreund (later Paul Muni), Julius Garfinkle (later John Garfield) and Marion Levy (later Paulette Goddard).[1] The mogul Samuel Goldman is said to have told the actor Danny Kaye that he could not hire him for a role because he looked 'too Jewish' and recommended that he get a nose job.[2]

There was naturally a context for this assimilationism, reflecting the cinema's domestic and international status, as well as the personal motives of the studio bosses. The moguls, like the current generation of American Jews, were only too well aware of the deep and lingering antisemitism within their society. As a result, they sought to hide or downplay their ethnic origins, which were often seen as a source of embarrassment, and promote themselves as patriotic Americans. They were also intoxicated by the new found possibilities of modern life and sought to embrace the country's democratic and liberal values. That meant shedding the outer garb of religious life and adopting the faith of the American dream instead.

There was also a business aspect to consider. The moguls were primarily interested in considerations of power and profit and knew that films had to have a broad appeal, rather than cater to parochial tastes, to be truly successful. The studios also had overseas markets for their films that the moguls did not want to jeopardize. They knew that films with Jewish characters, or even actors who had starred as Jews in previous roles, might be censored and banned in Germany, one of the most valuable of those markets. A film that openly avowed a Jewish theme would be financially risky.

One can see an example of this egregious censorship in the case of famous screenwriter Herman J Mankiewicz. Mankiewicz hit upon the idea of making a film to highlight the suffering of Jews in Germany and penned a play, *The Mad Dog of Europe*, about the destruction of a Jewish family under the Nazis. However, no studio was willing to touch it. It also raised the ire of Joseph Breen. He wrote:

---

[1] Paulette Goddard was of partial Jewish ancestry through her father.

[2] Giora Goodman and Tony Shaw, "Wooing a Star: Israel and Danny Kaye," University of Herts, January 27, 2021,https://uhra.herts.ac.uk/id/eprint/8883/1/Journal_of_M_Jewish_Studies_revised_article_27_Jan_2021_sent_to_journal_1_.pdf, accessed October 15, 2021.

> Because of the large number of Jews active in the motion picture industry in this country, the charge is certain to be made that the Jews, as a class, are behind an anti-Hitler picture and using the entertainment screen for their own personal propaganda purposes. The entire industry, because of this, is likely to be indicted for the action of a mere handful.[1]

Louis B Meyer specifically declared 'We have interests in Germany; I represent the picture industry here in Hollywood; we have exchanges there; we have terrific income in Germany and, as far as I am concerned, this picture will never be made.'[2] If the Jewish movie moguls had sought to capture Jewish interests at the expense of any other group, they went about it in a most hidden manner. As Friedman points out, the studio heads faced 'a cruel financial dilemma,' namely how to 'depict the momentous events taking place in Europe and still remain sufficiently apolitical so as not to jeopardize their vast foreign markets.'[3] As war approached, the last accusation that the moguls wanted to face was that they were highlighting the plight of the Jews in order to drag their country into an unpopular war, and one that would be pursued for 'parochial' interests. What resulted from this set of national and international factors was the creation of characters who were 'nationless, raceless and religionless.'[4]

The 'religion of assimilation' cemented the representation of Jews in the following decade, so much so that notions of religious particularism and ethnic difference were downplayed for the most part. War films tend to show Jews as part of a larger group of people fighting a common cause, namely the protection of their nation from barbarous foreign enemies. Jews are scarcely denigrated in those films but neither is their status and identity as Jews highlighted. Jewish solders serve patriotically, as do those from other minorities, but they are rarely mouthpieces for parochial causes and they do not highlight Jewish wartime suffering.[5]

In Lewis Milestone's *The Purple Heart* (1942), a group of American pilots are convicted in a Japanese show trial after being subjected to torture and ill treatment. Among their number is Lt. Wayne Greenbaum, a highly

[1] David Denby, "Hitler in Hollywood," *The New Yorker*, September 9. 2013.
[2] Ben Urwand, "How Hollywood Helped Hitler (Exclusive)," *The Hollywood Reporter*, July 31, 2013.
[3] Friedman, *The Jewish Image*, 79.
[4] ibid., 84.
[5] ibid., 96-7.

articulate defendant who is more than a match intellectually for his captors. Yet he is first and foremost an American patriot and the differences between the men, who come from various backgrounds, are submerged for the sake of promoting national unity.

After the war, Hollywood dealt with the problem of antisemitism in American society through two films, *Crossfire* (1947) and *Gentleman's Agreement* (1947). The latter, made against the objections of Jewish studio heads, was critically acclaimed at the time and won a raft of Academy Awards, including best picture. The film provides a surface understanding of anti-Jewish prejudice but it is a film told through gentile perspectives, rather than through the understanding of Jews themselves. As one critic writes, with antisemitism, 'contemporary social mores seemed to require a non-Jew to explain, codify, and present it.'[1]

Indeed, Jews are not only relegated to minor roles, they often say things that are unhelpful to confronting antisemitism. Professor Fred Lieberman, played by Sam Jaffe, admits that being a Jew is a matter of stubborn pride, given that neither religious nor racial considerations are of any relevance to him while Miss Havoc, a secretary to the lead character, complains that some Jews ('the kikey ones') 'give us all a bad name.' That Peck, a figure whose moral rectitude and seriousness embodied American dreams, could pass as a Jew reveals the extent to which the assimilationist ideology held sway. It was the sameness of Jews that was highlighted, not their differences, leading one critic to argue that these films 'so neutralized their Jewish characters as to deprive them of all reality.'[2] But the demand for assimilated, monocultural Jews merely reflected the changing socio-economic position of the new generation of American Jews, many of whom had become suburbanized, professionally successful and increasingly middle class.

By 1950, American Jews had lived through the era of the Holocaust and the rebirth of the state of Israel, the two most seminal developments of modern Jewish history. Yet those subjects were scarcely touched by Hollywood in the ensuing decade. *The Juggler* (1953) combined both elements in its story of a Holocaust survivor, played by Kirk Douglas, who resettles in Israel after the war and adjusts to life despite the psychological scars of his wartime experience. It stands out for its depiction of the Jewish state as a restorative

---

[1] Saul Austerlitz, "When Hollywood Was Scared To Depict Anti-Semitism, It Made 'Gentleman's Agreement,'" *Tablet Magazine*, May 15, 2014.
[2] Abrams, *The New Jew*, 5.

haven and a sanctuary for lost Jews. But if Hollywood Jews wanted to promote Jewish interests as the antisemites claim, the studios would have been pumping out films on both subjects. In fact, films with the most memorable screen Jews rarely reflect on their religious identities. This is especially true of Biblical epics like *Samson and Delilah* (1953), *The Ten Commandments* (1956) and *Ben Hur* (1959), all of which feature rugged, masculine gentile actors in Jewish parts. The films scarcely reference the religious heritage of the lead figures, contradicting the idea that Jewish moguls sought to enhance the religious narratives of their brethren, as opposed to bringing spectacular entertainment to the public.

One explanation for Hollywood's reticence was that the moguls were concerned at the accusation that they were promoting left wing, 'un-American' causes through their films. At the height of the second Red Scare, the House un–American Activities Committee (HUAC) investigated alleged Communist activity in the film industry. A number of friendly actors appeared before the committee, among them Gary Cooper and Ronald Reagan, with their testimony forcing others to be subpoenaed. When the 'Hollywood Ten' refused to answer the committee's questions, they were charged with contempt and jailed. The moguls feared being tarnished as communists, sensing that in the febrile Cold War atmosphere, such a charge would turn American public opinion against them. After all, many of those subpoenaed were Jewish and thus it was seen as essential to downplay the Jewishness of screen characters so as to avoid the antisemitic charge that Hollywood was promoting Jewish interests over American ones. Hollywood wanted a safe product that did not compromise its status in the eyes of HUAC and other conspiracy addled organizations, and which did not delve into complex areas of debate and controversy.

It was the 1960s that brought Jews to life on Hollywood's screens in a period marked by maturing ethnic consciousness. The unifying identity symbolized by the concept of the Great Melting Pot (though it excluded many) gave way to an intense individualism which prized markers of ethnic, cultural and religious identity. Some films had characters whose ethnically Jewish features were openly celebrated, among them *Funny Girl* (1968) and *Hello Dolly* (1969). *Funny Girl* is a biopic of the legendary comedienne Fannie Brice, which turned debut performer Barbara Streisand into a global star. The character's accent, movements and mannerisms are an exuberant evocation of Brice's Jewishness, making little effort to 'normalize' the star. *The*

Pawnbroker (1965) was perhaps the first film to properly confront the horrors of the Holocaust, though it was made some twenty years after the liberation of the death camps. Crucially, this decade saw two major films about the rebirth of Israel, namely *Exodus* (1960) and *Cast a Giant Shadow* (1966). *Exodus* is justly remembered for evoking the pioneering spirit of Israel's founding generation, a generation that lived through and suffered from the barbarities of Hitler's merciless persecution. It also features one of the most stirring soundtracks of any film from that era. Yet *Exodus* and *Cast a Giant Shadow* feature Jews who have assimilated into solider stereotypes, shedding their ancestry so that they could adapt to modernity. That meant fair physical features, rugged masculinity, a traditional family background and intense patriotism. These Jews dissolved into intensely bland figures whose ethnic and religious markers largely disappeared to sanitize them for an American audience.

It is not until the 1970s that Jewish American life takes centre stage with the films of Woody Allen and Paul Mazursky. Woody Allen's films deal with many of the central features of modern American Jewish life. They present a cast of urban Jews whose waywardness and neuroticism sets them apart from wider society. These are the anxiety ridden little men at odds with their environment whose physical attributes mark them out as schlemiels, that is, Jewish losers who are forever in awe of women and who are all too aware of their own shortcomings. They are often highly intellectual and bookish but physically scrawny, afraid to confront an aggressor, an attribute that plays to the stereotype of Jewish weakness and cowardice. Naturally, these self-deprecating portraits are heavily influenced by generations of Jewish humour and are not intended to portray Jews in a negative light. Indeed, the characters are often warm, genial and positive.[1]

The most famous 'Jewish' film of the period was *Fiddler on the Roof* (1971), based on the short stories by Sholem Aleichem about Tevye the Milkman and his family in Ukraine. It is a beautiful exploration of Jewish traditions, and the power those traditions have to shape the destinies of a community. In the film, Tevye sings a lyrical melody about tradition and tries to instil its importance in his five daughters, some of whom are of marrying age. However, three of his daughters, Tzeitzel, Hodel, and Chava, find the 'traditional' idea of a matchmaker less enticing than their father and find

[1] Friedman, 283.

themselves guided more by their heart than their father's wishes. Tzeitel wishes to marry a childhood friend, Motel the tailor, and little cares that he is neither rich nor well educated. Hodel falls in love with a radical Jewish student, Perchik, who revels in his defiance of traditions and the rulings of religious authority while Chava does the unthinkable by falling for a young Christian man, Fyedka. Tevye is forced to adjust his opinions about tradition, accepting the decisions made by two of his daughters but firmly drawing the line at intermarriage. Thus, he gives his blessing to the marriages of the first two daughters but shuns Chava and declares that she is 'dead' to him. While offering a sympathetic portrayal of Tevye, the film's guiding message is the triumph of love over tradition, that cleaving to outdated (and un-American) values is unacceptable in the modern age. It is arguably yet another message about assimilation.

One might have thought that films about the Holocaust, which reached a mass audience from the 1980s onwards, would be an antidote to negative portrayals of Jews. But even here, things are hardly clear cut. Though one cannot generalize about an entire sub-genre, it is clear that some noted films about Nazi persecution simply reinforce long standing tropes of Jewish passivity and meekness. The hero of *Schindler's List*, Hollywood's most famous Holocaust film, is a non-Jew who was transformed from a Nazi sympathizer to a righteous gentile who saved Jewish lives. The film's Jews play an assigned role as an undifferentiated and monolithic collection of undeserved victims whose lives are dependent on the behaviour of gentiles. However, other films refuse to assign Jews the role of pure victim. Productions like *Escape from Sobibor* (1987), *The Pianist* (2002) and *Defiance* (2008) feature Jewish protagonists who exercise their autonomy to resist the Nazis and defy the oppression to which they have been subjected. They do not depend on gentiles for their rescue.

Other films problematize the nature of Jewish victimhood, suggesting that the guilt of the accused is less clear cut than one might imagine. Thus, *The Reader* (2008) draws a contrast in the lives of a well to do Holocaust survivor, Ilana Mather, and the aging SS guard Hanna Schmitz. The latter has lived a life of despair, loneliness and poverty, having spent many years in prison for a crime that she falsely confessed to masterminding. The film encourages the audience to view Hanna as a victim and to criticize Ilana for refusing to forgive her tormentor after so many years. A similar refusal to draw moral distinctions between Jews and Germans resonates in *The Boy with the Striped*

Pyjamas (2008). In this British war film, a young German child Bruno, the son of a Nazi commandant, is drawn towards a Jewish child who is currently languishing in a concentration camp. They develop a friendship and Bruno, innocently failing to grasp the threat to his friend, joins him in the camp, with both wearing the same striped uniform. As they suffer a common fate inside a gas chamber, the camera focuses on Bruno's grieving parents, suggesting that both Jewish and gentile children are equally victims in the Holocaust.

While many films feature positive portrayals of Jews, Hollywood has also not shied away from depicting Jewish characters in a negative light. One classic example from the 1990s was *Glengarry Glen Ross* (1992), a film with a Jewish producer and screenwriter, about two days in the life of four American property salesmen. The salesmen are ruthless rip off artists in a cut-throat world who peddle worthless real estate to clients. But now they are threatened with unemployment unless they convert a series of leads into sales, leading them to devise desperate measures to ensure their survival. The film makes no attempt to hide their willingness to exploit others, and be exploited, as they cheat, lie and steal to conclude these sales and preserve their livelihoods. At least one of these morally eviscerated characters (Shelley Levene) is Jewish. Other memorable Jews of dubious morals include the gun-toting and somewhat disturbed Vietnam veteran Walter Sobchak in *The Big Lebowski* (1998), a film made by the Jewish Coen brothers, Walt 'Teach' Cole in *American Buffalo* (1996) and Harry Block in *Deconstructing Harry* (1997). Special mention can also be made of the cavalcade of physically unattractive, socially awkward and professionally unsuccessful Jews in the films of Judd Apatow. These include Cal in *The Forty Old Year Virgin* (2005) and Ben Stone in *Knocked Up* (2007), both played by the somewhat clunky Seth Rogen.

What is clear from this brief survey of Hollywood's representation of Jews is that the period in which Jews held sway most decisively (1930s to 1950s) was one in which the studios were the least fixated on dealing with Jewish themes and subjects. Jews were a hidden minority whose ethnic features were never highlighted on film, nor were issues central to the Jewish experience depicted on celluloid. Israel and the Holocaust received little attention in the 1940s and 1950s and it was only in the following decade, with its willingness to explore issues of ethnic identification and difference, that films started to address them. The reason was simple: the Jewish movie moguls were businessmen, attentive to the shifting climate of national and international opinion, and highly distanced from their ethnic and religious origins. They thought as movie entrepreneurs, not as Jews.

6. The Jews have invented the Holocaust

Charge

One of the most insidious lies spread by conspiratorial antisemites is Holocaust denial. Holocaust denialists spread the belief that the systematic genocide of six million Jews during the Second World War by the Nazis and their collaborationist allies was a myth or fabrication promoted by world Jewry for its own sinister ends. They charge Jews with inventing the story of their own persecution and using their 'lies' to manipulate governments into accepting blame for events that never happened. At its core, it is a conspiracy theory which alleges that, due to Jewish control of the press, academia and government, the world has become seduced by a myth of genocide that helps promote Jewish interests, enable Israel's persecution of Palestinians and induce a false sense of guilt among western nations. Not all Holocaust deniers state that 'no Jews' were killed by the Nazis and their allies. Some try to downgrade the number of Jews who were slaughtered, perhaps down to less than a million. They too distort and twist historical facts to suit their purposes and should be called deniers, rather than revisionists.

Holocaust denial started to spread in academic and pseudo-scholarly circles from the 1970s onwards with institutions such as the Institute for Historical Review (the IHR). The IHR was co-founded in 1978 by Willis Carto, a far right American nativist and populist who spread virulent antisemitic conspiracy theories and advocated for white supremacy. Described as 'a reclusive behind-the-scenes wizard of the far-right fringe of American politics'[1], Carto headed the organization Liberty Lobby, which had a mailing list of 400,000 at one point, and founded *Noontide Press,* a publishing house which promoted numerous antisemitic works, including Ford's *The International Jew*. But the IHR, with its associated Journal of Historical Review, was perhaps his most influential contribution to Holocaust denial. At the IHR's first conference, they offered $50,000 for verifiable 'proof that gas chambers for the purpose of killing human beings existed at or in Auschwitz.' A Czech born Auschwitz survivor, Mel Mermelstein (1926-

[1] Douglas Martin, "Willis Carto, Far-Right Figure and Holocaust Denier, Dies at 89," *The New York Times*, November 2, 2015.5.

2022), proceeded to provide such proof in the form of a notarized account of his experiences at the death camp in 1944, only to be turned down by the IHR for providing insufficient proof. After lengthy litigation, the IHR were ordered to pay him $90,000 and write a letter of apology, both of which he received.

The 1970s also saw the publication of *The Hoax of the Twentieth Century: The Case Against the Presumed Extermination of European Jewry* (1975) by Arthur Butz (1933-), an associate professor of electrical engineering at Northwestern University. Butz, a member of the editorial board of the Journal of Historical Review, argued that there was no evidence of gas chambers in the death camps and that the notion that six million Jews were killed in the Holocaust was a fabrication. He claimed that Zyklon B, the deadly gas used at Auschwitz and other camps, was an 'insecticide' rather than a deadly weapon used to kill Jews; dismissed the gas chambers as a hoax; stated that deaths at Belsen were because of a 'typhus epidemic' and claimed that evidence for an extermination program at other death camps was 'fairly close to zero.'[1]

Another figure who questioned the existence of gas chambers was Ernst Zundel (1939-2017), a Canadian neo-Nazi pamphleteer who published Holocaust denial literature and campaigned to ban films about the Holocaust. In 1974, he published *Did Six Million Really Die?,* a pamphlet which employed various pseudo-scholarly arguments to counter the accepted death toll in the Holocaust. The Supreme Court of Canada brought a prosecution against Zundel and as part of his legal defence, the publisher commissioned a report from an American technician, Fred Leuchter. The so called Leuchter Report was an attempt to investigate whether Jews had been gassed at the death camps in Poland, specifically focusing on Auschwitz. He argued that the absence of the pigment Prussian blue meant that the death camps could not have been used to gas people, findings that were deemed unreliable by Polish forensic scientists. They pointed out that Prussian blue was not an unconditional outcome of people being exposed to cyanide.

For many years, British writer David Irving claimed that he was not a Holocaust denier, even filing a libel suit against Deborah Lipstadt and

[1] Arthur Butz, *Hoax of the Twentieth Century: The Case Against the Presumed Extermination of European Jewry* (Uckfield: Historical Review Press, 1975), 215.

Penguin Books for publishing the British edition of Lipstadt's *Denying the Holocaust*. Lipstadt had called Irving a Holocaust denier, falsifier and bigot, and claimed that he manipulated and distorted real documents. At the libel trial, the judge, in his summing up, concluded that 'no objective, fair-minded historian would have serious cause to doubt that there were gas chambers at Auschwitz and that they were operated on a substantial scale to kill hundreds of thousands of Jews,' further, that 'Irving's denials of these propositions were contrary to the evidence.'[1]

Another figure associated with the IHR and its Journal was British born French academic Robert Faurisson (1929-2018). After Faurisson publicly questioned the authenticity of Anne Frank's dairy, he wrote an article in *Le Monde* in which he debated whether gas chambers existed during the Holocaust. He was later fined by a French court for declaring: 'Hitler never ordered nor permitted that anyone be killed by reason of his race or religion' and adding that the Holocaust was a 'lie, which is essentially of Zionist origin,' which had 'permitted a gigantic politico-financial fraud of which the State of Israel is the principal beneficiary.' After several further convictions and fines, Faurisson was branded by a French court as a 'professional liar' and a 'falsifier of history.'[2]

Today, many Holocaust denial books are freely available in parts of the Middle East, and nations like Iran sponsor denial conferences that are attended by devotees from around the world. Holocaust denial is far from a fringe belief held only by lunatics or the extreme right. A global poll taken by the Anti-Defamation League in 2014 found that among those who had heard of the Holocaust, nearly one third (32%) believed that it was either a myth or had been greatly exaggerated. The countries surveyed included nine of the ten most populous countries on earth.[3]

It is also alarming that so many younger people claim never to have heard of the Holocaust. According to a survey commissioned by the Conference on Jewish Material Claims Against Germany, roughly half of all Britons did not know that 6 million Jews were murdered during the Holocaust, and less than a quarter thought that 2 million Jews or fewer were killed. The survey did find

---

[1] *Irving v Lipstadt* (2000), Paragraph 13.98.

[2] Paul Berman, "The Grand Theorist of Holocaust Denial, Robert Faurisson," *Tablet Magazine*, April 26, 2018.

[3] "46% of Adults Worldwide Hold Significant Antisemitic Beliefs, ADL Poll Finds," *ADL*, January 14, 2025.

that nearly 90% had heard about the Holocaust.[1] Meanwhile, the *U.S. Millennial Holocaust Knowledge and Awareness Survey,* the first-ever 50-state survey on Holocaust knowledge among Millennials and Gen Z, found truly shocking levels of ignorance and conspiracism among young Americans. Some 63 percent of all national survey respondents did not know that six million Jews were murdered, 36 percent thought that 'two million or fewer Jews' were killed during the Holocaust and staggeringly, nearly half of all respondents could not name a single concentration camp from the war. Another disturbing finding was that 11 percent of U.S. Millennial and Gen Z respondents believed that Jews had caused the Holocaust.[2] In an age of conspiracy theories, anti-establishment thinking and virulent Jew hatred, it is not hard to see why Holocaust denial has caught on among certain sections of the population, especially in the Middle East.

Refutation

For starters, the Holocaust is one of the most well documented crimes of the modern world. The treasure trove of evidence, which includes photographs and video footage of Nazi atrocities carried out against Jews, footage of the liberation of death camps clearly showing the extent of the genocidal campaign against Jews, eye witness testimonies to shootings and beatings, documents of conferences that planned the extermination, physical evidence from occupied territories and diaries of the perpetrators, was presented first at the Nuremberg trials, which were held from 1945 onwards. Far from being a simple case of victor's justice, as it is sometimes portrayed, Nuremberg attempted to prove the guilt of the accused by using their own words and documents.

The Allied armies captured millions of items of evidence and presented tens of thousands of these at the trials. These included records from the German Foreign Office, records kept by Heinrich Himmler, the Chief of the police, as well as those from the German Army High Command. The tribunals were also presented with reports from the Einsatzgruppen, the special action

---

[1] "The First-Ever 8-Country Holocaust Knowledge And Awareness Index Shows Growing Gap In Knowledge About The Holocaust, Especially In Young Adults," Claims Conference, https://www.claimscon.org/country-survey, accessed August1, 2024.

[2] "First Ever 50 State Survey on Holocaust Knowledge of American Millennials and Gen Z Reveals Shocking Results," Claims Conference, https://www.claimscon.org/millennial-study, accessed August 9, 2024.

squads that were assigned to butcher Jews *en masse* in the occupied Soviet Union, the Stroop report which documented the suppression of the Warsaw Ghetto uprising and the minutes of the Wannsee conference of 1942 in which plans for the 'Final Solution' were drawn up. The defendants never doubted the authenticity of the documents but instead, claimed that they had no responsibility for what was done by their nation's leaders. Some Nazi leaders confessed to their crimes, among them Rudolf Hoss, who testified that one million Jews had been gassed at Auschwitz. While the deniers usually claim that such figures were tortured to confess to their crimes, they provide no evidence to this effect. The demographics of European Jewry provide a layer of depth to prove that the genocide did indeed occur. The figures of those killed vary from 5.7 to over 6 million Jews and include more than three million in Poland, more than two million in the USSR and over a quarter of a million in Romania. Again, the SS kept meticulous records of those who were deported, simply destroying the credibility of the case for Holocaust denial.

Some claim that the perceived lack of Jewish resistance is proof that the Holocaust did not occur. They argue that if the Jews knew of the mass extermination facilities, they would never have willingly got on deportation trains and their failure to resist is proof that they knew they were in no danger. Note first that this contradicts the antisemitic assertion that Jews are weak, cowardly and individualistic. Secondly, it is certain that many Jews did not know of the fate that lay in store for them or, if they did, that they were too powerless to resist it. Thirdly, we know that Jews did resist the Nazi war machine whenever they could. There were multiple revolts in the death camps (Auschwitz, Sobibor, Treblinka), uprisings in ghettos and Jewish partisan activity across Europe.

Others argue that the absence of a written document signed by Hitler ordering the extermination of 6 million Jews somehow proves that this genocide could not have occurred. The absence of a written document is not in itself surprising. The Nazi regime had a well-documented history of secrecy, cover ups and deception, especially in regard to their infamous crimes. Thus, when it became public knowledge that the Nazis had implemented a plan (T4) for involuntary euthanasia, there was an outcry, forcing the program to be cancelled, at least in public. It made Hitler wary of signing formal documents that admitted to heinous state policies, especially the Holocaust. That is why Himmler, in 1943, said of the Holocaust that 'We will never speak of it publicly…I mean the evacuation of the Jews, the extermination of the Jewish race.' He went on to say that the 'elimination of the Jews' was 'a page of glory in our history which has never been written and is never to be written.' Orders to carry out mass murder were more likely to have been transmitted orally, a point that is supported by statements made by Nazi leaders.

Hoss wrote that in the summer of 1941, he was summoned to Himmler's offices where he was told: 'The Fuhrer has ordered that the Jewish question be solved once and for all and that we, the SS, are to implement that order.'[1] The diary entries of Joseph Goebbels also indicate that in their regular conversations, Hitler was determined to implement a plan to eradicate European Jews. Here is one such entry:

> 14 February 1942: The Führer once again expressed his determination to clean up the Jews in Europe pitilessly. There must be no squeamish sentimentalism about it. The Jews have deserved the catastrophe that has now overtaken them. Their destruction will go hand in hand with the destruction of our enemies. We must hasten this process with cold ruthlessness.[2]

One might also ask the following question: If the Holocaust was a Jewish lie, what would that involve? It would require a grand plan in which thousands upon thousands of forged documents were planted that purported to speak of a genocide. The Jews would have had to concoct a vast array of documents which purported to give evidence of the atrocity. First and foremost, this would have to include the speeches of Hitler himself, such as his chilling call to exterminate the Jews of Europe in 1939.[3] They would have had to forge all the evidence of the 1942 Wannsee conference at which the final solution was decided. They would have had to forge the chilling diaries of key players like Himmler and Goebbels, both of which provide important evidence about the planning and implementation of the Holocaust. Indeed, it is a matter of luck that Goebbels' diaries were even found, given that they were about to be sold as 7,000 pages of scrap paper before being discovered. Such sloppiness is hard

---

[1] Source: Documents on the Holocaust, Selected Sources on the Destruction of the Jews of Germany and Austria, Poland and the Soviet Union, Yad Vashem, Jerusalem, 1981, Document no.164. pp.350-353.

[2] Joseph Goebbels' Diaries: Excerpts, 1942-43 - Part 2 of 2, The Nizkor Project, https://www.nizkor.org/joseph-goebbels-diaries-excerpts-1942-43-part-2-of-2, accessed April 7, 2025.

[3] Extract from the Speech by Adolf Hitler to the Reichstag: 30 January 1939.

to explain when one considers the magnitude of what is inside. For example, on February 14, 1942, he wrote that 'the Fuhrer once again expressed his determination to clean up the Jews in Europe pitilessly.' He added that 'The Jews have deserved the catastrophe that has now overtaken them' and that 'Their destruction will go hand in hand with the destruction of our enemies.' He adds on March 27, 1942 that 'about 60 per cent of them (Jews) will have to be liquidated.' Why would such damning evidence nearly be lost to history?[1]

Moreover, if deniers really claim that Jews forged documents of Nazi complicity, it remains bizarre that they overlooked the most important one of all, namely a confession from Hitler himself that he had ordered the destruction of the Jews. To date, no such document has ever been found, making it easy for deniers to claim that Hitler had no knowledge that any Jews were being killed. If the Jews were such great master forgers, able to duplicate with surgical exactness the handwriting of Nazi leaders that they had never met, why could they not forge a Hitler document that would provide final confirmation that the Fuhrer ordered the extermination?

If the Holocaust was a Jewish lie, then the Jews would have had to get a vast number of people, alleged survivors, to tell a similar atrocity story to try to convince the world that non-existent crimes had taken place. Given that Jews lived thousands of miles apart and were scattered across great stretches of Europe, given too that they spoke a variety of languages, it would be a tall order indeed to reach such a vast multitude in an effort to ensure that a uniform lie was created. Moreover, they would have to hope that none of the countless thousands of the survivors who were willing accomplices to this lie would dare to speak out and reveal the scale of this deception.

But this is only to scratch the surface of what such a gigantic Jewish hoax would look like. One of the most salient facts about the Holocaust is the testimonies of the *perpetrators*, not just the victims. Hundreds of key Nazi figures confessed to carrying out their unspeakable crimes against the Jewish people. Among those who did were Hans Frank, Hitler's personal lawyer and the Gauleiter of Poland during the Second World War. In his final confession he declared:

> *I myself have never installed an extermination camp for Jews, or promoted the existence of such camps; but if Adolf Hitler personally has*

[1] Joseph Goebbels' Diaries: Excerpts, 1942-43 - Part 2 of 2 - Nizkor.

laid that dreadful responsibility on his people, then it is mine too, for we have fought against Jewry for years; and we have indulged in the most terrible utterances.[1]

Quite how the Jews were able to extract such confessions is not made clear by the deniers. One cannot forget that in the interrogations of leading Nazis, not one claimed that the Holocaust did not occur, not one that it was a fabrication by the Jews themselves designed to smear or demean their beloved Germany. Given that their lives were at stake, it remains highly odd that Nazi leaders would not resort to such a defence. The deniers will retort that the Jews were central to the Allied interrogations and that they extracted forced confessions from the Nazi leaders. What undermines that argument is that such confessions have continued to be made in the decades since the Holocaust. In the 1980s, Nazis such as Franz Suchomel and the medical doctor, Dr. Hans Münch, confessed that they were present when the Nazis' factories of death were operating. One wonders why they were prepared to confess to supposedly non-existent crimes decades after the Nuremberg tribunal when they had no need to.

The Holocaust is also a terrible stain on Germany's reputation as a civilized state. In today's world, there is no worse crime than genocide and those who perpetrate it are pariahs among the nations. If the deniers are right, then a truly Orwellian situation exists whereby the modern German state confesses its guilt to a series of heinous crimes without parallel that it knows it has not committed. A sovereign state that cared for its historical integrity would do the utmost to challenge such lies and defamations rather than subject itself to enduring calumny. It is even more strange that far right groups in modern Germany, such as the AFD, do not challenge the idea that the Holocaust happened, instead claiming that it should not be prioritized in the nation's historical memory. One wonders if the Jewish fabricators have tortured the German far right too.

Of course, one finds a similar pattern of behaviour among most European states. In recent decades, there have been an endless stream of apologies from governments across the Continent, lamenting the deportation of Jews at the hands of their nationals. Such apologies are accompanied by the creation of artefacts of historical memory, including museums, memorials and

[1]Michael R Marrus, "The Holocaust at Nuremberg," Shoah Resource Centre, https://wwv.yadvashem.org/odot_pdf/microsoft%20word%20-%203220.pdf, accessed May 9. 2025.

exhibitions dedicated to the Jewish dead. One has to wonder why so many governments have expended so much energy on remembering crimes that they 'know' did not occur and thus for which they do not bear responsibility. The deniers have no answer to this.

Deniers argue that Jews deceive and manipulate others to believe their lies. But if Jews had such fiendish powers, one wonders why they spectacularly failed to persuade pre-war politicians to abandon their policies of appeasement towards Nazi Germany and the Arab world. After all, the White Paper of 1939 left millions of European Jews to their fate by ensuring that the number of immigrants to Palestine would be severely limited just at the moment when a new destination out of the continent was needed. The Evian conference of 1938 similarly witnessed an abject display by dozens of nations that were keen to keep unwanted Jews out of their countries. Why did the arch manipulators and controllers within world Jewry not intervene to produce a better result for their beleaguered brethren? Could they not have forged documents to sway the opinion of policymakers, just as the deniers claim that Jews forged documents after the war to manipulate world opinion. Moreover, the fanciful nature of the deniers' claims falls apart when one observes the widespread belief in Holocaust denial. If the Jews really did control the organs of the global media, a necessary component of spreading the Holocaust idea, why is it that such vast multitudes across the globe still believe either that it did not happen or that it has been hugely exaggerated. Surely the 'manipulative' and 'controlling' Jews would ensure that every organ of society was dedicated to fostering the 'myth' of genocide. Like so many other forms of antisemitism, Holocaust denial founders, not just on its aversion to facts and truth, but on its outright denial of logic. When tested against both the facts and reason, it is exposed as absurd nonsense.

Holocaust distortion is slightly different to Holocaust denial but no less serious. It can take a number of forms, including minimising the number of those killed, blaming the Jews for their own destruction, and exaggerating the collaboration between Jews and Nazis before the war.

7. The notion of Jewish collaboration with the Nazis

Charge

Some forms of Holocaust denial are more subtle. A variation of the belief that the Holocaust was a Jewish or Zionist concocted fairy tale is the idea that, though it happened, it was the Zionists who bear a great deal of responsibility for the Jewish tragedy. The claim so often made is that the prewar Zionist movement collaborated with the Nazis in a bid to gain control of Palestine, effectively condemning fellow Jews to slaughter at the Nazis' hands. A number of figures have made this argument, ranging from PA President Mahmoud Abbas, the Trotskyist historian Leni Brenner and former London Mayor, Ken Livingstone.

In April 2016, Livingstone gave an interview in which he defended a Labour MP, Naz Shah, who had been suspended for vitriolic anti-Israeli sentiments. He went on to declare: 'When Hitler won his election in 1932, his policy then was that Jews should be moved to Israel. He was supporting Zionism before he went mad and ended up killing six million Jews.'[1] He doubled down on these comments as the furore over his interview grew worse. In the *Independent*, Livingstone said: 'His (Hitler) policy was originally to send all of Germany's Jews to Israel and there were private meetings between the Zionist movement and Hitler's government which were kept confidential, they only became apparent after the war, when they were having a dialogue to do this.'[2] He then tried to exonerate himself from the charge of antisemitism by claiming: 'Someone who is antisemitic isn't just hostile to the Jews living in Israel, they're hostile to their neighbour in Golders Green, or the neighbour in Stoke Newington.'[3]

The basis for Livingstone's claim was the well documented Ha'avara agreement between the Palestinian Zionist movement and Nazi Germany in 1933. This agreement allowed Jews to transfer roughly half of their wealth in the form of German goods if they immigrated to Palestine. For Livingstone as for others, this alleged collaboration between Zionism and Hitlerism was proof that the movement for Jewish liberation was discredited, tarnished by association with the worst regime in modern history.

Refutation

There are many distortions and untruths in Livingstone's views, some of which can be traced back to the distortions found in Brenner's book *Zionism*

---

[1] "Ken Livingstone stands by Hitler comments," *BBC News*, April 30, 2016.

[2] Paul Bogdanor, "An Antisemitic Hoax: Lenni Brenner on Zionist 'Collaboration' With the Nazis," *Fathom*, Summer 2016.

[3] Paul Bogdanor, "Ken Livingstone and the myth of Zionist 'collaboration' with the Nazis," *The Tower*, April 23, 2017.

in the Age of Dictators. For starters, there was no Israel for Hitler to send Jews to in 1932, merely the British Mandate of Palestine. It is also wrong to state that Hitler's policy was to send Jews to mandatory Palestine when he came to power. Initially, the regime's aim was to expel Jews from the Reich, regardless of the country they fled to. As Richard Evans says, the 'principal aim of the Nazis in those years was to drive the Jews out of Germany and preferably out of Europe.'[1]

The Nazis agreed to this deal, not primarily because of any conviction in the rightness or viability of the Zionist movement, but because it presented a golden opportunity to render Germany *Judenrein*.[2] Palestine was merely the convenient vehicle for achieving the Nazis' demented dreams of German racial purity rather than a means by which Nazi and Zionist ideologies became congruent. In addition, it held economic benefits because it enabled the expansion of German export markets and helped relieve the strain on Germany's strained foreign currency reserves.[3]

The significance of the agreement for Jewish emigration should not also be overestimated. Between 1933 and 1938, 39,839 German Jews left for Palestine, though this figure was dwarfed by the 80,653 Polish Jews who came in the same period.[4] Palestine was a chosen destination simply because other countries, including the USA, had chosen to limit the number of Jewish entrants who could emigrate. Nor was it true that the Ha'avara agreement was secret. It engendered considerable public debate within the Zionist movement and while one can retrospectively criticize those who signed it for lamentable judgment, their motives had nothing to do with ideological sympathy for Nazism and everything to do with seeking to rescue German Jewry.

Livingstone is completely wrong to say that Hitler supported Zionism, even if there was a short period in which pragmatism dictated that the Nazis work with the Zionist movement. As Jeffrey Herf points out, 'Hitler despised Zionism,' seeing in Jewish Palestine 'part of the broader international

---

[1] Richard Evans, *The Third Reich in Power, 1933 - 1939: How the Nazis Won Over the Hearts and Minds of a Nation*, (New York: Penguin, 2005), 557.

[2] Bogdanor, An Antisemitic Hoax. An Antisemitic Hoax: Lenni Brenner on Zionist 'Collaboration' With the Nazis" (2016). www.academia.edu/26091910/An_Antisemitic_Hoax_Lenni_Brenner_on_Zionist_Collaboration_With_the_Nazis

[3] Yehuda Bauer, *Jews For Sale: Nazi-Jewish Negotiations, 1933-1945* (New Haven: Yale University Press, 1994), 10-12.

[4] Samuel Miner, "Planning the Holocaust in the Middle East: Nazi Designs to Bomb Jewish Cities in Palestine," *Jewish Political Studies Review*, vol. 27, no. 3/4, 2016, pp. 7–33. *JSTOR*, http://www.jstor.org/stable/44510568.

conspiracy which his fevered imagination presented as a dire threat to Germany.'[1] The project to build a Jewish national home clearly fed the fanatical Nazi belief that there was an international Jewish conspiracy allegedly determined to prevent the German Volk from achieving its destiny. This view is supported by comments made by German Foreign Minister Konstantin von Neurath when he penned a circular to German diplomatic offices in response to Lord Peel's partition proposal in Palestine. In the circular von Neurath wrote:

> The formation of a Jewish state or a Jewish-led political structure under British mandate is not in Germany's interest, since a Palestinian state would not absorb world Jewry but would create an additional position of power [power base] under international law for international Jewry, somewhat like the Vatican State for political Catholicism or Moscow for the Comintern.[2]

It is also a reason why the Ha'avara agreement was terminated in 1937, given Nazi fears that Palestine was becoming a burgeoning centre of Jewish life.

Further proof of the Nazis' demented hatred for the Zionist project comes from observing that, had Rommel overrrun the Allied positions in North Africa and captured Egypt, an Einsatzgruppe would have been activated in Palestine with the express intention of murdering its Jewish inhabitants. Instead, Rommel suffered defeat at the Second Battle of El Alamein and the Allied landing in French North Africa prevented that plan from being put into action. In 1943, the Luftwaffe also considered a proposal to bomb Tel Aviv and Jerusalem on the anniversary of the Balfour Declaration, but it was rejected on logistical grounds. In sum, the Nazis saw no distinction between Zionists and non-Zionist Jews. In their genocidal mindset, Jews were Jews regardless of their political affiliation so any temporary accommodation with the group was based on historical expediency and short-term advantage. Attempts to blacken Zionism by over egging a short term deal with Hitler should be seen as an egregious misuse of history.

---

[1] Jeffrey Herf, "Hitler and the Nazis' Anti-Zionism," *The Middle East Forum*, May 5, 2016.
[2] Samuel Milner. Planning the Holocaust in the Middle East: Nazi Designs to Bomb Jewish Cities in Palestine': The Jewish Political Studies Review, 27, 3-4 (2016). 2016, Jewish Political Studies Review.

8. Jews are trying to engineer the genocide of white people

Charge

In August 2017, hundreds of white nationalist protestors turned out for a 'Unite the Right' rally in Charlottesville, Virginia. The event was organized by a 'pro white' alt right activist and member of the Proud Boys, Jason Kessler, to protest the planned removal of a statue of confederate general Robert Lee. White supremacist sympathizers, including the Ku Klux Klan, marched and brawled and one such supporter, James Alex Fields Jr, drove a car into protestors, killing one person (Heather Heyer) and injuring others. At the rally, various alt-right groups chanted 'Jews will not replace us' and 'White lives matter.'[1] The former chant, misinterpreted at the time as an allegation that Jews were trying to replace white people in their communities, was a fundamental expression of 'the Great Replacement Theory.'

The theory states that white people are being gradually replaced by immigrants, Muslims and other people of colour in a deliberate process of engineering by sinister forces, often identified as Jews. French theorist Renaud Camus popularized the term in his 2011 book *Le Grand Remplacement*. He argued that native white European populations were being replaced in their countries by an influx of non-white, largely Muslim immigrants coming from Africa and the Middle East. He believed that the comparatively higher birth rates of Muslims compared to white Europeans were a direct threat to the demographic composition of those countries.[2] Some decades earlier, his co-patriot René Binet (1913–1957), had railed against the 'colonization of Europe' by 'negroes' and 'Mongols' and called for the 'union of former communist resistance fighters and the Waffen-SS in order to build 'the European nation.' Binet was in doubt who was responsible for the race problem confronting the Continent. In one piece he wrote: 'We accuse the Zionists and anti-racists of the crime of genocide because they claim to be

---

[1] Adam Gabbatt, "'Jews will not replace us': Vice film lays bare horror of neo-Nazis in America," *The Guardian*, August 16, 2017.

[2] Lara Bullens, "How France's 'great replacement' theory conquered the global far right," *France 24*, August 11, 2021.

imposing on us a crossbreeding that would be the death and destruction of our race and civilization.'[1]

The phrase 'white genocide' was bandied about by neo-Nazi groups in the decades after the war and came into prominence with the publication of *The Turner Diaries* (1978) by William Luther Pierce. The novel consists of the fictional diaries of an Earl Turner, which purport to cover a revolution by white supremacist group *The Organization* against *The System*, a network of political, media and social institutions which are run by Jews. The book sets forward the argument for the violent overthrow of democratic governments and encourages antisemitic and anti-black worldview. Also influential are the writings of David Lane, a member of a terrorist organization *The Order*. The concluding words of his White Genocide Manifesto have proved immensely influential: 'We must secure the existence of our people and a future for white children.'[2] Lane spoke of a 'Zionist conspiracy to…exterminate the white race,' as well as the threat posed by 'the unnatural act of homosexuality, and 'miscegenation' to the future of white populations.

The notion of white genocide has become a rallying cry for perpetrators of mass violence ever since. In July 2011, Norwegian terrorist Anders Breivik murdered 77 people, most in a shooting rampage on Utoya Island that targeted teenagers engaged in political activism. In his 1,500-page manifesto, titled 2083: A European Declaration of Independence, Breivik justified his actions by arguing that he was protecting 'white' Europe from a Muslim takeover and from the treacherous forces of liberalism and multiculturalism.[3] In 2018, Robert Bowers entered the Tree of Life synagogue in Pittsburgh and shot dead eleven people. Prior to carrying out the deadliest antisemitic shooting in American history, Bowers posted a message on an alt tech social network Gab, condemning the Hebrew Immigrant Aid Society and, referencing the arrival of Central American migrants, claimed: 'HIAS likes to bring invaders in that kill our people. I can't sit by and watch my people get slaughtered. Screw your optics, I'm going in.'[4] When he was apprehended, Bowers expressed the view that he 'wanted all Jews to die' because '[Jews] were committing genocide to

---

[1] Mark Davis (25 Jan 2024): 'Violence as method: the "white replacement," "white genocide," and "Eurabia" conspiracy theories and the biopolitics of networked violence.' Ethnic and Racial Studies, DOI: 10.1080/01419870.2024.2304640.

[2] James Ridgeway, "Fourteen Words that spell racism," *The Guardian*, October 28, 2008.

[3] "'Breivik manifesto' details chilling attack preparation," *BBC News*, July 24, 2011.

[4] Rita Katz, "Inside the Online Cesspool of Anti-Semitism That Housed Robert Bowers," *Politico Magazine*, October 29, 2018.

his people.'[1] His remarks betrayed the core ideas at the heart of the white genocide accusation. He accused Jews of enabling 'invaders' to enter American territory so that those people could destroy the lives of 'white' Americans in their traditional homeland. In other words, he was arguing that Jews were engineering the mass displacement of whites by an immigration and demographics policy, justifying their slaughter in that synagogue.

On March 15, 2019, Brenton Tarrant massacred 51 people in two mosques in Christchurch, New Zealand. In his manifesto, Tarrant accused liberal politicians of engineering the genocide or replacement of White Westerners through mass immigration of non-Whites, and was associated with the far right.[2] A month later, John Earnest killed one person in a synagogue in Poway, California. In an online letter, he argued that Jews were behind a 'white genocide,' adding: 'Every Jew is responsible for the meticulously planned genocide of the European race. They act as a unit, and every Jew plays his part to enslave the other races around him—whether consciously or subconsciously.'[3] Most recently in 2022, Payton S. Gendron, the killer of ten people at a supermarket in Buffalo, New York, was a racist believer in great replacement and referenced the Jews in his murderous testimony. In his 180-page manifesto, he argued that there was a 'crisis of mass immigration and sub-replacement fertility' which represented 'an assault on the European people' and one which, if not combated, would 'result in the complete racial and cultural replacement of the European people.'[4]

White supremacists blame Jews for this 'dilution of whiteness' because they assume that racial minorities are incapable, intellectually and organizationally, of advancing in society on their own, itself a deeply racist trope. They assume that those minorities need the guiding hand of the "cunning," "malevolent" Jews, depicted as a particularly dangerous group because of their 'adjacency to whiteness and a desire to destroy it.'[5] This reinforces the notion that while Jews are demonized and vilified in the minds

---

[1] Alex Amend, "Analyzing a terrorist's social media manifesto: the Pittsburgh synagogue shooter's posts on Gab,"| Southern Poverty Law Center, October 28, 2018.

[2] Michael McGowan, "Christchurch shooter was active with Australian far-right groups online but escaped police attention," *The Guardian,* December 8. 2020.

[3] Josh Kaplan, "The antisemitic roots of the Great Replacement theory explained," *The Jewish Chronicle*, May 20, 2022.

[4] Andrew Buncombe, "Inside the data that debunks the 'Great Replacement' theory," *The Independent*, May 16, 2022.

[5] Lavin, *Culture Warlords*, 25.

of the supremacists, they are secretly feared, maybe even admired, for their cunning, intelligence and organization. It helps ensure that Jew hatred is a quite unique form of racism.

While many of these individuals were likely radicalized online, they were arguably encouraged by political figures who engaged in the demonization of immigrants and who stoked fears about the demographic threat purportedly posed by minority groups. One such figure is the reactionary right winger Patrick Buchanan, author of the book *Death of the West*. Buchanan wrote: 'How does the West, America included, stop the flood tide of migrants before it alters forever the political and demographic character of our nations and our civilization?'[1] Among others one could cite are President Trump[2], Steve Bannon, Rep. Marjorie Taylor Greene, Victor Orban, Geert Wilders, Giorgia Meloni, Marine Le Pen and Heinz-Christian Strache of the Austrian Freedom Party. Outside of Europe and America, the Australian neo-Nazi group, Antipodean Resistance, has been fanning the flames of hatred against immigrants and Jews, using much of the same rhetoric as their European and American counterparts.[3]

Meanwhile, a number of American figures have spread a lighter version of this theory, arguing that mass immigration is a political tool designed for partisan purposes. Thus, Senator Ted Cruz once said: 'They believe each illegal alien is a potential Democrat voter.'[4] His views were echoed by Fox News' Tucker Carlson, a right-wing broadcaster who said: 'I know that the left and all the little gatekeepers on Twitter become literally hysterical if you use the term 'replacement,' if you suggest that the Democratic Party is trying to replace the current electorate — the voters now casting ballots — with new people, more obedient voters from the Third World, but they become

---

[1] Ronald Bailey, "We Are in the Midst of the Third Bogus 'White Extinction' Panic in Just as Many Centuries," *reason.com*, June 28, 2016.

[2] Amanda Marcotte, "Donald Trump's "white genocide" rhetoric: A dangerous escalation of racism," *salon.com*, August 27, 2018.

[3] Danny Tran, "Antipodean Resistance Neo-Nazi group trying to sway Australia's same-sex marriage postal vote," *ABC News*, September 4, 2017.

[4] "Sen. Cruz Blasts Biden Executive Action to Give Amnesty to Illegal Aliens", April 18, 2024, https://www.cruz.senate.gov/newsroom/press-releases/sen-cruz-blasts-biden-executive-action-to-give-amnesty-to-illegal-aliens, accessed May 10, 2025.

hysterical because that's what's happening, actually. Let's just say it. That's true.'[1]

Today, the great replacement theory is scarcely a fringe movement. Some 32% of British people thought that the theory was either 'definitely true' or 'probably true,' according to a June 2023 poll conducted by King's College, London.[2] A poll by the University of Massachusetts Amherst poll also found that one third of Americans, and two thirds of American Republican voters, believe in some tenets of the theory.

Refutation

The theory founders when its arguments are closely examined. It is neither true that white people are about to be replaced in America, or other western countries, nor is it true that those minorities will automatically vote for left wing parties. Above all, there is no Jewish guiding hand attempting to engineer such subversive and malignant designs on white majority societies.

Let us start with the demographics of America, the country in which the great replacement theory enjoys perhaps its strongest support. According to US Census Bureau data for 2020, the racial breakdown of America indicates that 76.5% of the population are white, if one includes those of Hispanic origin, while 57.8% are white alone. Those who are black or African American are 12.1% of the population, with the remaining population made up of American Indians, Alaska natives and other minorities.[3]

A series of demographic estimates purport to show that by the middle of the twenty first century, white Americans will no longer be a majority (49.9%) in the country, with other minorities (Hispanics – 24.6%, Blacks – 13.1%) having a boosted share of the population.[4] This has created a degree of alarm which has only been exacerbated by the amount of immigration to the US from non-white communities. It led the neo-Nazi National Alliance to

---

[1]"The Great Replacement: An Explainer," Anti-Defamation League, April 19, 2021, https://www.adl.org/resources/backgrounder/great-replacement-explained, accessed May 10, 2025.

[2] "Conspiracy belief among the UK public and the role of alternative media," *The Policy Institute*, June 2023.

[3] U.S. Census Bureau QuickFacts: United States

[4]Projecting Majority-Minority, United States Census Bureau, https://www.census.gov/content/dam/Census/newsroom/releases/2015/cb15-tps16_graphic.pdf, accessed September 16, 2025.

describe whites as 'Earth's Most Endangered Species.'[1]

But such figures can be misleading. For one thing, the changing figures for white Americans owe much to the Bureau's shift in coding, one which allows respondents to choose more than one race to describe themselves. Second, even if non-Hispanic whites cease to be an absolute majority in America, they are still by far the largest single demographic bloc if one does not lump together all other groups in a homogenous whole. They would be several times larger than the white Hispanic population, the African American population and the Asian American population. The fear of white extinction is thus a perverse form of moral panic based on misleading data, logic and evidence. The notion that there is a political incentive to increase the immigrant population is also flawed because it assumes, in the case of America, that all newcomers will automatically vote Democrat. In fact, there are considerable percentages of new immigrants who have warmed to the Republican cause, with little evidence to suggest this will stop.[2]

Quite simply, there is no imminent threat to the demographic or economic status of white American or European populations. No shadowy force is trying to eliminate the white societies of these countries and replace them with immigrants, refugees, Muslims or other people of colour from foreign countries, no matter how much that might seem to be the case. Demographic shifts in the racial composition of any society occur over many years and are the result of an array of factors, including immigration, changes in fertility, intermarriage and identity choices. Even with immigration, policies are made by many people in multiple administrations over lengthy periods. Thus, the belief that there is one single factor in the changing racial dynamics of white societies, namely immigration, is much too simplistic.

Of course, the great replacement theory is flawed too because it is based purely on data from current trends and does not take into account the impact of future government policies, a factor which, by definition, no one can predict. Such policies depend on the current political mood of any nation, the impact of future wars or economic crises, the make-up of the country's political parties, as well as their political priorities, and a variety of other

---

[1] Ryan Lenz, "Following the White Rabbit," Southern Poverty Law Center, August 21, 2013.

[2] Alex Nowrasteh and Krit Chanwong, "Naturalized Immigrants Probably Voted Republican in 2024," Cato Institute, March 25, 2025.

factors. The mistake made with projections which extrapolate from existing data is that they cannot take these unknown factors into account.

The term 'white genocide' is itself a misnomer. White people are not being massacred or even deliberately targeted by Jews or anyone else. No one is trying to extinguish them from society in Europe or elsewhere. White people are free to marry who they like, have as many children as they like and move where they like. If many among them choose to emigrate, remain single, intermarry with minorities or have fewer children with their partners, all of which reduces their overall demographic share of the population, that remains the free choice of those people.

But the idea that the guiding hand is a Jewish one can only reflect one of the most persistent and insidious of all anti-Jewish tropes: the belief that Jews are conspiring to rule the world for their own selfish purposes, combined with the 'cultural Marxism' thesis, the idea that Jewish intellectuals have sought to undermine, degrade and ultimately destroy white European culture by promoting equality, human rights, feminism and other causes. That should not be surprising in this context, given that Jews have always been the number one target for white supremacists in every country.

It is of course true that many prominent Jews were involved with the struggle for racial equality in the middle of the twentieth century. During the struggle for Civil Rights between the 1940s and 1960s, many Jewish voices were raised in support of black equality and desegregation and in opposition to the Jim Crow laws and militant violence. In South Africa, it is equally true that Jews were the most prominent white group in advocating for the end of apartheid and for political change. Many white American segregationists were also antisemitic as a result. But none of this proves that Jews were seeking to dilute the white majority population. It simply shows that they wished to live in a society shorn of prejudice and discrimination, one where political rights and economic opportunities were open to people regardless of their racial and ethnic background. Inevitably this meant empowering minorities who were excluded and subjugated, affording them the chance to rise up the social ladder and assert rights that they were previously denied. In short, Jews wanted to live in a society where white people lacked a set of unjust privileges that consigned people of colour to second class status. Moreover, the legislatures that engineered cultural changes, including more liberal values and racial tolerance, were not 'Jewish dominated' in any western country. Those who see the guiding hand of the chimerical Jew in modern social change have fallen prey to age old foundational paradigms about Jewish control and manipulation.

9. Jews are the enemies of black people

Whereas the far-right blames Jews for conspiring to undermine the 'white race,' much of the far left, under the guise of modern identity politics, depicts Jews as part of a privileged white establishment that controls the fate of minorities. It is this curious mixture of attitudes that leads the British writer David Baddiel to talk of Jews as 'Schrodinger's whites,'[1] namely that their degree of whiteness depends entirely on who is looking at them. Among those whose fates Jews are alleged to control are black people, especially African Americans.

The notion that Jews are bloodsuckers and exploiters of black people, especially in the United States, has become a staple of black nationalism in recent decades. In 1991, the Nation of Islam (NOI) produced a three-volume study called *The Secret Relationship Between Blacks and Jews.* The first volume peddled the view that Jews initiated and were the prime benefactors of the transatlantic slave trade, citing the names of those Jews who were involved in this nefarious industry in the eighteenth and nineteenth centuries. Subsequent volumes claim that this pattern of Jewish exploitation of black people continued after the abolition of slavery, right down until the present day.

For NOI, Jews appeared as exploiters in a number of guises: they were spiteful and venal store owners, cruel and oppressive landlords, school teachers responsible for infecting young minds with pernicious ideas, insensitive social workers and activists opposed to affirmative action. *The Secret Relationship* produced a clear message about Jews, namely that they were the enemies of black people and of the black liberation movement. If there was a guiding hand that kept black people oppressed and which robbed them of life chances, it was a Jewish one.

Since then, the pronouncements of leaders within the NOI have only given further voice to the trope of illegitimate and insidious Jewish control. In November 1993, NOI official Khalid Muhammad asked the question 'Who are the slumlords in the Black community?' He responded by saying that they were 'the so-called Jews.' He went on to ask: 'Who is it sucking our blood in

[1] David Baddiel, *Jews Don't Count*, (London: TLS Books, 2021), 51.

the Black community?' His reply was: 'A white imposter Arab and a white imposter Jew.'[1] Louis Farrakhan, two years later, made comments alluding to the same idea: 'Many of the Jews who owned the homes, the apartments in the black community, we considered them bloodsuckers because they took from our community and built their community.'[2]

The artist known as Ye (formerly Kanye West) amplified these explosive claims in 2022, reproducing longstanding tropes of antisemitic control and global influence. He claimed that 'Jewish people have owned the Black voice' and that the Jewish community, especially in the areas of music and entertainment, 'take us and milk us till we die.'[3] He has looked at the 'black musicians signed to Jewish record labels,' ones which 'take ownership not only of the publishing…but also ownership of the culture itself,' likening this to 'modern day slavery.'[4] He has gone on to claim that '90% of black people in entertainment — from sports, to music, to acting, are in some way tied into Jewish businesspeople.'[5] Similar inferences about the Jewish exploitation of black people in the entertainment industry were made by the British rapper Wiley. In one post he wrote: 'If you work for a company owned by 2 Jewish men and you challenge the Jewish community in anyway of course you will get fired.'[6]

Refutation

There is an element of truth in the idea that the modern relationship between blacks and Jews in America has been far from uniformly positive. In places like Harlem, it is true that many of the landlords, grocery store owners and pawn shop owners were Jewish, with relations marked by animosity. The words of the philosemite Martin Luther King are instructive:

> *When we were working in Chicago, we had numerous rent strikes on the West Side, and it was unfortunately true that, in most instances, the persons we had to conduct these strikes against were Jewish landlords… We were living in a slum apartment owned by a Jew and a number of*

---

[1] Robert D McFadden, "Islamic Figure In New Tirade Against Jews," *The New York Times*, February 28, 1994.
[2] "Farrakhan Remarks Stir Anger," *The New York Times*, October 15, 1995.
[3] Ye, *Twitter Post*, 16 October 2022.
[4] Ye, *Twitter Post,* 17 October 2022.
[5] Ye, *Twitter Post***,** 24 October 2022.
[6] Ben Beaumont-Thomas, "Wiley posts antisemitic tweets, likening Jews to Ku Klux Klan," *The Guardian*, July 24, 2020.

others, and we had to have a rent strike. We were paying $94 for four run-down, shabby rooms, and .... we discovered that whites ... were paying only $78 a month. We were paying 20 percent tax.[1]

Undoubtedly, there were examples of racist Jews whose interactions with black people left a stain in places like Harlem and Chicago. But that did not define the limits of such interactions. The Jewish influence in the music industry was also extensive during this period. Jews were highly represented among Tin Pan Alley songwriters and publishers and they played a dominant role in the world of vaudeville and minstrelsy. Much of the popular music at the time incorporated caricatures of African-Americans, including so called 'coon songs' in which black people appeared 'not only ignorant and indolent, but also devoid of honesty or personal honor, given to drunkenness and gambling, utterly without ambition, sensuous, libidinous, even lascivious.'[2] The illustrated covers of black song sheet music contained defamatory images of black people and the use of the N word while some Jewish entertainers performed in blackface. Today, blackface is seen as a grotesque form of racism and offensive caricature. But for the Jews who performed this way, blackface was not intended to offend. It was their way of identifying with the despised and lowly 'other,' the authentic world from which they had come, just as they were punching up the social scale and losing touch with their ethnic roots.[3]

Jews continued to play a major role during the jazz age, both as singers (Al Jolson, Eddie Cantor, Fanny Brice and Sophie Tucker), night club owners, music executives and label owners. Some of those label owners and musical executives were accused of exploiting black musicians and taking advantage of their art. Among them was Herman Lubinsky, the founder of Savoy Records.

But perhaps the single biggest reason why tensions existed between the two communities in America was their changing socio-economic status in society. As the twentieth century progressed, Jews experienced a remarkable

---

[1] Justin Joffe, "The Music Industry's Long History of Dividing Blacks and Jews," *Observer*.com, February 9, 2017, https://observer.com/2017/02/music-industry-history-dividing-blacks-and-jews, accessed September 15, 2025.

[2] James M. Dormon, "Shaping the Popular Image of Post-Reconstruction American Blacks: The 'Coon Song' Phenomenon of the Gilded Age." *American Quarterly*. 1995. 40 (4): 450–471. doi:10.2307/2712997. JSTOR 2712997 (p. 455).

[3] Steve Lipman, "Jews And Blackface: A Complicated History," *New York Jewish Week*, February 6, 2019.

level of upward mobility and economic success. They moved out of black inner-city areas into more prosperous suburbs. They were well represented in the higher professions (education and academia, law, medicine and journalism), enjoyed a rising level of income and wealth and some were prominent in the political establishment. Jews assimilated and acculturated successfully, while African Americans were largely left in their wake. Fundamentally, Jews were seen as being on the wrong side of the great racial dividing line in America: between whites and blacks. Jews were viewed as having all the privileges of being white, added to which they experienced declining levels of both structural and institutional racism while for black Americans, that prejudice and racism was all too real. As Professor Cornell West put it: 'Black anti-semitism is a form of underdog resentment and envy, directed at another underdog who has made it in American society.'[1]

While these interactions and perceptions led to fraught relations between many blacks and Jews, there can clearly be no justification for imbibing western tropes of Jewish power and conspiratorial control. The narratives of Kanye and Farrakhan move away from specific grievances about individual Jews (which may or may not have been justified) to disseminating malign falsehoods about Jewish control and exploitation. In the case of Farrakhan, these narratives are accompanied by defamatory charges of Jewish immorality and celebration of Hitlerism. This is not so much 'black antisemitism' as a case of black nationalists adopting a slew of harmful antisemitic tropes that have damaged community relations.

But this is not all there is to say about black-Jewish relations in the twentieth century; far from it. Jews were well represented within the Civil Rights movement throughout the twentieth century. Among the founders of the National Association for the Advancement of Coloured People (NAACP) was the civic leader and activist Henry Moscowitz (1879-1936). Joel Elias Springarn (1875-1939), a Jewish American educator and lifelong campaigner for the cause of racial justice, joined the NAACP after it was founded, then served as Chairman of the Board (1913-19), Treasurer (1919-30) and finally President (1930-39). He established the Springarn medal in 1914, instituting 'an annual award for the highest or noblest achievement' by a black American during the preceding year/years.

---

[1] Larry Aubry, "Anti-Semitism and Blacks," *Los Angeles Sentinel*, February 4, 2016, https://lasentinel.net/anti-semitism-and-blacks.html, accessed January 10, 2024.

His brother, Arthur Springarn (1878-1971), was another 'leader in the struggle for equal rights.' He became head of the NAACP's National Legal Committee as well as vice President in 1911. In 1940, he succeeded his brother as President of the organization, serving until 1965. Thurgood Marshall, a Supreme Court Justice, said that 'If it had not been for Arthur Spingarn, we would not have an N.A.A.C.P. today.'[1] Following Springarn's death, the organization's new President was Kivie Kaplan (1904-1975), vice-chairman of the Union of American Hebrew Congregations (which is now the Union for Reform Judaism) and a leading figure in the American Jewish community. This meant that for the majority of its first sixty-five years, the guiding lights of an organization dedicated to justice for black Americans were Jewish activists.

Some Jewish lawyers offered their services to the NAACP during its early years, among them Louis Marshall (1856-1929), a constitutional lawyer who was a champion of Jewish communal rights but who was also passionate about securing rights for all minorities. Felix Frankfurter, later a Supreme Court Justice, served on the NAACP's National Legal Committee and Louis Brandeis, another Supreme Court justice, planned the legal battle against Jim Crow laws in the South. Another powerful voice for Civil Rights came from the pulpit, namely that of Rabbi Stephen Wise (1874-1949). He was inspired by the ethical ideals of Judaism: 'The supreme declaration of our Hebrew Bible was and remains, "Justice, justice shalt thou pursue," whether it be easy or hard, whether it be justice to white or black, Jew or Christian.'[2]

It was thanks to the business magnate Julius Rosenwald (1862-1932), that major advances were made in African American education. His donations helped to create a vast number of black schools (known as Rosenwald schools), of which there were eventually some 5,000 in southern states educating 700,000 black children.[3] It was said that the Rosenwald schools fostered a genuine community spirit and sense of solidarity among black people and encouraged the virtues of self-help and autonomy, precisely the aim of Rosenwald's approach to welfare capitalism.

Throughout these years, however, the violence meted out to black Americans continued in the form of lynchings, a form of extrajudicial mob violence in which the victim would be hanged in front of a large crowd. A

---

[1] "Springarn's Work Hailed at Rites," *The New York Times*, December 6, 1971.

[2] Stephen Wise, *Challenging Years*, (New York: Putnam's Sons, 1949), 110.

[3] Michael J Solender, "Inside the Rosenwald Schools," *Smithsonian Magazine*, March 30, 2021.

powerful progressive voice was needed to highlight their savagery and that voice was provided by Louis Isaac Jaffe (1888-1950), the editor of the *Virginia Pilot* from 1919 to 1950. In 1929, he received the Pulitzer Prize for editorial writing for *An Unspeakable Act of Savagery.*

A galvanising anthem was also necessary for the anti-lynching cause. That was dutifully provided by the Jewish song writer Abel Meeropol (1903-1986). In 1937, he saw a photograph that haunted him: it showed the lynching of two African American men in 1930 whose bodies dangled before a jeering crowd. He published a poem called *Bitter Fruit* in *The New York Teacher* magazine and later set it to music with the changed name *Strange Fruit.*[1] The song reportedly came to the attention of Jewish immigrant Barney Josephson (1902-1988), who founded and ran *Cafe Society*, the first integrated nightclub in New York. Billie Holliday sang *Strange Fruit* at the venue in 1939 and continued to sing it thereafter. Her attempts to release the song foundered on fears of negative reactions in the south and after some rejections, she turned to record producer Milton Gabler (1911-2001), whose parents were Jewish immigrants from Europe. He was said to have been moved to tears by the song and released the recording on his own record label, Commodore Records. As Meeropol put it, 'People had to remember *Strange Fruit*, get their insides burned by it.' In 1999, *Time Magazine* named it the 'song of the century.'[2]

Historian Howard Sachar has written that 'Nowhere did Jews identify themselves more forthrightly with the liberal avant-garde than in the Civil Rights movement of the 1960s.'[3] Sachar would have been the first to admit that this did not imply a unified Jewish response, given that the majority of activists came from outside the orthodox community. The pivotal legal case of the 1950s was *Brown v the Board of Education* (1954) in which the father of a black child (Oliver Brown) who had been denied entrance to an all-white school filed a law suit against the Board of Education in Topeka, arguing that the restrictions she faced violated the equal protection clause inherent in the fourteenth amendment.

Yet the case might never have happened without the intervention of

---

[1] Aida Amoako, "Strange Fruit: The most shocking song of all time?" *BBC Culture*, April 17, 2019, https://www.bbc.co.uk/culture/article/20190415-strange-fruit-the-most-shocking-song-of-all-time, accessed September 16, 2025.

[2] Dorian Lynskey, "Strange Fruit: the First Great Protest Song," *The Guardian*, February 16, 2011.

[3] Howard Sachar, "Jews in the Civil Rights Movement," myjewishlearning.com. accessed November 18, 2025

another Brown, a Jewish woman called Esther Brown (1917-1970). In 1948, she had seen the inadequate conditions in a dilapidated all black school in Kansas, noting that students had no principal, only two teachers and had to walk home for lunch. Determined to ensure that black and white students could attend a new, 'all white' school on an equal basis, she raised money for a legal battle, hiring black attorney Elisha Scott to pursue a case against the South Park district. Her efforts paid off when, in 1949, the Kansas Supreme Court, declared in *Webb vs School District No. 90* that black people had the right to attend the new South Park School, previously designed to be off limits for black students. After that success, she then turned to Topeka in an attempt to integrate the city's elementary schools. She later sought litigants for what would become the landmark *Brown v Board of Education* case, among them Oliver Brown, and her efforts led the secretary of the Topeka NAACP to declare: 'I don't know if we could have done it without Esther Brown.'[1]

Presiding over the case for the NAACP in the Brown case was Thurgood Marshall, later the first black Supreme Court Justice, and his co-counsel, Jack Greenberg (1924-2016), a Jewish lawyer born in New York and a 'courthouse pillar of the Civil Rights movement.'[2] He was one of a number of lawyers to present vital oral arguments in the Brown case, one which altered American history. Undoubtedly another unsung legal hero was the civil rights activist William L Taylor (1931-2010), a behind the scenes fighter both in courtrooms and on Capitol Hill, advising and lobbying political figures and helping draft legislation over a period that spanned more than half a century. Among his achievements was to help draft the legal brief for the Supreme Court case (Cooper v Aaron) that compelled Little Rock, a school in Arkansas (and others), to desegregate in 1958. The NAACP called Taylor 'a staunch advocate for educational equity throughout his storied legal career.'[3]

Paralleling the legal challenges to segregation and unjust discrimination was a campaign of grass roots activism led for a decade by Martin Luther King. Jewish ministers from within the Reform movement were among the leading white figures rallying around King and providing him with moral and

---

[1] Lawrence Bush, 'May 17: Esther Brown v. Board of Education,' *Jewish Currents*, https://jewishcurrents.org/may-17-esther-brown-v-board-of-education, accessed November 18, 2025.
[2] Richard Severo and William McDonald, "Jack Greenberg, a Courthouse Pillar of the Civil Rights Movement, dies at 91," *The New York Times*, October 12, 2016.
[3] Douglas Martin, "William Taylor, Vigorous Rights Defender, Dies at 78," *The New York Times*, June 30, 2010.

material support for his case. Among them was Polish born Rabbi Abraham Heschel (1907-1972), a Jewish theologian whose activism was inspired by his 'lifelong study of the Biblical prophets.'[1] For Heschel, the prophetic message enjoined Jews to feel the pain of others and gave them a moral obligation to respond to the evils of society. Heschel struck up an intensely personal bond with King and the two spoke and appeared together at public events. Other Jewish clerics who rallied to the cause included Rabbi Joachim Prinz (1902-88) of the American Jewish Committee, a Berlin born theologian who had preached against Nazism and was a powerful advocate for Civil Rights in the US. One of King's key advisors was the American lawyer and businessman Stanley Levison (1912-1979). A lifelong supporter of progressive causes, Levison teamed up with Bayard Rustin and Ella Baker to form *In Friendship*, an organization which raised money for civil rights activists. They believed it was necessary to set up a Congress of Organizations which would fight for non-violent mass action, the genesis of what became the Southern Christian Leadership Conference (SCLC).

The Freedom Riders were a group of black and white American protestors who boarded southbound buses to challenge segregationist Jim Crow laws. They sat together in segregated bus stations and went to segregated diners where they were attacked and abused by racist patrons. It has been estimated that Jews made up at least one third of the Freedom Riders. Finally, honourable mention should be made of Michael Schwerner (1939-1964) and Andrew Goodman (1943-1964) who, together with African American James Chaney (1943-1964), travelled to Mississippi in 1964 as part of a voter registration drive for the organization CORE. All three were murdered by the KKK and all three received a posthumous Presidential Medal of Freedom. The words of Martin Luther King still remain important: 'Our Jewish friends have demonstrated their commitment to the principle of tolerance and brotherhood in tangible ways, often at great personal sacrifices.'[2]

While the post 60s landscape has been marked by disagreement, tension and prejudice, it is important to remember that there are many organizations that fight for racial justice and oppose prejudice faced by black people in America. They include: The Black Jewish Entertainment Alliance, an organization that was launched 'to bring the two communities together in

[1] Norman H Finkelstein, *Heeding the Call: Jewish Voices in America's Civil Rights Struggle*, (Philadelphia, Jewish Publication Society, 1997), 148.
[2] Finkelstein, *Heeding the Call*, 172.

solidarity, to support each other in their struggles, and to better understand each other's plight and narratives'; Black Jewish Alliance ADL, which was forged in 2017 to 'galvanize Black communities and Jewish communities to fight racism, antisemitism and all forms of hate in the Philadelphia region'; AJC's Atlanta Black/Jewish Coalition, which brings together black people and Jews for the purposes of education, outreach and advocacy; The Jewish Council for Racial Equality, an organization set up in 1976 to provide a Jewish voice on race and asylum issues; Jews for Racial and Economic Justice and the Institute for Black Solidarity with Israel.

Such organizations give hope that the common cause between Jews and black people more than a century ago can continue to be renewed in future generations. The final words belong to Martin Luther King, extolling the alliance between American blacks and Jews: 'Our unity is born of our common struggle for centuries, not only to rid ourselves of bondage, but to make oppression of any people by others an impossibility.'[1]

[1] From an address delivered by King at the National Biennial Convention of the American Jewish Congress, May 14, 1958.

Chapter 4

Anti-Zionist Antisemitism

1. Zionism is an inherently racist and illegal philosophy

Zionism, the founding political ideology behind the modern state of Israel, is regularly traduced within academia, the media and the NGO community, to say nothing of mainstream Arab and Palestinian politics. Zionism is condemned as a racist, illegitimate, expansionist, colonialist and genocidal ideology which is responsible for the repression of the Palestinians and the wider abuse of human rights in the Middle East. Ideological anti-Zionism, far from being a recent political trend, is rooted in the anti-western politics of the Soviet Union.

For decades, the Soviet system had promulgated the view that Zionism was a poisonous ideology based on anti-Communism, anti-Sovietism and chauvinism. After the Six Day War, the regime portrayed Zionists using Nazi like imagery and discourse, claiming that they were engaged in a global conspiracy along the lines of the *Protocols* and were disseminating a fascistic ideology that undermined national and international interests. Zionists were accused of facilitating Nazi aggression against the Soviet Union and of colluding in the murder of European peoples. From 1967 on, the Soviet anti-Zionist campaign, with its hundreds of books, thousands of articles and cartoons and countless films, lectures and broadcasts, succeeded in transforming the understanding of Zionism from being a Jewish liberation movement to one akin to 'racism, fascism, Nazism, genocide, imperialism, colonialism, militarism and apartheid.'[1]

In 1975, the UN General Assembly adopted resolution 3379 which stated that 'Zionism is a form of racism and racial discrimination.' The resolution followed a prior one (resolution 3151 G (XXVIII) of 14 December 1973), which recalled 'the unholy alliance between South African racism and

[1] Izabella Tabarovsky, 'Soviet Anti-Zionism and Contemporary Left Antisemitism,' *Fathom Journal*, May 2019.

Zionism.' Resolution 3379 came about because of a concerted effort by an Arab/Muslim/Third World bloc within the UN to delegitimize the Jewish state in the aftermath of defeat in the Yom Kippur war. The US Ambassador to the UN, Daniel Patrick Moynihan, declared that 'a great evil has been loosed upon the world' and that his country would 'never acquiesce in this infamous act.' In 1991, under US pressure, the resolution was rescinded with a substantial majority among UN member states, but the damage had been done. The UN resolution helped to inspire a generation of academics and activists in their relentless quest to demonize and isolate the Jewish state.

Noam Chomsky, the grandfather of the anti-Israel movement, has long argued against the very idea of a Jewish state on the grounds that the said state is inherently racist and discriminatory. 'Embodied in the political institutions of a Jewish state,' he argues, are 'concepts of purity of nation and race which can prove quite ugly.'[1] He has gone on to say that in such a state, there can be 'no full recognition of basic human rights... Such limitations are inherent in the concept of a Jewish state that also contains non-Jewish citizens.'[2]

British political activist Ben White has echoed these sentiments. In a piece written for *The New Statesman*, White has written: 'Despite declaring the regime as democratic, ethnicity (and not territorial citizenship) is the main determinant of the allocation of rights, powers, and resource ... [and] the logic of ethnic segregation is diffused into the social and political system.' He adds that a number of Israel's laws, such as its right of return, have 'shaped an institutionalized regime of ethno-religious discrimination by extending Israel's "frontiers" to include every Jew in the world (as a potential citizen), at the same time as explicitly excluding expelled Palestinians.'[3]

Judith Butler has railed against the perceived constitutional illegitimacy of a Zionist state. Her book *Parting Ways* draws a connection between Zionism's 'hegemonic control' over Jewishness and the 'colonial subjugation (it) has implied for the Palestinian people.' She argues that it is only by 'an end to political Zionism, understood as the insistence on grounding the State of Israel on principles of Jewish sovereignty,' that the region can come to realize 'broader principles of justice.' Judith Butler's critique of the right of return is couched as a critique of a wider issue: 'It would be unjust for any

---

[1] Noam Chomsky, *Peace in the Middle East, Reflections on Justice and Nationhood* (New York: Pantheon Books, 1974), 119.

[2] ibid. p. 17.

[3] Ben White, "Is Israel a democracy or an ethnocracy?" *New Statesman*, February 5, 2012.

state to insist on one religious and ethnic group maintaining a demographic majority to create differential levels of citizenship for majority and minority populations.'[1]

The Guardian columnist Seumas Milne has offered a similar analysis: 'Those who insist there can be no questioning of the legitimacy of the state in its current form - with discriminatory laws giving a "right of return" to Jews from anywhere in the world, while denying it to Palestinians expelled by force - are scarcely taking a stand against racism, but rather the opposite.'[2]

For philosopher Michael Neumann in *The Case Against Israel*, the assignment of territory and political power on ethnic lines is tantamount to 'advocating the political supremacy of an ethnic group.' Citing a host of failed attempts at self-determination on ethno-national lines (Yugoslavia, Rwanda, Algeria), he says that the 'the self-determination of peoples has been a smokescreen for bitter religious or class warfare' and has led to the production of 'racially pure enclaves.' He thinks this is true of Zionism which, far from producing a pure form of self-determination, has created a crude nationalist state in which non-Jews are forced to live 'at the good pleasure of the Jews.'[3] Historian Tony Judt makes the same point. Israel, he says, 'is an oddity among modern nations...because it is a Jewish state in which one community, Jews, is set above others, in an age when that sort of state has no place.'[4]

A related critique is that Zionism is a colonialist movement designed to usurp an indigenous population in favour of a western implanted one. This has been central to the critiques of several academics and political thinkers, among them the French Marxist Maxime Rodinson in his book *Israel: A Colonial Settler State?* The South African anti-apartheid activist Ronnie Kasrils has declared Israel 'guilty of an illegal and immoral colonial project' and cited a report by South Africa's Human Sciences Research Council confirming that 'the everyday structural racism and oppression imposed by Israel constitutes a regime of apartheid and settler colonialism.'[5] The journalist Nir Rosen agrees with this assessment, viewing Israel as the world's last colonialist state

---

[1] Judith Butler, *Parting Ways: Jewishness and the Critique of Zionism*, (New York: Columbia University Press, 2013), 118.
[2] Seumas Milne, "This Slur of Antisemitism is Used to Defend Repression," *The Guardian*, May 9, 2002.
[3] Michael Neumann, *The Case against Israel*, (Petrolia: Counterpunch, 2006), 16-20.
[4] Tony Judt, ""Jewish State" has become anachronism," *Los Angeles Times*, October 10, 2003.
[5] Ronnie Kasrils, "South Africa's Israel boycott," *The Guardian*, September 29, 2010.

that, like other such states, uses its own civilians strategically to 'claim land and dispossess the native population, be they Indians in North America or Palestinians in what is now Israel and the Occupied Territories.'[1] Apologists may claim that these critiques are of Israeli policy in the West Bank, one which is often compared to that of colonial powers. But for anti-Zionists, there is no difference between Zionism on either side of the 1967 lines. The Jews of Israel, wherever they live, are depicted as illegitimate settlers who have been strategically implanted at the behest of foreign powers and who have displaced the 'rightful' population of the land.

The discourse of anti-Zionist demonization suggests that Israel is not a normal country. Instead, it is a pariah state that deserves opprobrium, vilification and delegitimization.

Michael Neumann says that 'Israel stands out among other unpleasant nations in the depth of its commitment to gratuitous violence and nastiness.' He goes on: 'This you expect to find among skinheads rather than nations.'[2] In July 2013, the German newspaper *Süddeutsche Zeitung* depicted Israel as a hideous Moloch, utilising the kind of images that were commonplace in Nazi Germany. On the far right, Israel is described as a 'sadist, sociopath Jewish state'[3] while for Gideon Levy, the country's population are in a state of 'psychosis.'[4] The chairman of Amnesty's Finnish division has said that Israel is a 'scum country'[5] while for comedian Alexei Sayle, Israel has become 'the Jimmy Saville of nation states.'[6] The former Independent columnist Johann Hari could not think of modern Israel without the 'smell of shit,' a reference to the raw sewage that he claimed was being pumped across Palestine by vicious settlers.[7] It was a linkage that was part of an infamous rant by French Ambassador, Daniel Bernard, who served as a diplomat in the UK from 1998 to 2002. He was quoted at a dinner party in 2001 as saying: 'All the current

---

[1] Nir Rosen, "Gaza: The logic of colonial power," *The Guardian*, December 29, 2008.

[2] Michael Neumann, "What's so bad about Israel," *Counterpunch*, July 6, 2002.

[3] http://www.judeofascism.com/2011/09/sadist-sociopath-jewish-state-fears.html, accessed March 10, 2024.

[4] Gideon Levy, "Israelis' Ideal State: A Country Without Criticism," *Haaretz*, May 23, 2010.

[5] Joshua Muravchik, *Making David into Goliath: How the World Turned Against Israel*, (New York: Encounter Books, 2014), 193.

[6] Alexei Sayle, "Israel is the Jimmy Saville of nation states," *Belfast Telegraph*, July 16, 2014.

[7] Johann Hari, "Israel is suppressing a secret it must face," *The Independent*, April 28, 2008.

troubles in the world are because of that shitty little country Israel. Why should the world be in danger of World War III because of those people?'[1] There is seemingly no limit to the lurid demonology with which the Jewish state is depicted by normally sane, mainstream commentators.

Some argue that a secular world cannot accommodate a nation state that prioritizes people of a religious faith. Palestinian writer Susan Abulhawa has written that a Jewish state is a dangerous and reactionary anachronism. She wrote: 'As if citizens of disparate cultures, nationalities, languages and locations constituted a singular race or ethnicity by virtue of their shared religion.'[2] She is not the first person to make this critique. Edwin Montagu, a leading British Jewish politician who served in the wartime cabinets of Herbert Asquith and David Lloyd George, was deeply opposed to Zionism, calling it 'a mischievous political creed, untenable by any patriotic citizen of the United Kingdom.' He denied that there was a cohesive Jewish nation and argued that Jews from different countries would scarcely be able to communicate with each other. He railed against the idea that Jews were anything other than members of different nations with a separate and distinct religious faith.

Refutation

We need to understand what Zionism is, and what it is not. In essence, Zionism is a movement for Jewish national liberation, national self-determination and sovereignty in the land of Israel, the historic and ancestral homeland of the Jewish people. The Jewish connection to the land of Israel has long been embedded in Jewish culture, tradition and liturgy. Jews have lived in the land for three millennia, first attaining independence and sovereignty under King David and, since their violent expulsion by the Romans, have yearned for a return. Zionism is not equivalent to the policies of any particular Israeli government that happens to be in power. It is not the same as endorsing the building of settlements or the occupation. It cannot be identified with religious affiliation, even just among Jews, and it covers a full spectrum of political views, including moderates, progressives and hawks. Zionism is not politically homogenous and counts among its numbers such diverse figures as Theodore Herzl, Ahad Ha'am, Menachem Begin and Meir

[1] "Daniel Bernard," *The Daily Telegraph*, May 3, 2004.

[2] Susan Abulhawa, "The Balfour Declaration: Enduring colonial criminality," *Middle East Eye*, November 9, 2017.

Kahane. Zionists include the left-wing activists of Peace Now and the right-wing hilltop settler youth. Zionism is a blend of Likud and Labour, secular and religious, left and right, dove and hawk. Zionism is more a symphony of voices than a flat tune with a shrill message. It also does not preclude, and has never precluded, the creation of a Palestinian state alongside Israel.

There is nothing either racist or illegal about Zionism as a movement. The right of self-determination is enshrined in international law, specifically in Article I of the Charter of the United Nations, which talks of the 'principle of equal rights and self-determination of peoples.' It is another important part of the Declaration of Principles of International Law Concerning Friendly Relations and Co-operation among States (1970) which states that the 'principle of equal rights and self-determination of peoples constitutes a significant contribution to contemporary international law.' It is also mentioned in the Helsinki Final Act adopted by the Conference on Security and Co-operation in Europe (CSCE) in 1975, the Vienna Declaration and Programme of Action of 1993 and the Committee on the Elimination of Racial Discrimination. Zionism is just one of the many movements for liberation and national sovereignty that are legitimized by these international instruments and statutes

Some may argue that Zionism is invalidated by the fact that the Palestinians in the West Bank and Gaza do not have their own state, a purported denial of their right of self-determination. Yet there is nothing in the history of Zionism to suggest that an independent Palestinian state living next to Israel was not possible. That was why, even before the establishment of the State of Israel, the pre-state Jewish leadership accepted the principle of partition on two separate occasions. In 1937, the Peel Commission, in investigating the causes of unrest the previous year, recommended the partition of the land of mandatory Palestine into an Arab and a Jewish state. The Jewish state would compromise roughly 17% of the total area, the Arab state some 75% with the remainder being a mandated zone under British control. It was accepted that there would be exchanges of population to make the states viable. There was disagreement among the Zionist factions though it is argued that there was an acceptance of partition in principle, with further negotiations necessary to improve the size of the Jewish state. The Arab leadership in Palestine bitterly rejected the proposal.

A decade later, the UN recommended partition of mandatory Palestine into an Arab and Jewish state, this time with different allocations of land. The

Zionist leadership accepted the proposals while the Palestinian Arab leadership, together with many allies throughout the Arab world, denounced them outright. The State of Israel offered to create a sovereign Arab Palestinian state on other occasions, most recently in 2000, 2001, 2008 and 2019. These offers were predicated on the Palestinians accepting the legitimacy and sovereignty of the Jewish state, something that was on each occasion refused by their leadership. The primary reasons for that rejection hinge on the belief in the right of return and a refusal to accept an end to the conflict, both of which are tantamount to a continuing declaration of war against the Jewish state. The failure to create a separate Palestinian state is the result of obstinacy, revanchism and rejectionist sentiment by successive Palestinian leaders, their outright refusal to accept the permanence of Jewish sovereignty in the region, a necessary condition of such an agreement.

What of the argument that Zionism has created a state with specifically ethnic features? It is certainly true that Israeli nationality is centred around and defined by its dominant religious tradition: Judaism. The core cultural characteristics of the state are Jewish, including its flag, its national anthem, its official holidays, its majority language and its immigration laws (the law of return). The right of return, its central immigration policy, favours one ethnoreligious group, namely Jews, though non-Jews can and do become citizens. That does not imply that non-Jews have reduced rights compared to Jewish citizens. Non-Jewish Israelis can vote, receive every level of education, serve in Parliament, the army and other institutions, use public facilities, appeal to the Supreme Court, practice their faith and engage in public protest. But the cultural flavour of the country is unmistakably Jewish.

Yet if a 'Jewish state' is inherently racist on this account, why are other countries which cleave to religious traditions not similarly traduced in the court of opinion? Many countries in Europe have established themselves on national lines and have defined themselves by reference to Christian tradition, heritage or symbolism. Similarly, Muslim countries have produced constitutions which place the principles of Islam at the core of their self-definition and their legal systems, but this does not merit the charge of racism or discrimination. Israel is not alone in putting religion or ethnicity at the heart of its self-definition. Further, while there are cities in Israel with a degree of ethno-religious homogeneity (Tel Aviv), there are many other cities with more mixed populations, such as Haifa, Jerusalem and Acre.

Both Montagu and Abulhawa are wrong in their arguments against

Zionism. Jews are not just members of a religious community like Catholics or Protestants, bound to a set of faith commitments but lacking any further sense of social solidarity. They are a people in the fully civilizational sense of the term, with a common culture, a set of traditions and a sense of belonging, regardless of their geographic dispersion, levels of religiosity or separate languages. To deny Jews a state in which they can collectively flourish and cement their future is to assail their identity and attack their collective rights as a nation.

Finally, Zionism cannot be considered as a colonialist movement, as a western implant in the region designed to further the aims of expansionist powers. Colonialism implies that a state uses its power to dominate another country economically, politically and militarily, and to settle its own population as part of a land grab. This is exactly what European powers did when they carved up 90% of the African continent in the last decades of the nineteenth century. Those who were sent to these far-flung regions of the world had no prior connection to them and many were, in the truest sense, interlopers and exploiters.

Yet the Jews who went to Palestine from the 1880s onwards were not sent by a foreign power. Instead, they were refugees from other powers, such as Tsarist Russia, Poland or Romania. They were not beholden to or agents of a foreign despot so much as pioneers seeking an independent life in a new land. That is why we do not see names like New Moscow or New Vilnius or New Bucharest in the newly emerging Jewish cities of Palestine. Jews were not trying to replicate the towns from which they came but to build new ones in the spirit of a national home.

There was no certainly no enticing economic benefit from migrating to Palestine. Contemporary accounts from the late nineteenth century paint a picture of a desolate, swamp infested and malaria ridden outpost of the Ottoman Empire which required back- breaking effort to revivify. Unlike colonial settlers from European countries, the Jews acquired their land legally, buying it at hugely inflated prices from landlords that were keen to profit from such one sided transactions. It was, moreover, a land to which the Jewish emigrants could claim to have had a longstanding historical and religious connection. That was why the preamble to the 1922 League of Nations mandate for Palestine specifically recognized 'the historical connection of the Jewish people with Palestine' as well as 'the grounds for reconstituting their national home in that country.'

What is missed in the accusation of colonialism is that biblical Palestine was not foreign to the consciousness of world Jewry, much as the Congo might have been to the nineteenth century Belgians or Eritrea to the Italians. Instead, the land of Israel was, and remains, deeply embedded in the culture, rituals, beliefs and prayers of Jews the world over. The Biblical stories of the Jewish patriarchs and matriarchs are played out in that land, including the stories that are connected to Abraham, the first Jew in history. Naturally, the historical veracity of those accounts is open to question as any secular Jew would surely be the first to admit. Jews pray three times a day facing Jerusalem, the city that contains the remnants of the Holy Temple (the Wailing Wall), the holiest site for Jews anywhere in the world. Jews refer to their co-religionists living outside Israel as being in the galut (exile). If one discounts religious practice and bible stories, then one can point to the fact that King David made Jerusalem the nation's capital during the two centuries of Jewish independence there. Even after the Romans forced Jews into exile after 70AD, Jewish communities were formed in many towns in the new Palestine, including Tiberias, Safed and Jaffa. Before the waves of migration in the 1880s, there were already 10,000 Jews in the land, a number that would increase dramatically in the coming decades. This unbroken historical connection gives the lie to the idea that Zionism was colonialist by nature.

2. Israel is a genocidal state

Of all the accusations made against Israel today, none is so incendiary and malign as the one which accuses it of being a genocidal state. The racist twist in this foul charge is that Israel, a land populated by a substantial number of Holocaust survivors and their descendants, is depicted as a replica of Nazi Germany, the nation state that committed the mass extermination of European Jewry during the Second World War and was responsible for the single most destructive war in human history. In other words, Israel is viewed as the embodiment of utmost cruelty, bestiality, illegality and criminality on a truly psychotic scale. Law lecturer Lesley Klaff refers to this as 'Holocaust inversion,' namely 'an inversion of reality' whereby 'Israelis are cast as the "new" Nazis and the Palestinians as the "new" Jews.' As she puts it, such inversion tarnishes the memory of the Holocaust by trivialising the Nazi genocide and imposing on Israel a 'uniquely onerous moral responsibility.'[1]

A few representative examples will suffice. The Portuguese Nobel Prize winning novelist, Jose Saramago, while visiting Yasser Arafat's besieged compound in Ramallah, said that what was happening in Palestine was 'a crime we can put on the same plane as what happened at Auschwitz,' and accused the Israelis of being 'rentiers of the Holocaust.'[2] At the height of the Second Intifada, Northern Irish poet, essayist and academic Tom Paulin wrote a poem which included a reference to Palestinians being 'gunned down by the Zionist SS.'[3] In an interview with the Egyptian newspaper *Al Ahram* in 2002, he called for Jewish settlers in the West Bank to be 'shot dead,' adding, 'I think they are Nazis, racists, I feel nothing but hatred for them.'[4] In 2009, during the Gaza offensive, Yasmin Alibai-Brown asked, 'How many Palestinian Anne Franks did the Israelis murder, maim or turn mad?'[5] By her logic, Israel's targeting of Palestinians in that enclave was akin to the round up of innocent Jewish children by the Nazis in the war. It was a clear attempt to picture Gaza as an extermination camp that had been built on the memories of the last Holocaust.

For Richard Falk, UN Special Rapporteur for the 'Palestinian territories,' Gaza was akin to the Warsaw Ghetto. In his article from 2009 called 'Slouching towards a Palestinian Holocaust,' he wrote that the 'dire and worsening situation in Gaza threatens to produce a new holocaust' and denied that it was an 'irresponsible overstatement to associate the treatment of Palestinians in Gaza with this criminalized Nazi record of collective atrocity.'[6] At the height of the Gaza offensive in 2014, former Labour Deputy Prime Minister Lord John Prescott likened Gaza to a 'concentration camp' and in a subsequent telephone conversation with the author, claimed that the type of concentration camps he was referring to were actually those constructed by Britain in the Second Boer War. It was pointed out, to little avail, that few

---

[1] Lesley Klaff 'Holocaust Inversion and contemporary antisemitism' *Fathom*, Winter/ 2014.

[2] Julian Evans, "The militant magician," *The Guardian*, December 28, 2002.

[3] Tom Paulin, "Killed in Crossfire," *The Guardian*, February 18, 2001.

[4] Sarah Hall, "Death to Jewish settlers, says anti-Zionist poet," *The Guardian*, April 13, 2002.

[5] Yasmin Alibhai-Brown, "Israel's friends cannot justify this slaughter," *The Independent*, January 19, 2009.

[6] Richard Falk, "Slouching Towards a Palestinian Holocaust," *Countercurrents* (blog), July 7, 2007, https://www.tni.org/my/node/9132, accessed 19 April 2024.

would associate the term 'concentration camp' with the Boer War, as opposed to the Nazi constructed death camps.

Following the start of Operation Swords of Iron, comparisons of Israel and Nazi Germany were commonplace. Brazilian President Luiz Inácio Lula da Silva caused outrage when he said: 'What's happening in the Gaza Strip isn't a war, it's a genocide. It's not a war of soldiers against soldiers. It's a war between a highly prepared army and women and children.'[1]

Consistent with this demonization of Israel is the notion that its population has been transformed from the 'oppressed to oppressors,' to quote political theorist Alex Ryvchin.[2] The British children's author Roald Dahl was typical in this respect. In 1982 Dahl wrote a review for *Literary Review* in which he said this of Jewish people: 'Never before in the history of man has a race of people switched so rapidly from being much-pitied victims to barbarous murderers.'[3] Dahl may have tried to justify this in view of the perceived ruthlessness of the Israeli army in Beirut. In reality, he was simply venting his long-held prejudice against Jewish people.

For some, this alleged Nazi behaviour is particularly shocking because it represents a failure of Jews to comprehend their own suffering. These critics argue that the Holocaust should be seen as an eye opening educational opportunity in anti-racism at which the Jews had the privilege of a front row seat. By reincarnating themselves as Nazis, the Jews were missing the whole point of 1939-1945. Thus, the race relations activist Lee Jasper once declared that Israel had 'failed to learn the lessons of its own tragic history having evolved into a racist oppressor.' He added: 'Israel has...allowed itself to turn into the very thing that it despises the most, a political ideology that seeks to oppress people on the basis of race or religion.'[4] In 1982 the Nicaraguan delegate to the UN stated: 'It is difficult to believe that a people that suffered so much from the Nazi policy of extermination in the middle of the twentieth century would use the same fascist, genocidal arguments and

---

[1] Lazar Berman, "Israel livid as Brazil's Lula says Israel like 'Hitler,' committing genocide in Gaza," *The Times of Israel*, February 18, 2024.

[2] Alex Ryvchin, *The 7 Deadly Myths: Antisemitism from the time of Christ to Kanye West*, (Academic Studies Press, 2023), chapter 7.

[3] Megan McCluskey, "What to Know About Children's Author Roald Dahl's Controversial Legacy," *Time*, March 18, 2021.

[4] Jennifer Lipman, "Lee Jasper shows no respect for Israel or HMD," *The Jewish Chronicle*, January 24, 2013.

methods against other peoples.'[1] For these people, the Holocaust had to be seen, less as a tragedy for the Jews, and more as a learning experience in which 'ignorant' Jews came to utilize the dark arts of Nazi sadism so as to oppress the Palestinians.

Such malevolent discourse has been accompanied by equally perverse and graphic imagery, all designed to blacken Israel in the eyes of the public. In 1988, the Kuwaiti paper *Al-Rai Al-Aam* drew an image of an Israeli soldier (with a clearly visible Star of David on his helmet) shovelling a baby into a furnace, a clear allusion to the crematoria in the death camps.[2] This combined several ideas: that the Jewish nation was a child killing state, that it was a devilish state and that Jews were living Nazis.

In April 2002, a Greek paper showed a cartoon by Greek activist Stathis Stavropoulos in which a soldier (possibly Israeli) was screaming: 'Whoever was killed by bad Ariel Sharon and bad George Bush should go to the right...whoever was killed by good Shimon Peres and good Colin Powell should go to the left.'[3] In other words, Israel was re-enacting the gruesome selection process at the extermination camps though under the pretence that some of its leaders, unlike the Nazis, were deemed to be virtuous. Meanwhile the war started on October 7 spawned a vast outpouring of antisemitic cartoons from the Arab world, including ones that defamed Israel as a Nazi state.[4]

If Jews have failed to gain the essential insight into the Holocaust, it follows that the community's memorials to the dead, far from being honoured by non-Jews, can be attacked and desecrated to make a political point. In 2018, members of Students for Justice in Palestine at Columbia University chose to hold an anti-Israel demonstration opposite an event that marked Holocaust Memorial Day. Their protest aimed to 'show solidarity with the 30,000 Palestinians participating in the #GreatReturnMarch,' and students could be heard chanting: 'From the river to the sea, Palestine will be free.' Two years

---

[1] William Schabas, *Genocide in International Law: The Crimes of Crimes*. (Cambridge: Cambridge University Press, 2000), 454.

[2] Ian Black, "Cartoon symbols of the Israeli-Palestinian conflict," *The Guardian*, December 19, 2008.

[3] "Anti-Semitism in Greece: A Current Picture 2001-2002," *Eurac Research*, November 2022, http://miris.eurac.edu/mugs2/do/blob.html%3Ftype=html&serial=1044527060367.html, accessed May 5, 2024.

[4] "Antisemitism in Arab Cartoons during the Israel-Hamas War: A Chronology of Dehumanization of Jews and Demonization of Zionism and Israel," *Anti-Defamation League*, December 21, 2013.

later, a group of BDS activists in Germany interrupted an online memorial for Holocaust Remembrance Day with 'images of Hitler, pornographic content and anti-Israeli and antisemitic slogans.' In other words, 'anti-fascists' from a nation which perpetrated the Holocaust were prepared to interrupt and derail a solemn commemoration of the dead by tarnishing it with the very images of hatred and destruction that symbolized the catastrophe. Holocaust memorials across Europe were also defaced after the October 7 attacks. In one typical example, a statue of Anne Frank in Amsterdam was daubed with 'Gaza' graffiti, leading to a fierce condemnation from local Mayor Femke Halsema.[1]

These anti-Israel activists wish to attack the notion of Jewish victimhood and persecution because they feel it will undermine support for Israel and transfer it instead to Israel's 'victims,' the Palestinians. They cannot, in other words, simultaneously make the case for a safe and secure Jewish state, and argue for Palestinian rights. One thing has to cancel the other in a zero-sum game.

Refutation

Professor Alan Johnson is right to label this abuse of Holocaust memory 'a grotesque inversion of morality and truth.'[2] It is important to understand why the charge is baseless in fact, law and logic. Secondly, it will help to turn the tables on the accuser, showing why the genocide accusation can be levelled at Israel's worst critics in the region.

Genocide is defined by the 1948 UN Convention[3] as a series of acts that are committed with the 'intent to destroy, in whole or in part, a national, ethnical, racial or religious group.'[4] These acts include 'killing members of the group,' 'causing serious bodily or mental harm to members of the group,' 'deliberately inflicting on the group conditions of life calculated to bring about its physical destruction in whole or in part,' 'imposing measures intended to prevent births within the group' and 'forcibly transferring children of the group to another group.' Intent is critical; simply killing members of a particular ethnic or racial group is not per se genocidal. It is only when they

---

[1] Benjamin Brown and Teele Rebane, "Anne Frank monument defaced with 'Gaza' graffiti in Amsterdam," *CNN*, July 10, 2024.

[2] Alan Johnson, "Comparing Israel to the Nazis is a grotesque inversion of truth," *The Telegraph*, November 2, 2023.

[3] UN Convention on the Prevention and Punishment of the Crime of Genocide.

[4] The term genocide was coined by a Polish Jew, Raphael Lemkin, who lost most of his family in the Holocaust.

are killed *because* they belong to that group, and with an intention to destroy that group, that it is genocide.[1] Genocide is the 'crime of crimes' and the most unforgivable stain on any nation.

The Holocaust, an attempt to eradicate the biological basis of European Jewry, was an industrial genocide, carried out with all the instruments of modern science and technology and characterized by a terrifying level of organization and efficiency. It followed a period of six years in which the Nazi regime excluded Jews from public life, encouraged their humiliation in public, stripped them of citizenship, vilified them in the media, orchestrated acts of mass violence and coerced them to emigrate.

Another genocide occurred in Indonesia between 1975 and 1999 when tens (possibly hundreds) of thousands of Timorese were brutally murdered by the Indonesian New Order government and its military. The crimes committed against the people of east Timor included murder, forcible expulsion, starvation, kidnapping and forced birth control. In 1994, some 800,000 members of the Tutsi minority in Rwanda were slaughtered by militias and civilians from the dominant Hutu tribe. The killing spree of Tutsis was endorsed enthusiastically by the government, the military and the media following a wave of hate speech against a Tutsi population that had been likened to cockroaches. These genocides involved government planning, demonization, systematic preparation and eventual slaughter.

The charge of genocide does not apply to the conflict between Israel and the Palestinians on the basis of either demographic factors or intent. Whereas the Holocaust destroyed two thirds of European Jewry, reducing a prewar population of 9 million people to some 3 million, the Palestinian population has significantly increased since 1948. According to the Palestinian Central Bureau of Statistics, the Palestinian population in the West Bank stood at 690,000 in 1967 with some 340,000 Palestinians in Gaza. In 2022, according to the US State Department, there were over three million Palestinians in the West Bank and nearly two million in Gaza.[2] The demographics refute the charge that Israel has been engaged in a long-term campaign of genocide.

It is of course true that many Palestinians have been killed in the various conflicts with Israel over recent decades, especially since the disengagement from Gaza in 2005. Some of those killed, quite tragically, have been civilians,

---

[1] What is crucial is the dolis specialis (special intent) to destroy a group.

[2] "2024 Country Reports on Human Rights Practices: Israel, West Bank and Gaza—West Bank and Gaza," United States Department of State.

including children. It is estimated that since the inception of the Arab-Israeli conflict in 1920, over 91,000 Arabs and Palestinians have been killed during wars with Israel, with close to 25,000 Israeli fatalities.[1] Many of these are terrorists and fighters who were killed in war. If we add those who have killed after October 7, assuming that Hamas's figures are correct (there are many reasons to doubt this), the number rises to perhaps 150,000. This equates to some 1,500 killed per year since 1920, less than three deaths per day with a substantial percentage of those killed being armed combatants.

Given the vast military capabilities of the Israeli armed forces, a truly genocidal Israel would be capable of an ongoing killing spree that would by now have decimated the entire Palestinian population throughout the territories. The question of intent is also crucial in this context. The accuser has to prove that Israeli governments have always intended to eliminate Palestinian Arabs by various means ranging from violent attacks in war to starvation. Aside from the demographic arguments presented above, one problem for the accuser is the existence of an ethnically identical community to the Palestinian Arabs, namely today's sizeable Israeli Arab community. Today, the Arab community makes up 21% of the country's population according to the Israeli Central Bureau of Statistics. In absolute terms, this is a population of approximately 2.1 million, up from 156,000 in 1948. If there was a policy to make the country Arab-rein, why would the Arabs have multiplied in number so significantly? A truly genocidal nation would see such a population rise, with all the attendant civil rights that go along with it, as a spectacular form of negligence.

If the experience of Israeli Arabs was deemed equivalent to that of Germany's Jews before 1939, it would rewrite the history of Hitler's domestic policies. Nazi Germany would have had Jewish judges in its supreme court, Jews would have served in the Wehrmacht, often with distinction, Jewish policemen would have helped to enforce the law, Jewish doctors and nurses would have been allowed to treat Germans in hospitals right up to the start of the war, Jews and non-Jews would have voted on equal terms, both groups would have mingled freely on buses, restaurants and universities, German NGOs would have been allowed to defend Jewish rights against the state with legal immunity and laws against incitement would have been enforced

---

[1] "Total Casualties, Arab-Israeli Conflict 1860-Present," jewishvirtuallibrary, https://www.jewishvirtuallibrary.org/total-casualties-arab-israeli-conflict, accessed 17 September 2025. These figures do not include the casualty counts from the most recent war in 2023.

routinely. All of this would have happened against a backdrop of permanent terrorism from a Jewish community whose intent was to bring the German state to its knees. The comparison is not just inapt; it makes no sense at all.

Related to this is a question of Israel's conduct in recent wars with Palestinian terrorist groups. Taking the Swords of Iron war as an example, Israel has repeatedly warned Palestinian civilians to leave parts of Gaza due to impending military operations in the area. It has conducted leaflet drops and sent text messages to civilians warning of coming attacks,[1] leading to a mass evacuation of people. Israel delayed its ground invasion of Gaza by several weeks and had regular daily pauses to allow medicine and food to enter the Strip. One has to ask why such tactics would be used unless the intent behind them was to save lives.

The accusation of slow genocide, namely that Israel has sought to lower living standards of Palestinians living under their direct control to hasten their demise, is equally without merit. Examining policy towards the West Bank when it was most directly under Israeli rule (1967 to 1994), one sees a very different picture. From 1967, Israel spent hundreds of millions of dollars to improve roads, the sewer system, electricity and water facilities. This meant that within two decades, over 90 percent of the population in the West Bank and Gaza had electricity around the clock, as compared to one in five people in 1967; 85 percent had running water in dwellings, as compared to 16 percent in 1967 and 83.5 percent had electric or gas ranges for cooking, as compared to 4 percent in 1967. An increasing number of Palestinians had regular access to over 100 medical clinics, which also drastically raised living standards. From 1968 to 2000, Palestinian infant mortality fell from 60 to 15 per 1,000 live births and fatal diseases such as polio, whooping cough, tetanus and measles were eradicated.[2] Life expectancy for Palestinians increased from 48 in 1967 to 72 in 2000.

The irony of the genocide charge is that it can certainly be levelled at Israel's enemies, both those with some military capability in the region (Hamas, Hezbollah and Iran) and those without but who call for Israel's destruction. The starting point for Hamas is the Charter written in 1988. Article 6 of this document makes a clarion call to 'raise the banner of Allah over every inch of Palestine.' Article 11 states that Palestine is an 'Islamic

---

[1] Emine Sinmaz, "Israel drops leaflets warning people to flee southern Gaza towns," *The Guardian*, November 16, 2023.

[2] Efraim Karsh, "What occupation?" *Commentary,* July-August 2002.

Waqf [endowment]' which has been 'consecrated for future Muslim generations until Judgement Day.' It goes on to say that no part of it can be 'squandered' or 'given up.'

Article 19 of the *Hamas Principles and Policies* (2017) declares that 'There shall be no recognition of the legitimacy of the Zionist entity' while elsewhere, the Zionist project is described as 'racist, anti-human and colonial.' Khaled Mashaal, a leader in exile, has since declared that 'Palestine is ours from the river to the sea and from the south to the north' and that there will be 'no concession on any inch of the land.'[1] What this states with crystal clarity is that Israel as a Jewish state must be destroyed in its entirety if Hamas's demands are to be met. Those who doubt whether this involves murderous violence need only look at the hideous massacres of October 7.

The same is true for Hezbollah, which has revealed to the world its anti-Zionist position most unequivocally. In its 1985 manifesto, it talks of how its struggle with the 'Zionist entity' will end 'only when this entity is obliterated,' adding: 'We recognize no treaty with it, no ceasefire and no peace agreements, whether separate or consolidated.'[2] Hezbollah's aim is not just to 'liberate' Palestine but to annihilate world Jewry. Their leader, Hassan Nasrallah, has stated this brazenly enough when he said: 'If Jews all gather in Israel, it will save us the trouble of going after them worldwide.'[3]

Hezbollah is a client state and proxy of the Iranian regime. In recent decades, Iranian leaders have repeatedly used genocidal language towards the Jewish state as part of an ideology of annihilationism. Among those who call for Israel's destruction is Ali Khamenei, who has described Israel as a 'cancerous tumour' that must be removed.[4] Former President Ahmadinejad has extended the microbiological analogy by calling Israel a 'filthy germ.'[5] Akbar Rafsanjani, an alleged moderate, once extolled the advantages of an Islamic nuclear attack on Israel. He said: 'An atomic bomb would not leave anything in Israel but the same thing would just produce damages in the

---

1 "Doctrine of Hamas," *Wilson Center*, October 20, 2023, https://www.wilsoncenter.org/article/doctrine-hamas, accessed February 29, 2025.
2 Quoted in *As Safir*, February 16, 1985.
3 Quoted in *Lebanon Daily Star,* October 23, 2002.
4 Alex Spillius, "Iran's supreme leader vows to confront 'cancerous tumour' of Israel," *The Daily Telegraph*, February 3, 2012.
5 "UN Chief: Ahmadinejad's verbal attacks on Israel intolerable," *Haaretz*, February 21, 2008.

Muslim world.'[1] These leaders demonstrate the notion that irrational accusations against Israel are so often a form of projection, a confession of their own twisted desires for mass murder.

An even more perverse irony is that a nation which accuses Israel of genocide and seeks to carry out that act by all means possible also officially denies the genocide that its inhabitants suffered prior to the state's founding. On January 23, 1998, President Rafsanjani claimed that only 200,000 Jews were killed in the Holocaust.[2] In the same year, President Khatami lauded Roger Garaudy as a thinker and believer, even though Garaudy was a well-known Holocaust denier.[3] In 2001, Ayatollah Khamenei claimed that the number of Jews killed during the Holocaust was 'fabricated to solicit the sympathy of world public opinion, lay the ground for the occupation of Palestine, and justify the atrocities of the Zionists.'[4] In December 2005, in a speech broadcast on television, President Ahmadinejad claimed that the Jews 'created a myth in the name of the Holocaust and valued that higher than God, religion, and the prophets.'[5] In 2006, Iran announced a cartoon contest to mock the Holocaust, attracting some well-known Holocaust deniers and trivializers. In July 2011, its ambassador to Uruguay, Hojatollaji Soltani, mused thus in Montevideo: 'Maybe a few thousand died… but 2 million, 3 million, 6 million? This is a lie.'[6] As recently as 2025, Ayatollah Khamenei sparked outrage when he complained that in Europe, when 'a person expresses his objection to the myth of the Holocaust and announces that he does not believe in it, they throw him into prison.'[7]

The Iranian regime is thus in the grip of the most abhorrent form of genocide denial while both accusing Israel of genocide and plotting another one on the Jewish state. That the West remains in denial of all this is truly shocking and shameful.

---

[1] Emanuele Ottolenghi, *Under a Mushroom Cloud: Europe, Iran and the Bomb,* (London: Profile Books, 2019), 90-1.

[2] Dave Rich, "Holocaust Denial as an Anti-Zionist and Anti-Imperialist Tool for the European Far Left," *The Jerusalem Center for Security and Foreign Affairs*, January 9, 2008.

[3] Behnam Gholipour, 'Antisemitism and Holocaust Denial in Iran: A Review of State Narratives Since 1979,' *Iranwire*, November 29, 2021.

[4] Reuel Marc Gerecht and Ray Takeyh, "The real reason Iran Hates Israel," *The Wall Street Journal*, November 27, 2023.

[5] "Holocaust a myth, says Iranian president," *The Guardian*, December 14, 2005.

[6] "The Threat from Iran," *The Journal*, July 12, 2012.

[7] Amotz Asa-El, "Khamenei's Holocaust denial sparks outrage as Jews mark Purim," *The Jerusalem Post*, March 14, 2025.

3. The Israeli lobby controls western governments and policy makers

Charge

One of the most familiar antisemitic tropes in the anti-Israel movement is the notion that Israel controls the policies of western governments. The Jewish state is depicted as a troubling menace and strategic liability, as well as a national embodiment of political skulduggery in world affairs. For its critics, there is no end to Israeli manipulation. One minute it is seeking to undermine world governments with false accusations of antisemitism. The next it is plotting pro-Israel policies in other nations that bear no relation to those countries' real interests. For its critics, Israel invents spurious reasons why countries should declare war in the Middle East and manipulates nations into defending its own 'nefarious' behaviour. It purportedly carries out false flag attacks in western countries, and supports or creates terrorist groups to do its bidding, all designed to bring subservient western politicians to heel. There seems to be no end to the evil machinations, devious plotting and malevolent deception of the Jewish state.

At this stage, a quick caveat is required. One can certainly make legitimate criticisms about pro-Israeli lobby groups, whether in the UK, the US or elsewhere. A critic can claim that such lobbies are too sanguine in their view of Israel or too critical of Israel's enemies. They can challenge the claims made by groups such as BICOM and AIPAC that the West should deepen its ties with the Jewish state or argue that bilateral links with Israel harm western interests. Naturally, such arguments can be contested (they frequently are) but they are not necessarily antisemitic ones. In the same way, one can and should criticize the gun lobby (the NRA especially), the smoking lobby, the oil lobby and the food lobby. The arguments for and against the tactics and arguments of these groups are part and parcel of healthy, democratic debate and help inform the making of public policy. Criticising the views of AIPAC can be a legitimate exercise. What makes a claim about the Israel lobby antisemitic is the allegation of total manipulative control; the idea that Israel has octopus like tentacles which shape and determine the policies of another country and that its motives and interests in international statesmanship are always selfish, malign, devious and harmful to other nations.

If one glances at the recent political landscape in Britain and the US, one sees no shortage of conspiracy mongering about Israel's alleged control of global politics. Labour MP Tam Dalyell, a long-term opponent of British military intervention around the world, argued that Tony Blair had fallen under the spell of a 'cabal of Jewish advisers.' The three advisors that he had in mind were Lord Levy, Jack Straw and Peter Mandelson, and he went on to express his concern about Britain 'being led up the garden path on a Likudnik, [Ariel] Sharon agenda.'[1] The problem was that only one of these British advisors (Levy) was Jewish, though the other two had some Jewish ancestry. The word cabal is usually associated with secret plotting and intrigue, just the kind of language that one finds in the Protocols.[2]

But he was not the only fringe figure to be seduced by this type of conspiratorial thinking. Former Liberal Democrat politician, Baroness Jenny Tonge, complained at a party gathering that the pro-Israel lobby had 'got its grips on the western world, its financial grips' and they had 'probably got a grip on our party.'[3] This followed earlier remarks in which she said she would consider becoming a suicide bomber if she had been subjected to the kind of experiences faced by Palestinians.[4] Her political colleague, Chris Davies, warned in 2006 that he would 'denounce the influence of the Jewish lobby' that seems to have 'far too great a say over the political decision-making process in many countries.'[5] Former Labour MP Martin Linton, speaking before the 2010 elections, claimed in a meeting that there were 'long tentacles of Israel in this country who are funding election campaigns and putting money into the British political system for their own ends.'[6] The use of the term 'tentacle' to describe the machinations of global Jewry would not have been lost on figures like Edouard Drumont.

All these figures were alleging that the shaping of foreign and domestic policy was guided, unduly influenced or even controlled by an Israeli lobby. Sometimes, there is support for such views from within Israel itself, Thus, left-wing Israeli journalist Mira Bar Hillel denounced the 'guiding hand' behind the strategy of silencing British politicians who would otherwise be

---

[1] Nicholas Watt, "Dalyell may face race hatred inquiry," *The Guardian*, May 5, 2003.

[2] Dalyell later claimed that the lobby he was referring to was an American one, though there too, the key figures identified were Jews.

[3] 'Tonge condemned for Israel remark,' *BBC News*, September 21, 2006.

[4] Nicholas Watt, "Lib Dem MP; Why I would consider being a suicide bomber," *The Guardian*, January 23, 2004.

[5] David Hirsh, 'Revenge of the Jewish lobby?' *The Guardian*, May 5, 2006.

[6] Martin Bright, "MP: Israel's tentacles will steal the election," *The Jewish Chronicle*, March 29, 2010.

critical of Israeli policy were it not for fear of 'being accused of anti-Semitism.'[1] Another example came in 2020 following the murder of George Floyd. A faction within the UK BLM movement suggested that British politics had been 'gagged of the right to critique Zionism' amid a policy of colonialism in the West Bank.[2]

Others have focused on the idea that Israel has silenced Britain's mainstream media. To take just one example of many, former BBC Middle East correspondent Tim Llewellyn, speaking at a book launch hosted by Middle East Monitor in October 2012, claimed that the BBC was under enormous pressure from a 'careful, well-organized, assiduous propaganda campaign' by the UK's Israeli lobby. The pressure to silence the mainstream media's reporting on Israel came from 'the higher level of pro-Israel Zionists' who were 'scattered at strategic points throughout the British establishment.'[3] The Australian left wing journalist John Pilger voiced similar sentiments following the BBC's refusal to show his documentary, *Palestine is Still the Issue*. He claimed that the pro-Israel lobby 'intimidates journalists to ensure that most coverage remains biased in its favour.'[4]

The accusation that a 'pro-Israel' lobby was engineering US foreign policy, in a direct threat to that country's national interests, was made prior to the second Iraq war. In 2002, former German defence minister Rudolf Scharping commented that President Bush needed to overthrow Saddam Hussein, not because he had a personal stake in removing the dictator or because economic interests were predominant, but because he had to curry favour with 'a powerful – perhaps overly powerful – Jewish lobby' in the coming US elections. In somewhat smug fashion, he went on to say that his own country, in the absence of such a powerful lobby, could afford to stay out of the conflict.[5] Doubtless, this also reflected the strong anti-Americanism that typified the Schröder administration as it sought to distance itself from calls for war. But it was the Jewish element that stood out.

One lecturer at the University of California at Irvine, discussing the war, said: 'If you have any questions why we're in Iraq, ask the Jews in the

---

[1] Mira Bar Hillel, "The truth about the UK's pro-Israel lobbies," *The Independent*, September 1, 2014.
[2] #BlackLivesMatterUK, *Twitter Post*, 28 June 2020, 10:50.
[3] Melanie Phillips, "Assiduous Campaign? Where?" *The Jewish Chronicle*, October 26, 2012.
[4] John Pilger, "Why my film is under fire," *The Guardian*, September 23, 2002.
[5] William Safire, "The German Problem," *The New York Times*, September 19, 2002.

audience.'[1] This was a clear attempt to imply that Jews, all Jews, were effectively pawns in a global network of Israeli influence that was being extended to the realms of academia. Helen Thomas, part of the White House press corps, once declared that Jews possessed 'power over the White House, power over Congress,' claiming: 'It's real power when you own the White House.' She added: 'Everybody is in the pocket of the Israeli lobbies which are funded by wealthy supporters, including those from Hollywood.'[2] In a later speech, she said that 'Congress, the White House, Hollywood and Wall Street' were all 'owned by Zionists.'[3]

While Thomas might have considered herself left wing and progressive, others of a different ilk have imbibed the same theories. Thus, the accusation of a Jewish global conspiracy has been embraced by David Duke, the grand wizard of the Ku Klux Klan. In a YouTube video from 2014 called 'The Illustrated Protocols of Zion,' he argued that the document was not a forgery and that groups like AIPAC revealed the existence of a real Jewish conspiracy. He declared: 'The Protocols of Zion could have just as easily been titled "The Protocols of Zionism"... The modern elders are leaders of Zionism.'

Some influential European figures cannot avoid the temptation to indulge freely in this antisemitic conspiratorial thinking. Thus, Pertti Salolainen, a former minister in the Finnish government, stated that America found it 'difficult to take a more neutral stance on the Israel-Palestine issue because they have a large Jewish population who have a significant control of the money and the media' in the country. He described this as a 'sad truth about US politics.'[4] In one statement, Salolainen combined the idea that Jews controlled the US monetary system, the media and the political system. Even cruder were the views of Karel de Gucht, a European commissioner for trade and former Belgian foreign minister, a man who invoked the spectre of the Jewish lobby in attempting to show why peace talks in the Middle East were doomed. 'Do not underestimate the Jewish lobby on Capitol Hill. That is the best organized lobby, you shouldn't underestimate the grip it has on American politics - no matter whether its Republicans or Democrats.'[5] Such

---

[1] Kenneth L Marcus, *Definition of antisemitism*, (Wiley: OUP USA, 2015), 25.

[2] "Helen Thomas: Jews in total control of US," *Ynetnews*, March 19, 2011.

[3] "Helen Thomas' school scraps award over 'Zionists' remark," *CNN*, December 5, 2010.

[4] Benjamin Weinthal, "Finnish politician: Jews control money, media in US," *The Jerusalem Post*, December 1, 2012.

[5] Ian Traynor, "Anger at EU's chief Middle East outburst," *The Guardian*, September 3, 2010.

reductionist, monocausal and essentialist explanations are designed to simplify the complex process by which western foreign policy is made. They appeal to a segment of the public which wants to assign blame for the highly questionable decisions taken by successive political leaders. But in their defiance of the facts and logic, they fail to land with any force.

Refutation

The simplest proof that Israel does not control the organs of policy making in the West is listening to what politicians, media figures and policymakers outside of Israel actually say about the conflict. The UK is an interesting place to start, given that it was the progenitor of the Balfour Declaration in 1917. In some ways, the UK media is ground zero for western media criticism of Israel. Publications like *The Guardian*, *The Independent* and *The Economist* have printed a range of extremely hostile commentary on Israel, with some articles even questioning the country's right to exist and denouncing its policies in incendiary terms. Even more supportive publications, such as *The Times*, have questioned the Israeli narrative on some major issues and none could be described as mouthpieces for the Netanyahu government.

The BBC, the most influential broadcaster in the world, has refused to call Hamas a terrorist organization without attribution, accused Israel of targeting children and unfairly libelled Jewish victims of antisemitism in the UK. During Israel's recent wars in Gaza, the BBC has focused a great deal on Palestinian suffering in that enclave. Images beamed to western audiences, ones that feature dead bodies, shattered apartment blocks, scorched cars and damaged hospitals, suggest that Israel has used excessive and disproportionate force to achieve its objectives. These reports have implied that Israel had been engaged in a display of aggressive and destructive behaviour, targeting innocent civilians in a reckless killing spree. The BBC has also consistently fought against demands to publish in open the 2004 Balen Report, incurring significant legal expenses in the process.

Successive British governments, despite having positive relations with the Jewish state, have refused to move their embassy from Tel Aviv to Jerusalem despite a clear request from Israel that this be done. Despite friendly relations with Israel under the governments of Tony Blair, Gordon Brown, Theresa May, David Cameron and Boris Johnson, each of these UK administrations has made clear their opposition to Israeli settlements. For the

UK government, these settlements are not only deemed to be illegal but are widely seen as a major stumbling block to any negotiated peace with the Palestinians. In addition, Israeli pressure has been unable to budge the UK government's support for the Iranian nuclear deal (the JCPOA) and the two-state solution, as well as failing to shift many votes at the UN.

If the pro-Israel lobby controls the levers of power, one might also ask why it has had such little sway over the Foreign and Commonwealth Office. The FCDO has long been accused of an Arabist leaning, having advised British governments in the 1950s not to sell arms to Israel, rejecting an Israeli request to join the Commonwealth, supporting an Israeli withdrawal from all territory taken in 1967, criticising Israel during the 1982 Lebanon war and promoting the visits of HM Queen Elizabeth II to a succession of Arab countries but *never* to the Jewish state. The FCDO has long been aligned with the commercial and political interests of the wider Middle East and prioritized these interests over those of Israel.

There is a similar story in the US with two administrations proving the point here. There are many times when an Israeli administration has been unable to persuade its American counterpart to adopt a policy in line with Jerusalem's interests. It is worth revisiting the Iraq War (2003) at this point, as it has often assumed to have been started at Jerusalem's specific urging. In fact, Israel saw Iran as a bigger threat than Saddam's Iraq. Lawrence Wilkerson, who was Chief of Staff for Colin Powell, remembered the Israeli message to Bush in 2002: 'If you are going to destabilize the balance of power, do it against the main enemy.' He went on to describe this warning as 'pervasive' in Israel's communications with the administration, and that it was communicated by 'a wide range of Israeli sources, including political figures, intelligence and private citizens.'[1]

President Bush also protested Israel's use of American made helicopters that were being used for targeted killings, imposing an embargo on spare parts. In 2007, the Bush administration refused an Israeli request to bomb suspected nuclear sites in Syria, leaving the job to the government of Ehud Olmert. It also downplayed the extent of the Iranian nuclear threat in an infamous National Intelligence Estimate.

In 2015, President Obama refused an Israeli request to link Iran's recognition of Israel to the nuclear deal that was then under discussion.

[1] Gareth Porter, "Israel warned us not to invade Iraq after 9/11," *IPS*, August 28, 2007.

Instead, Obama said that the treaty would address Iran's nuclear weapons programme.[1] Obama had in fact spent years criticising the expansion of Israeli settlements, much to the chagrin of Israeli leaders, and his language and tone caused a perceived rift between the two capitals. It was a rift which only worsened when Netanyahu accepted an invitation to address the US Congress in 2015, an occasion used by the Israeli Prime Minister to urge a changed approach over the nuclear deal. In the end, the deal was signed by the US and its European partners against Israeli wishes. This administration, like others before it, defied Israeli requests to release Jonathan Pollard, the US spy convicted for passing secrets to Israel.[2]

Another salient feature of the Obama administration was the influence of Arabists within the State Department, an organ of foreign policy making whose Middle East views are often likened to those of the Foreign Office. One of the most famous of these Arabists was John Kerry, Secretary of State between 2013 and 2017, who famously declared that 'there will be no advanced and separate peace with the Arab world without the Palestinian process and Palestinian peace.'[3] In 2016, Kerry delivered a speech in which he lambasted Israel's government as 'the most rightwing coalition in Israeli history' and warned that the expansion of settlements in the West Bank meant that 'the status quo is leading toward one state and perpetual occupation.'[4] The hostility he showed recalled that of previous senior officials, among them James Baker and national security advisors Brent Scowcroft and Zbigniew Brzezinski.[5]

Others will argue that the pro-Israel lobby, or the Israeli government itself, pressures the US (Israel's main ally in the international community) into providing automatic support for the Jewish state at the UN. In particular, the US veto against anti-Israel resolutions is seen as a fixity in international diplomacy and a guarantee that all hostility towards Israel will be deflected. But it was not until 1972 that America first vetoed a UN Security Council

[1] The nuclear treaty was known as the Joint Comprehensive Plan of Action (2015).

[2] Pollard was finally released in 2015 and, -five years later, the former spy relocated to Israel.

[3] Joseph Wulfsohn, "John Kerry mocked for 2016 claim that 'there will be no separate peace' between Israel-Arab nations without the Palestinians," *foxnews.com*, September 16, 2020.

[4] Heather Stewart, "Theresa May's criticism of John Kerry Israel speech sparks blunt US reply," *The Guardian*, December 29, 2016.

[5] Gerald Posner, "How Obama flubbed his missile message," *The Daily Beast*, September 17, 2009.

resolution that was critical of Israel. Furthermore, American support for Israel in the Security Council is far from guaranteed anyway. From 1973 to 2006, America used its veto on roughly 40% of occasions, effectively endorsing anti-Israel resolutions through support or abstention nearly two thirds of the time.[1]

What is true of the US is even more true of other western allies, including in Europe. Between 2015 and the end of 2023, there have been 141 UN General Assembly resolutions against Israel while other countries have attracted far less attention (and opprobrium). In the same time period, there have been resolutions against Russia (23), Iran (7), North Korea (8), Syria (10), Myanmar (7) and 0 resolutions for China, Libya, Cuba, Turkey and Qatar. At the General Assembly, Germany, one of Israel's main allies in Europe, has voted for 71% of anti-Israel resolutions and only voted with Israel on 4% of the resolutions. France has voted against Israel on 73% of the resolutions and never voted even once with Israel. Poland too has never voted once with Israel but also supported 72% of anti-Israel resolutions.

Quite simply, if Israel really controlled western foreign policy, the US and the UK would have invaded Iran in 2003, potentially bringing down that regime. They would not have armed a number of Israel's Arab neighbours, especially Saudi Arabia, criticized settlement policy or ignored the threat from Syria. There would also be unanimous levels of support for Israel within the UN.

The reason for all this is that western foreign policy is the outgrowth of what is perceived to be in the national interest, not the interests of any one regional ally. Talking of the US, Secretary of State, George Schultz, said something of great importance: 'When we make a wrong decision – even one that is recommended by Israel and supported by American Jewish groups – it is our decision, and one for which we alone are responsible. We are not babes in the wood, easily convinced to support Israel's or any other state's agenda. We act in our own interests.'[2] American foreign policy interests in the Middle East are closely bound up with Israeli ones but this does not translate into automatic support.

America's strategic interests, such as the need to secure the flow of oil and sell arms and other goods, require friendly relations with a number of

---

[1] Mitchell Bard, *The Arab Lobby: The Invisible Alliance That Undermines America's Influence in the Middle East*, (Harper Collins, 2010), 195.
[2] Abe Foxman, *The Deadliest Lies: The Israel Lobby and the Myth of Jewish Control*, (New York: St Martin's Press, 2007), p. 17.

Arab regimes, principally the Saudis and Qatar. They need to station troops in friendly regimes, hence the ties to countries such as Bahrain, which hosts the fifth fleet, and Qatar, home to the largest US air base in the Middle East. Their economic, military and diplomatic interests ground their presence across the region and make the US sensitive to the concerns of their Arab allies. The same is true for European nations. They require oil imports from Arab countries and need to maintain access to energy resources. They are also keenly aware that conflict in that region spills over into migration and feeds unrest among their own domestic Muslim populations. These interests mean that there can never be a blank cheque for an Israeli security or political request, a factor well understood in Jerusalem.

4. Israel was behind 9/11 and the rise of ISIS

In the age of conspiracy theories, no single event seems to have catalysed the 'true believers' more than the 9/11 attacks on New York and Washington. There is a whole industry devoted to proving that the terrorist assault on that deadly morning was engineered, not by 19 members of al-Qaeda, but by the US government in cahoots with other elements of the deep state and external actors. In other words, 9/11 is depicted as a false flag attack, a hostile act designed to look as if it was carried out by another entity other than the one responsible. An alternate reading is that the government had foreknowledge of the attack but allowed it to proceed so as to give the US a pretext for pursuing an aggressive foreign policy in the Middle East. Some believe that the main actor was a hostile and aggressive US government whereas for others, the US was the lapdog of external forces, primarily Israel.

The antisemitic conspiracy theory usually goes something like this: Israel did 9/11, causing catastrophic harm to American civilians in order to force America to do its bidding in the Middle East. For Amin Hweidi, an ex-chief of the Egyptian Intelligence Service, Israel was 'the only beneficiary of all what [sic] has taken place' because they would 'shift attention from greater Israeli atrocities in the Palestinian territories.' Michael Collins Piper of *The American Free Press* stated that 'these hijackers could well have been Israeli-sponsored fundamentalist Jewish fanatics (posing as 'bin Laden Arabs') hoping to instigate an all-out U.S. war against the Arab world'[1] while Sheikh Muhammad Gemeaha, a former

[1] Michael Collins Piper was a talk show host who regularly spread conspiracy theories about JFK, 9/11 and Jews.

imam with the Islamic Cultural Centre in New York, lamented that Jews 'were behind these ugly acts [of Sept. 11], while we, the Arabs, were innocent.'[1] Former US Representative and Green Party Representative Cynthia MacKinney posted an image on Twitter in June 2021 about the 9/11 attack on the Twin Towers. It was in the form of a puzzle and included the message: 'The final piece of the puzzle…Zionists did it.'[2] Christopher Bollyn, who writes for conspiracy newspapers, has said that '9/11 and the War on Terror are the two sides of an Israeli dual-deception' and demanded that 'its perpetrators be brought to justice.'[3] Former CIA operative Philip Giraldi, co-head of the Council for the National Interest, claimed that Israel 'had detailed prior knowledge of what was to take place' on 9/11 and lamented that Israel was not included in the Commission Report 'in spite of obvious involvement in 9/11.'[4] Interestingly, Giraldi's obsession with conspiracy theories extends to the Hamas attacks on October 7, which he claimed were a 'false flag operation rather than a case of institutional failure on the part of the Israelis.'[5]

Part of the Israelcentric conspiracy theory involves American Jews being given pre-warning of the attack. This antisemitic smear, spread by Hezbollah's al-Manar channel, claimed that 4,000 Israelis did not turn up for work on the morning of the attacks. The theory was supported by Iranian President Mahmoud Ahmadinejad who, commenting on a purported lack of Jewish deaths, said: 'One day earlier they (Jews) were told not go to their workplace.'[6] The 4,000 missing Israelis trope was also repeated by Yorgos Karatzaferis, the leader of the far-right Greek Popular Rally Party. Karatzaferis sent a letter to the Greek Parliament 'asking the foreign minister if he was aware that the Israeli press had published articles claiming that Jews had not gone to work on Sept. 11 after they were forewarned about the attacks on the Twin Towers.'[7] Conspiracy theorists also claim that then Israeli Prime

[1] Marina Jiménez, "The radicalization of U.S. Muslims," *National Post*, November 17, 2001.
[2] "Former US Congresswoman Cynthia McKinney Tweets Zionists Responsible For 9/11 Attacks," *i24NEWS*, June 28, 2021.
[3] Christopher Bollyn, "The Dual-Deception of 9/11 and the War on Terror," https://www.bollyn.com/the-fraudulent-war-on-terror/#article_16017, accessed March 10, 2025.
[4] Philip Giraldi, "Israel's Role In 9/11," *The Unz Review*, May 28, 2019, https://www.unz.com/pgiraldi/israels-role-in-9-11, accessed May 11, 2024.
[5] Philip Giraldi, "Gaza Strikes Back," *The Unz Review*, October 15, 2023, https://www.unz.com/pgiraldi/gaza-strikes-back, accessed March 10, 2025.
[6] Robin Pomeroy and Ramin Mostafavi, "Iran President: Sept. 11 exaggerated," *Reuters,* August 7, 2010.
[7] "SWC to Greek Minister of Interior: 'Close Down Racist Politician's Television Mouthpiece

Minister, Ariel Sharon, had planned to be in New York for 9/11 and cancelled his trip, indicating that he knew what was going to take place in the city. Finally, conspiracy theorists point to the fact that five Israelis were arrested on 9/11 after being seen behaving strangely near the scene of the attacks. The men had been filming the aftermath of the assault and aroused suspicion because of their demeanour.

The far right have been no latecomers to the party. One of the racist conspiracy theorists, Kevin Barrett, described 9/11 as the 'granddaddy of all false flags' and said that it was 'a neoconservative Zionist coup d'etat orchestrated to hijack American policy and use the American military to destroy the countries around Israel in that region.'[1] David Duke has embraced the softer version of the conspiracy theory, as when he claimed that Israeli spies had penetrated 'American law enforcement and military facilities' and 'conducted intensive surveillance of al-Qaida operatives in the United States' but 'treacherously did not give American officials information that could have easily prevented the attack.'[2]

Antisemitism is the one type of prejudice that tends to unite so many disparate groups. Thus, we find Louis Farrakhan of the NOI saying that it was 'apparent that there were many Israelis and Zionist Jews in key roles in the 9/11 attacks.'[3] He has united in this respect with fundamentalist Christian preacher Rick Wiles, founder of TruNews, who said that the attacks were a 'wildcard' carried out by the 'Israeli Mossad.'[4]

Israel has also been blamed for the rise of the Sunni terror group, Islamic State (ISIS), and for carrying out its attacks. Often, anti-Israel activists believe that one of Israel's purposes in inventing terror groups and staging attacks is to further the reach of anti-Muslim prejudice. One of those who made this claim was Iran's Deputy Foreign Minister, Hossein Amir Abdollahian, who said in 2014 that Israel had created Islamic State in order to tarnish Iran's image.[5] This was also the charge made by Yasmina Haifi, a senior employee of the Dutch Justice Ministry's National Cyber Security Centre, who said in

---

of Hate,'" Simon Wiesenthal Centre, 11 October 2002

[1] Kevin Barrett, Interview on Press TV, September 2019.

[2] "Unveiling Anti-Semitic 9/11 Conspiracy Theories," Anti-Defamation League, 2003.

[3] Tamar Pileggi, "Farrakhan: 'Lying, murderous Zionist Jews' behind 9/11," *Times of Israel*, March 6, 2015.

[4] "Antisemitic Conspiracies About 9/11 Endure 20 Years Later," *Anti-Defamation League*, September 9, 2021.

[5] "Senior Iran Official: Israel's Mossad created ISIS," *Haaretz*, November 4, 2014.

2014 that ISIS was 'part of a plan by Zionists who are deliberately trying to blacken Islam's name.'[1]

The Israeli origin of ISIS meme was also expressed by left wing figures within the UK Labour party. One such activist claimed that ISIS was 'run by Israel' and that the only reason why the terror group had not attacked the Jewish state was 'because the dog doesn't bite its own tail.'[2] The evidence for this bizarre assertion was that country after country that had recognized 'Palestine' had seen its citizens attacked by ISIS. A Labour Councillor posted a video on Facebook which was titled 'ISIS: Israeli Secret Intelligence Service,' adding: 'I've heard some compelling evidence about ISIS being originated [sic] from Zionists!'[3] Perhaps they took their cue from Jeremy Corbyn, then a backbench MP and later leader of the Labour party. In discussing an attack carried out by jihadis that killed 16 Egyptian soldiers, he suggested the hidden hand of Israel was behind the atrocity. He asked 'In whose interests is it to destabilize the new government in Egypt...other than Israel. I suspect the hand of Israel in this whole process of destabilization.'[4]

On March 22, 2024, ISIS claimed responsibility for a major terror attack on the Crocus City Hall in Moscow where the Russian band Picnic was playing. Four gunmen carried out a mass shooting that killed 203 people and injured many hundreds more. Despite all the signs pointing to an attack by ISIS fanatics, the conspiracy theorist Daniel Haqiqatjou said that the incident had coincided with 'the Jewish festival of Purim,' one that celebrated the killing of 75,000 'enemies of the Jews.'[5] He thus sought to draw some linkage between Jews and ISIS.

Refutation

The starting point for refuting all 9/11 conspiracy theories is the 9/11 Commission, which went through the painstaking process of examining over two and a half million documents, including classified national security

---

[1] "Senior Dutch gov't employee: ISIS a Zionist conspiracy," *The Times of Israel*, August 13, 2014.

[2] Will Worley, "Labour Party member Bob Campbell denies suspension over Israel and Isis comments," The *Independent*, March 28, 2016.

[3] Tom Marshall, "Beinazir Lasharie: Ex-Big Brother contestant suspended from Labour Party over 'anti-Israel' Facebook posts," *Evening Standard*, October 19, 2015.

[4] Juliane Helmhold, "Jeremy Corbyn's top ten outrageous anti-Israel moments this month," *The Jerusalem Post*, August 27, 2018.

[5] Daniel Haqiqatjou, *Twitter Post*. March 22, 2024, 6:17.

papers, as well as carrying out some 1,200 interviews. It found that 15 of the 19 young Arab hijackers, all members of al-Qaeda, were from Saudi Arabia with others coming from Egypt, the UAE and Lebanon. The report went on to outline the brief history of Islamist terror prior to 9/11, a key period during which al-Qaeda posed an increasing threat to western interests, especially those of the US. It highlighted intelligence failures, specifically a culture of secrecy preventing effective communication between the CIA and FBI, as well as the need for diplomacy in the war on terror.

The major conspiracy theories associated with 9/11 have similarly been demolished time and again.[1] This includes the claim that the towers were damaged before the airplanes struck, something directly contradicted by a report from the National Institute of Standards and Technology; the notion that steel could not burn at a temperature such as to bring the Towers down (similarly debunked); that explosions occurred inside the buildings and that a missile brought down the Pentagon, a claim eviscerated by the ASCE Pentagon Building Performance Report.[2] Conspiracy 'truthers' say that the US administration had foreknowledge of the attack but the evidence shows that the intelligence received in August 2001 pointed to a general danger from al Qaeda, rather than a specific threat. The evidence points most clearly to the idea that this was a terrorist attack perpetrated by al Qaeda, the success of which was aided by American agencies' lack of preparedness and problems within the intelligence community.

In view of all this, the notion that either America or Israel somehow engineered the attack is palpably absurd. But did Israel have some foreknowledge of the attack and withhold it? In fact, Mossad had warned the FBI that not only did al Qaeda pose a threat, but it was planning a major operation. The head of Mossad, Ephraim Halevy, revealed that his organization '*had* sent several warnings in the week prior to September that an attack was coming' and cited 'credible chatter' that Mossad agents had picked up in Afghanistan, Pakistan and Yemen.[3] Both the CIA and the FBI knew that al Qaeda posed a growing danger and that one of its operatives had

---

[1] For a comprehensive refutation of 9/11 conspiracies, see: David Dunbar and Brad Reagan (eds), *Debunking 9/11 Myths: Why Conspiracy Theories Can't Stand Up to the Facts*, (Hearst, 2006).

[2] "The Pentagon Building Performance Report," ASCE Library, https://ascelibrary.org /doi/book/10.1061/9780784406380, accessed July 6, 2024.

[3] Gordon Thomas, "Mossad and 9/11," The History Reader, https://www. thehistoryreader. com/military-history/mossad-91, accessed September 19, 2025.

been stopped from flying a plane into the Eiffel Tower. The growing conflict between the two agencies led to a sense of paralysis that scuppered effective intelligence gathering at the time. But crucially, there was no exact intelligence that would have pinpointed the location and time of any attack.

It is relatively easy too to refute the notion that 4,000 Israelis were forewarned of the attack and thus chose to stay away from the Twin Towers. The source for the story was a concern from the Israeli government, picked up by outlets such as *The Jerusalem Post*, for approximately 4,000 Israelis who were in New York on the day of the attacks, though only a small number actually worked at the World Trade Centre. This led to the idea that 4,000 Israelis were forewarned and to the further assumption that not a single Jew was killed on 9/11 because those with insider knowledge (the planners of the attack) had told them to stay away from the danger zone. When a delegation from the British Royal College of Defence Studies visited Damascus, they were reportedly told by Syrian Defence Minister Mustafa Tlass that Mossad had planned the aerial assault on the Twin Towers as part of a Jewish conspiracy.[1]

In fact, the attacks were a leveller, killing people of multiple denominations and backgrounds. According to an article in the October 11 2001, *Wall Street Journal*, roughly 1,700 people had listed the religion of a person missing in the WTC attacks; approximately 10% were Jewish. As for Ariel Sharon's non-appearance in New York, it is indeed true that he had planned to visit the city but not until September 23, where he would have taken part in a pro-Israel rally. But the trip, like many events in New York, was cancelled in the aftermath of 9/11.

Finally, it is true that five young Israelis in their 20s were arrested that day after reports of suspicious activities, including the men filming the towers collapsing. These 'dancing Israelis' were found with passports, cash and some box cutters. But they had not been part of a shadowy intelligence operation to follow al Qaeda. Instead, they were in the country working for a fellow Israeli's delivery company, Urban Moving Systems, and their job involved the use of box cutters. The men admitted violating immigration law and were promptly sent back to Israel. Some of the men were later believed to be part of an Israeli intelligence operation but they were thought to be targeting fund raising networks in the city that were channelling money to Hamas and

[1] Linda Grant. "The Hate that will not die," *The Guardian*, December 18, 2001.

Islamic Jihad.[1] Israeli sources denied this. An FBI investigation determined that 'none of the Israelis had any information on prior knowledge regarding the bombing of the World Trade Center' and that 'none of the Israelis were actively engaged in clandestine intelligence activities in the United States.'[2]

The most rudimentary knowledge of the rise of Islamic State refutes any idea that it had an Israeli origin. The Islamic State, also known as Daesh and later, the Islamic State of Iraq and Syria, emerged from the death throes of al Qaeda in Iraq, a Sunni terror group that was founded by Abu Musab al Zarqawi in 2004. In 2014, this group launched an offensive on two Iraqi cities (Mosul and Tikrit) and announced the creation of a caliphate that stretched from Aleppo in Syria to Diyala in Iraq. As ISIS expanded into other countries, it carried out a series of terror attacks, including the downing of a Russian plane, killing 224 people, and murdering 130 people in a series of attacks in Paris. A US led coalition led the fightback, removing the Islamic State from its strongholds in Mosul and Raqqa and capturing towns in eastern Syria. By the end of 2019, the terror group had lost all its territory and its leader was killed in an airstrike. To claim that ISIS was backed or created by Israel is not just absurd on the surface, it also denies the agency of Muslims in acting upon a theocratic ideology that strives to revivify medieval Islam.

5. Israel is a strategic liability to the west

Charge

The notion that Jews pose a mortal threat to the world is reflected in many of the tropes already identified. A nation of Christ killers who plot to kidnap and murder young children for their blood, poison wells, seize the levers of global finance and usurp the will of national leaders, all to further their own interests instead of their own countries, can only be seen as constituting a grave peril that no civilized country could ignore. The notion that 'Jews are our misfortune' finds resonance in the words of Heinrich von Treitschke, a German historian who wrote these sinister words: 'The international Jew, hidden in the mask of different nationalities, is a disintegrating influence; he

[1] "Were the Israelis Detained on Sept 11 spies?" *ABC News*, June 20, 2002.

[2] Josh Kaplan, "Dancing Israelis 9/11 conspiracy theory: Why do people believe Mossad did 9/11," *The Jewish Chronicle*, September 9, 2023.

can be of no further use to the world.'[1] Today, the trope might well be called 'Israel is our misfortune.'

A number of modern day von Treitschkes have lined up to tell the world that Israel is a malign threat to global stability and a mortal danger, not just to the Middle East, but to the West more widely. They depict Israel as a ticking time bomb, a nation whose unresolved conflicts imperil an otherwise stable world and portend an era of global conflict. This catastrophising narrative was most famously expressed by the former French Ambassador to London, Daniel Bernard. At a dinner party hosted by journalist Conrad Black, he was quoted as saying: 'All the current troubles in the world are because of that shitty little country Israel...Why should the world be in danger of World War III because of those people?'[2] For this diplomat, Israel was no ordinary country caught up in conflict but the national embodiment of a grave and lethal liability to the planet. For Bernard, it was the tiny Jewish state that threatened to rock the globe, not Iran, Russia, China or any of the other dangerous and destabilising autocracies.

His comments were echoed with chilling hatred by the antisemitic Greek composer Mikis Theodorakis. He declared in a television interview that 'everything that happens today in the world has to do with the Zionists' and that 'American Jews are behind the world economic crisis that has hit Greece also.' He said in 2003 that 'Jews were "the root of all evil" and, referencing a visit by delegates from the Conference of Presidents of Major American Jewish Organizations to Greece, declared that his country was 'in danger.'[3] Such a view suggests that Jews are a poison within global bodies and that their 'evil' threatens civilized values.

The views of Theodorakis and Bernard were certainly extreme, but were they representative of wider European opinion? One piece of evidence suggesting they might have been came from a poll of 7,500 Europeans in 15 countries that was conducted by the European Commission in 2003. It asked whether or not specific countries presented a threat to peace in the world and found that Israel was ranked higher than any other country.[4] Among the

[1] Alfred Andrea and James Overfield, ed. (2011). *The Human Record: Sources of Global History, Volume II: Since 1500*. Cengage Learning. pp. 294–95.
[2] "Daniel Bernard," *The Telegraph*, May 3, 2004.
[3] "I am an anti-Semite," famous Greek composer admits, *World Jewish Congress*, February 10, 2011.
[4] Peter Beaumont, "Israel outraged as EU poll names it a threat to peace," *The Guardian*, November 2, 2003.

countries judged as a lesser threat were Pakistan, Syria, Libya, Saudi Arabia, China, Russia and Somalia. Of course, all the usual caveats need to be made about this opinion poll: it might have been influenced by poorly chosen questions; it represented a snapshot of opinion; it may not have been answered by all sections of the population and it did not necessarily reflect a considered or nuanced opinion about global politics. Nonetheless, it was a sign of how Israel was perceived internationally by a large number of people in many different nations. Were the same poll to be conducted in the aftermath of the October 7 attacks, it is likely to yield a similar result.

At the time, Europeans were living in the immediate aftermath of 9/11 and the eruption of war in the Middle East. It was often assumed that the global Islamist threat was, in part, centred on Israel's perceived failure to make peace with the Palestinians, with the West bearing the brunt for its support of Israel. British columnist Polly Toynbee once declared that Palestine was 'the rallying cry for the terrorism that hurled itself at the World Trade Centre' and stated that Israel's failure to make peace had 'turned (it) into a lethal liability.'[1] Caroline Lucas, leader of Britain's Green party, commented about how grievances over Palestine were at the heart of the Mumbai attacks in 2008. She said: 'I think that the situation in Palestine for example, with the ongoing Israeli occupation with the absolute strangulation of Gaza with this siege on Gaza - essentially this economic blockade - is really feeding so much anger right across the world and it means that there is more of a fertile breeding ground then for extremists to flourish.'[2]

During a speech in the House of Lords during the Strategic Defence and Security Review, Liberal Democrat Jenny Tonge talked of how the 'treatment of Palestinians by Israel' was 'the root cause of terrorism worldwide.' She added that she felt 'sorry for the people of Israel' as 'their government's policies have made that country the cause of a lot of the world's problems, yet now they are seen as the remedy and the base for the West to fight back.'[3] And in the *Guardian* on August 22 2005, Madeleine Bunting wrote that 'the main inspiration for British Muslim extremists' was 'not local mosques but

[1] Polly Toynbee, "Say it loud: no more support until Israel agrees to pull out," *The Guardian*, October 24, 2001.

[2] Lucas made those remarks in a debate on BBC Radio 4 that was chaired by Jonathan Dimbleby on November 28, 2008, https://www.bbc.co.uk/radio4/news/anyquestions_transcripts_20081128.shtml, accessed September 11, 2025.

[3] Elad Benari, "British MP says Israel is "cause of terrorism,"" *Arutz Sheva*, November 23, 2010.

television footage of Palestine and Iraq,' implying that western foreign policy was the prime factor that was aggravating radicalized Muslims.[1] In a meeting with the Jordanian embassy in London around 2016, the author was assured that Israel was the primary cause of all the ruptures and conflicts engulfing the Middle East, past and present, and the view was echoed in a similar meeting with Jordan's Ambassador to the UN Human Rights Council.

The accusation that Israel is ultimately liable for Islamist terrorism or other forms of extremism is not necessarily a species of political antisemitism, though it is, at the very least, an intellectually feeble and morally questionable argument. But it undoubtedly feeds into antisemitic ways of thinking when it shifts the blame from the perpetrator and organizer of terror attacks to a blameless party and, in addition, blames the Jewish state for those who attack its citizens (victim blaming).

Refutation

The argument that Israel is a strategic liability comes apart when one considers two salient points. Firstly, Islamist terrorism is predicated primarily on attacking the secular west for its 'un-Islamic' nature and seeking to impose sharia law upon the land of 'unbelievers.' It is not a response to Israeli wrongdoing and thus Israel should not be considered as indirectly responsible for anti-western terror attacks. Secondly, Israel turns out to be a valuable strategic asset to the West, especially in the war on terror.

Radical Islam: The ideology of radical Islam is not centred on the Palestinian issue or any one specific grievance with Western foreign policy. Its primary emphasis is on rescuing Islam, and the global Muslim community generally, from the perceived harmful effects of Westernization, modernization and secularism. Islamists reject the Western model with its fundamental division between state and church, individual freedom, democracy, religious tolerance, sexual liberalism and equality for non-Muslims. Islamism is anti-Western, anti-democratic, authoritarian, racist, homophobic and sexist to the core.[2] One can thus see Islamism as, less a cry of distress from the poor and oppressed, and more an outraged response from

---

[1] Madeleine Bunting, "Throwing mud at Muslims," *The Guardian*, August 22, 2006.

[2] Daniel Pipes, *Militant Islam reaches America*, (New York, WW Norton, 2003), 39-42 and 64-5.

those whose sense of identity has been assailed by the experience of modernity.[1]

Due to the perceived toxicity of western influence, Muslims in both the Arab world and the secular west are believed to be living in a state of perpetual war with unbelievers. It is believed that unless those 'kuffar' are destroyed or brought to heel, Islam will suffer a permanent decline. Islamism thus seeks to purge existing (especially Muslim) societies of purportedly corrupt, decadent and immoral influences, replacing them with societies ruled by Islamic (Sharia) law. Islamists truly believe that the only valid rules for governing society are the Islamic Sharia laws, which are 'as accurate and true as any of the laws known as the "laws of nature"....'[2] Yet for this model to reign supreme, the apostate states, initially in Muslim lands, must be defeated and replaced with a single and unified Muslim state, the restored Caliphate, ruled by Sharia law and answerable alone to the Islamic divinity. Like Hitler, they too demand an empire, albeit an Islamic one, which would be purified by the purging of secular influence.

Naturally, there is little that the West can do to stave off this threat, short of complete submission to the tyranny of religious fanatics. But how does Israel fit in? It might be tempting to argue that, while authoritarian, medieval dogma animates the fanatical leaders of Islamist movements, the issue of Palestine is an endemic sore that attracts converts to the terrorist cause. The problem with this argument is that the 'endemic sore,' both for radical and ultra-conservative Muslims, is not Israel's real or alleged transgressions so much as the state itself, and what it represents. The issue is what Israel is, not what it does.

Historically, the Jew was assigned a cosmic role within the Muslim world - as a subservient, humble figure who was forever watchful of his Islamic overlords. The Jew was a dhimmi, offered the protection of a Muslim state in return for financial penalties and social discrimination. Yet Israel is perceived as a threat to that cosmic order. It is charged with violating a fundamental tenet of Islamic law, namely that the Jew cannot attain independent status or sovereignty within the Muslim world. Jewish sovereignty is, as Raphael Israeli observes, 'an insult...to the holy tradition of Islam.'[3] As Robert

---

[1] Roger Scruton, *The West and the Rest*, (London: Continuum, 2002), 131.
[2] Sayyid Qutb, *Milestones*, (New Delhi: Islamic Book Service, 2001), 88.
[3] Raphael Israeli, *War, Peace and Terror in the Middle East*, (London: Frank Cass, 2003), 64.

Wistrich puts it, the Jews are seen as an 'insidious and permanent enemy,' with the battle against them part of a wider battle to 'throw back the diabolical conspiracy sapping the foundations of the true faith.' In this fight, 'no compromise is possible.'[1] That Israel should come into existence and then survive repeated onslaught by the forces of Islam is a further grievous blow, a sign that Islam and the civilization accompanying it, once in the ascendant in the world, are now in crisis. Moreover, the rhetoric of Islamists is deeply antisemitic to the core and involves archetypes of the Jew as traitor, deceiver, controller and usurper.

It has been argued that 'Palestine' is the main recruiting sergeant for today's militant Islamists. In a way, that is a strange argument because the terrorist threat actually increased in the 1990s at a time when Israel was taking great strides to make peace with the PLO. That decade saw the Oslo accords, Oslo II, the Wye agreement and the talks at Camp David and Taba. Yet throughout the 1990s, Bin Laden planned and launched a devastating series of attacks against Western targets, including the first attack on the World Trade Centre in 1993, the bombings of the US embassies in 1998 in Kenya and Tanzania, the attack on the USS Cole in 2000 and 9/11. Moreover, Hamas, Hezbollah and Iran have already made it clear that nothing short of the total destruction of Israel will ever satisfy their Jew hating urges.

The Islamists are fundamentally aggrieved at the existence of Israel, which represents to them a formidable barrier to a restored Caliphate and an un-Islamic intrusion in the Muslim world. A peace deal either with the Palestinians or surrounding Arab states, valuable as those things are, would not fundamentally alter the desire of Islamists to attack the West. They have no interest in improved rights for the Palestinians per se or in addressing Israeli human rights abuses where they occur. They are solely interested in removing any regime that is seen as insufficiently Islamic and in ensuring the creation of an empire run on Sharia principles. No Israeli state in any form could ever reach that threshold, nor could any secular state in the West.

Sadly, any peace settlement with Israel would buttress the Islamists' argument that terror brings territorial gains and compromise from its weakened enemies. As Michael Gove puts it so aptly, Israeli concessions are viewed as 'a vindication of violence, a reward for those who issued threats,

---

[1] Robert Wistrich, *Hitler's Apocalypse: Jews and the Nazi Legacy*, (London: Weidenfeld & Nicolson, 1985), 192.

and a promise that future threats would yield yet greater rewards.'[1] Thus, Israel is not responsible for the threat that the West still faces from Islamist actors that range from al-Qaeda and ISIS to Hamas and the Taleban. Israel is on the front line against Islamism and has helped to inflict mortal blows on many of its most violent actors.

Israel as a strategic asset to the West

Far from being a lethal liability, Israel is a fundamental asset to the West in so many ways. The West's primary interests in the Middle East are to prevent the proliferation of weapons of mass destruction, contain the threat from radical regimes in the region, secure the free flow of energy supplies, promote liberal, democratic forces and reap the fruits of science and technology.[2] In recent decades, Israel has played a key role in securing, or at least not interfering with, all of these objectives.

Prevent WMD proliferation: Israel has certainly helped to prevent radical and tyrannical regimes from acquiring weapons of mass destruction. The bombing of the Osirak nuclear plant in 1981, also known as Operation Opera, prevented Saddam Hussein from being a rogue nuclear armed dictator, something that made possible his defeat in the 1991 Gulf War. Israeli intelligence also played an important role in helping UNSCOM to 'penetrate Iraq's concealment mechanism and to dismantle Iraq's residual WMD programs in the mid to late 1990s.'[3] The destruction of the Syrian nuclear reactor at Deir al-Zour in 2007, known as Operation Orchard, required meticulous planning and intelligence and prevented the Syrian Civil War (2011 onwards) from becoming an even more destructive and dangerous episode in the Middle East's bloody history.

Today, the greatest danger from WMD comes from Iran's attempt to join the nuclear club with its clandestine programme now two decades old. A number of intelligence operations linked to Mossad slowed down the nuclear operations, including mysterious explosions that rocked the nuclear facilities at Arak and Isfahan, the targeting of leading nuclear scientists in targeted assassinations and the sophisticated cyber-attack (Stuxnet) in 2010. In 2025,

[1] Michael Gove, *Celsius 7/7*, (London: Weidenfeld & Nicolson, 2006), 52.

[2] Aaron David Miller, "The Politically Incorrect Guide to US Interests to Middle East," *Foreign Policy*, August 15, 2012.

[3] Michael Eisenstadt and David Pollock, *Asset Test: How the United States Benefits from its Alliance with Israel*, The Washington Institute.

during the 12 days war, Israel carried out a wave of strikes against Iran's main nuclear facilities, including Natanz, Isfahan and Fordow. These strikes, in combination with those of the US in Midnight Hammer, caused considerable damage to the nuclear infrastructure at those locations though not terminating the programme altogether. Doubtless, further negotiations are needed to fully ensure that the Islamic Republic can never obtain weapons of mass destruction but it is Israel's willingness to use force that has given teeth to the West's demands. A side benefit is that Israel's targeted destruction of the Russian made S300 air defence anti-missile system in Iran, carried out in a wave of strikes in 2024 and 2025, has helped to demonstrate the weakness of Putin's military arsenal compared to its western counterparts, thereby showcasing the vacuity of the Russian leader's threats to the West.[1]

These cases show that Israel has exerted a chilling effect on rogue regimes and their plans for nuclear proliferation. Retired US Air force intelligence chief Major General George F. Keegan once said that 'the ability of the U.S. Air Force in particular, and the Army in general, to defend whatever position it has in NATO owes more to the Israeli intelligence input than it does to any other single source of intelligence, be if satellite reconnaissance, be it technology intercept, or what have you.' He claimed that it was worth 'Five CIAs.'[2]

War on terror: Israel has played an important role in the war on terror and against jihadism. Israel invented the modern unmanned aerial drone that is now being used in Afghanistan for intelligence gathering and combat warfare. The American navy has benefited from a defensive gun system developed in Israel which provides defence against terrorist dinghies and other hostile small vessels. From 2016, a sophisticated Israeli helmet mounted display system has been 'part and parcel of all American stealth aircraft produced.'[3] Israel is also America's most sophisticated partner in the field of rocket and missile defence.[4] Joint US-Israeli drills help protect against the threat of ballistic

[1] "Israel took out primary Iranian air defenses, left it 'essentially naked' – report," *The Times of Israel*, October 30, 2024.

[2] Wolf Blitzer, *Between Washington and Jerusalem: A Reporter's Notebook*, (Oxford: Oxford University Press, 1985), 89.

[3] Udi Etsion, "F-35s to carry Israeli developed helmet display," *Ynetnews*, October 13, 2013.

[4] Eisenstadt and Pollock, *Asset Test*, xi.

missiles.[1] America also made use of Israeli military innovations from its experience battling Palestinian terror, such as checkpoints, IED detection dogs and roadblocks, during the Iraq insurgency.[2] The American military has also used the emergency bandage, invented by Israeli Bernard Bar Natan, which stops potentially fatal bleeding from traumatic injuries,[3] and used a recuperation method known as Prolonged Exposure, which is designed to alleviate the symptoms of battle induced post-traumatic stress disorder.[4] Israel has also led the way in improving airline defence, with its use of armed sky marshals, profiling and metal doors to protect the cockpit, being of great importance.[5]

Britain too has benefited from the fruits of Israeli military technology. The British army's manual for tackling suicide bombers in Afghanistan is based on Israeli advice given to Colonel Richard Kemp, former commander of British forces in Afghanistan, who also received help from Israeli contacts after 7/7. The *Hermes 450*, an aircraft designed by Israel's Elbit Systems, has been used extensively in Afghanistan and credited with being vital in protecting British lives.[6] London's metropolitan elite firearms unit SO19 has used techniques derived from Israel's counter terror agencies while Israeli technology has been used to safeguard Buckingham Palace and Heathrow Airport.[7]

Israel has also played a part in ramping up European security with the sale of such weapons as the Spike anti-tank portable missile system and the unmanned aerial drone, the latter credited with saving the lives of European troops in places like Afghanistan, Mali and Libya. An Israeli company was tasked with protecting athletes during the 2004 Athens Olympics[8] while the country has also conducted joint training exercises and missile defence drills

---

[1] Vasudvan Sridharan, "US and Israel Hold Anti-Missile Defence Drill Juniper Cobra," *International Business Times*, May 18, 2014.
[2] *Asset Test*, 16.
[3] David Horowitz, "The guy with the bandage," *The Jerusalem Post*, April 29, 2011.
[4] Jeffrey Kluger, "Edna Foa," *Time 100*, April 29, 2010.
[5] Daniel Wagner, "What Israeli Airport Security Can Teach the World," *Huffington Post*, March 17, 2014.
[6] "Hermes 450 reaches 70,000 hours in Afghanistan," *UK Ministry* of Defence, September 19, 2013.
[7] Report: "*Added Value: Israel's strategic worth to the EU and its member states*," Henry Jackson Society, 2014, 10.
[8] Dina Craft, "Israelis help secure Olympic Games," *Jewish Telegraphic Agency*, July 29, 2004.

with the armed forces of European nations. Israel and Germany have also been reported to be working on a secret project for differentiating nuclear tipped from decoy missiles in the event of a nuclear war. Amid growing concerns over people smuggling, the EU mandated Airbus and two Israeli air and space companies to fly drones over the Mediterranean Sea so they could monitor migrant smuggler ships.[1]

Energy supplies: The argument that a strong western relationship with Israel potentially jeopardizes the supply of energy to the West was long ago exploded. Arab oil producing nations have been selling 'black gold' to the world's richest nations despite the lack of long term peace between Israel and some of her neighbours and the lack of a Palestinian state specifically. The Abraham Accords proved that energy rich Arab countries were prepared to align their interests with Israel in pursuit of common political interests and goals, including the need to confront the Shia power of Iran. Yet the agreements were not conditioned on the creation of a Palestinian state. The prospect of a normalization agreement between the Jewish state and Saudi Arabia, the region's biggest oil producer, remains the jewel in the crown of regional diplomacy though it has been delayed due to the ongoing fallout from the Israel-Iran wars that started on October 7. Few doubt that in the long term, such an accord could be created even if there is no permanent settlement of the conflict. It also reflects a fact that is lost on so many self-proclaimed experts in Middle East politics: the Saudis' prime interests, apart from selling oil, are to guarantee their own long-term survival. Previous decades have seen potent threats coming from Nasser's Egypt, Saddam Hussein's Iraq and, most recently, the Islamic Republic of Iran. Like Bahrain, the UAE, Egypt and Jordan, Saudi national self-interest is paramount, rather than any abstract concern for the rights of fellow Arabs. This was why, in 1979, Jimmy Carter stated that he had 'never met an Arab leader that in private professed the desire for an independent Palestinian state.'[2]

Promotion of liberal and democratic values: It is not hard to see how Israel upholds the fourth western interest in the region: the promotion of liberal, democratic values. Israel is a multi-party democracy, based on free and fair elections, a relatively open press, an independent judiciary, sexual equality and the right to protest. It has a strong record on women's rights and, in recent

---

[1] Benjamin Haddad, "How Europe Became Pro-Israel," *Foreign Policy*, May 20, 2021.
[2] Bard, *The Arab Lobby*, 351.

years, on gay rights too. Israel protects its religious minorities, something which explains why the Baha'is, a religious minority persecuted for their beliefs in Iran, have found safe haven in Israel, as have the moderate Ahmadiyya sect of Islam. A variety of NGOs openly scrutinize the country's record on human rights and publish searching critiques of government policy. Some aspects of Israel's democracy have come under strain recently, due to plans by the government for a judicial overhaul that would neuter the Supreme Court's independence. But the strength of the popular backlash, and international opinion abroad, suggests that these reforms may be scuppered.

Science: Finally, Israel has been a world beater in the areas of scientific progress, medical advancement and technological innovation. Its contributions span a full range of fields, ranging from electric car technology to fish farming, stem cell research to desalination, airline security to crop protection and green energy to earthquake relief. In medicine alone, Israeli doctors have worked on life saving research into diseases such as Parkinson's, multiple sclerosis, Ebola, cancer and asthma. Israelis have invented a vast number of medical devices, including the optical heartbeat monitor, BabySense, which helps to prevent crib death, Spine Assist, a robotic tool for performing spinal surgery and ReWalk, which has given mobility to those who would otherwise be paralysed[1]. Israeli companies have also produced innovative methods of drip irrigation and an environmentally friendly means of eliminating mosquitos. Israeli achievements are even more impressive in the field of high tech. The technology behind voicemail, text messaging and the transmission of pictures and movie clips has come from Israeli engineers, as has anti-virus software. It is the reason why dozens of American companies, including the giants Intel, Google and IBM, have set up major research and development centres in Israel. Quite simply, Israel has become an indispensable ally to the West, and western leaning nations, instead of the threat and liability that its enemies pretend it to be.

6. Israel and Israelis deserve to be boycotted because of their 'apartheid' state

Charge

It has become a commonplace among Israel's foes that the Jewish state is

[1] Raizel Druxman, "Israeli invention the ReWalk suit helps people to walk again," *The Jewish Chronicle*, July 11, 2018.

an instantiation of apartheid and thus a pariah country within the international community. Critics liken Israel's policies towards the Palestinians to South Africa's treatment of black people, arguing that it is a constitutionally and structurally racist state.

Archbishop Desmond Tutu often likened the position of the Palestinians under Israeli rule to that of black people in apartheid South Africa. In 2007, Tutu wrote: 'What do I see and hear in the Holy Land? Some people cannot move freely from one place to another. A wall separates them from their families and from their incomes. They are arbitrarily demeaned at checkpoints and unnecessarily beleaguered by capricious applications of bureaucratic red tape. I have to tell the truth: I am reminded of the yoke of oppression that was once our burden in South Africa.'[1]

Tutu's fellow anti-apartheid campaigner, Ronnie Kasrils, evidently agreed. He gave a speech in 2009 at an Israel apartheid week event where he claimed that, 'In its conduct and methods of repression, Israel came increasingly to resemble apartheid South Africa at its zenith – even surpassing its brutality in the scale of removal of communities, targeted assassinations, massacres, imprisonment and torture of its opponents.'[2]

In June 2022, the Catalan Parliament passed a resolution which stated that Israel was committing 'the crime of apartheid against the Palestinian people' and recommended ending any support for the country.[3] This position was supported by the Mayor of Barcelona, Ada Colau, who announced that her city's twinning policy with Tel Aviv was being suspended, citing concerns over apartheid.[4]

Some faith groups have not been afraid to make this accusation, among them the General Synod of the United Church of Christ, which claimed that Israel was operating an apartheid system of laws and legal procedures.[5] A number of Israeli public figures have supported this charge. Former attorney general, Michael Ben-Yair, concluded that his country had 'sunk to such

---

[1] Desmond Tutu, "Realizing God's Dream for the Holy Land," *The Boston Globe*, October 26, 2007.

[2] Ronnie Kasrils, "Apartheid in duplicate," *Middle East Monitor*, January 29, 2014.

[3] "Catalan parliament considers Israeli treatment of Palestinians 'equivalent to apartheid,'" *Catalan News*, June 17, 2022.

[4] Jackie Hajdenberg, "Barcelona mayor severs ties with twin city of Tel Aviv, 'apartheid,'" *The Jerusalem Post*, February 9, 2023.

[5] Tiffany Vail, "Synod delegates approve resolution decrying oppression of Palestinian people," *United Church of Christ*, Jully 19, 2021.

political and moral depths that it is now an apartheid regime.'[1]

Just as apartheid South Africa faced an onslaught in the form of boycotts and sanctions, so too Israel faces a relentless campaign to isolate it through the so called BDS (boycotts, divestment and sanctions) movement. In recent years, BDS campaigners have sought to demonize and delegitimize Israel by targeting its academics, journalists, scientists, musicians, writers and sportsmen. They argue that singling out these groups is essential because they all plan a role in the 'apartheid system' of the state, as well as function within its military. Its supporters claim that their movement is politically legitimate, aimed at ending the perceived oppression and racism inherent in the Jewish state and restoring equality to all of the country's citizens. They firmly reject any charge that the BDS movement is antisemitic in intent or outcome.

Refutation:

Yet these arguments are specious in the extreme. This is not only because the apartheid charge is an abhorrent calumny, baseless in both fact and law, but because BDS is deeply antisemitic: the aims of the movement are racist (they wish to destroy Israel) while its tactics have had deeply discriminatory consequences for Jews.

The charge of apartheid is mendacious, libellous and unsupported by the factual evidence. Apartheid refers to the racial discrimination and segregation enforced on the black majority of South Africans by white minority rule over a 46-year period. Black people were denied voting rights and political citizenship, could not marry white people under the Prohibition of Mixed Marriages Act and the Immorality Act and were forced to use separate public facilities. Racial segregation was enforced under the Reservation of Separate Amenities Act, which reserved municipal areas for certain races and separated public institutions, such as hospitals and beaches, on racial lines. This was constitutional, not institutional, racism.

Within pre-1967 Israel, minorities, including the Arab community, are citizens of the state. They can and do vote, a right guaranteed under the Basic Laws, and are represented in the Cabinet, the civil service and in the Supreme Court. Members of minority communities have served as diplomats as well as the army and police service. They can also have sexual relationships with non-Jews though such marriages are not performed in Israel for religious reasons,

[1] "Former AG of Israel: With great sadness I conclude that my country is now an apartheid regime," *The Journal,* February 10, 2022.

affecting every community. Jews and Arabs attend schools and universities together, work and receive treatment in the same hospitals and use buses and public facilities on an equal basis. In 1978, the Supreme Court stated that the prohibition of discrimination on the grounds of race, religion, nationality or belief was a key constitutional principle. Indeed, it is a criminal offence under Israeli law for any public body to discriminate on the basis of either race or religion.[1] No such comparable set of laws protected the black majority in apartheid South Africa. It is true that Israeli Arabs are not mandated to do military service, owing to the possible conflict of interest that some may face in conflict zones. The reality is that thousands of Israeli Arabs can and do serve in the Israeli army, often with distinction.

It is undeniably the case that the Arab community suffers from a certain level of social discrimination and inequality, with Arabs underrepresented in the university system and disproportionately represented among the poorer and unemployed classes of Israeli society. In 2023, 42.4% of the Arab population lived below the poverty line, which was more than double their share in Israel's population.[2] Their communities also face difficulties in regard to infrastructure, housing and access to municipal services. Poorly funded schools leads to lower levels of educational attainment and reduced employment prospects. In addition, making the choice not to enlist in the army disadvantages Arabs by failing to make important connections with fellow Israelis.[3] Social prejudice and occasional incitement from nationalist elements is also a problem for the community. Nonetheless, Israeli Arabs still enjoy a range of political benefits and socio-economic opportunities not found elsewhere in the Middle East.

The apartheid label does not apply to Palestinians either. While it is true that they cannot vote in Israeli elections, this is because they vote instead for Palestinian parties in the West Bank and Gaza, though democratic institutions have been hollowed out in the last two decades amid increasing corruption. Palestinians also face restrictions in moving around the West Bank with its array of checkpoints and roadblocks, as well as the security barrier (called the 'apartheid wall'). These have caused undeniable hardship, as conversations

---

[1] Prohibition of Discrimination in Products, Services and Entry into Places of Entertainment and Public Places Law (2000).

[2] "Israel's Arab Population is at Risk," *Washington Jewish Week*, April 7, 2025.

[3] Kali Robinson, "What to know about the Arab citizens of Israel," *The Council on Foreign Relations*, October 26, 2023.

with Palestinians will show. But they exist to provide a level of security for Israelis, given both the past terrorism instigated during the Second Intifada and the current wave in the West Bank. The security barrier was created because of the threat from suicide bombing, which claimed hundreds of lives in the 1990s and 2000s. Thus, describing it as a form of apartheid makes no sense, as it is not a way of separating people along racial grounds. It is as much a security device as the Saudi barrier with Yemen and the Moroccan barrier in Western Sahara. Israeli Arabs can still travel in the West Bank along 'Israeli only roads' (not Jewish only roads).

Fundamentally, Israel has offered a settlement with the leadership of the Palestinian people over several decades, one that would have yielded a sovereign state of their own with all the cultural, economic and social opportunities afforded by statehood. Sadly, the Israeli overtures were rebuffed on multiple occasions by bad faith Palestinian political actors such as the Mufti of Jerusalem, Yasser Arafat and Mahmoud Abbas.

The aims of the BDS movement are also undeniably racist and thus lack any form of political legitimacy. This is because they seek the eradication of Israel from the map and its replacement with a Palestinian state. For this reason, Omar Barghouti has said that he opposes a Jewish state 'in any part of Palestine,'[1] Ahmed Moor has declared that BDS 'does mean the end of the Jewish state'[2] and Ronnie Kasrils has declared that 'BDS represents three words that will help bring about the defeat of Zionist Israel and victory for Palestine.'[3] The BDS author and scientist John Spritzler has said that the BDS movement 'will gain strength from forthrightly explaining why Israel has no right to exist.'[4]

What these ideologues have in common is a strongly held belief that there can be no just resolution of the conflict with one party (Israel) allowed to exist.

---

[1] David M Halbfinger, Michael Wines and Steven Erlanger, "Is B.D.S Anti-Semitic? A Closer Look at the Boycott Israel Campaign," *New York Times*, July 27, 2019.

[2] Ahmed Moor, "BDS is a long-term project with radically transformative potential," *Mondoweiss*, April 22, 2010, https://mondoweiss.net/2010/04/bds-is-a-long-term-project-with-radically-transformative-potential/. Accessed on November 1, 2025

[3] "Ronnie Kasrils Speech at Israeli Apartheid Week 2009," *BDS Movement*, accessed 16 October 2020, https://bdsmovement.net/news/ronnie-kasrils-speech-israeli-apartheid-week-2009.

[4] John Spritzler, "Norman Finkelstein's Criticism of BSD: Wrong, But with a Germ of Truth," *Truthout*, accessed February 1, 2020, https://truthout.org/articles/norman-finkelsteins-criticism-of-bds-wrong-but-with-a-germ-of-truth/, accessed September 9, 2024.

Barghouti thus rejects both a binational state and also a two-state solution, simply because both are predicated on the idea of two nations with equal claims to the land. He calls for a one state solution in which all Palestinians displaced in 1948, together with their descendants, would be allowed to return to their homes. But he knows that this would mean the demographic destruction of the Jewish majority. Denying the Jews the right of self-determination while advocating it for others smacks of a terrible double standard, and yet another calumny against the Jews. Moreover, there is a chilling echo in the incessant calls to boycott the Jewish state with the resonance of the German economic boycotts in the 1930s still fresh in the historical memory.

Naturally, that does not mean that all those who join the BDS marches are antisemitic themselves, or that they make antisemitic demands. People can demand a boycott of Israel because they believe it has committed great wrongs, whether related to the occupation, settlement activity, the conduct of war in Gaza or elsewhere. Though their arguments are often one-sided, unfair or illogical, they may reasonably believe that supporting this movement is the way to force Israel to change course. Nonetheless, the *movement* is clearly predicated on a desire to eradicate Israel.

The final problem with the BDS movement, and the strongest argument for it being antisemitic in effect, is that its activities have involved a quite deliberate discrimination against Jewish and Israeli celebrities, performers and students, a double standard that amounts to racism. That this should be so seems to flow logically from the movement's interpretation of Israel as a bastion of colonialism, racism and genocidal apartheid. Such a state cannot exist in a world framed by human rights, international law and civilized decency. It cannot be part of the international order and must be rendered a pariah among the nations.

But so too the Zionists, by allying themselves with such a 'noxious' state, are deemed to be supporters of all the things that progressives hate (colonialism, racism, apartheid) and thus must be hounded out of the 'community of the good.' As Jews have the closest connection to Israel, BDS advocates believe that they must disavow their links to Israel or face being ostracized and vilified. They must face a loyalty test: do they primarily subscribe to a world of Palestinian 'resistance' and 'liberation' by condemning Zionism (and Jewish communal rights), or do they implicitly support Israel through their silence and thus defile the progressive movement's 'safe space'? If it is deemed the latter, the result is that Jews are silenced, Jewish institutions are shuttered (or feel under assault) and antisemitism thrives.

In 2015, BDS Pais Valencia demonstrated just how easily their anti-Zionist narrative could segue into wider antisemitism. It centred on an invitation extended by the Spanish Rototom Sunsplash festival to the Jewish-American reggae singer, Matisyahu. The local BDS chapter objected to this invitation, arguing that Matisyahu was a Zionist who defends 'a state — Israel — that practices apartheid and ethnic cleansing.' The organizers, stating that Matisyahu's previous statements of support for Israel did not imply support for every Israeli policy, ignored the request to ban the singer. Two days later, the festival head demanded that Matisyahu clarify his position on the conflict, something the singer refused to do. His concert was then cancelled, with the stated reason being that he had failed to 'clearly declare himself regarding the war and in particular the right of the Palestinian people to have their own State.'[1] Following a howl of justified outrage, he was then re-invited to perform. Matisyahu was no supporter of extremism or racist views towards Palestinians.[2] In fact, his preferred position was apolitical, refusing to discuss the minutiae of the conflict as he was a musician seeking to 'bring people together.' Yet the fact that he had expressed even vague support for Israel, that he did not denounce the state, was enough to brand him a militant advocate for apartheid and ethnic cleansing. Even worse, Matisyahu was not an Israeli, he was a Jew. Holding Jews to account for the actions of the State of Israel is itself an antisemitic canard.

But there is a bigger problem going on here. Matisyahu was the only performer who was asked to clarify his political position prior to being invited or disinvited from the festival. No Chinese performer was asked about Tibet, no Russian about the occupation of Georgia, no Australian about the Aborigines, no Turk about the Copts and no American about Guantanamo Bay. No one demanded to subject the political views of other nationalities to cross questioning. This loyalty test smacked of an egregious double standard, the kind of double standard to which Jews have long been subjected throughout their history.

A similar double standard was evident in 2014 when the Tricycle Theatre

[1] Zack Beauchamp, "The Matisyahu Israel boycott controversy, explained," *Vox*, August 19, 2015.

[2] "Matisyahu row: Jewish singer invited back to festival," *BBC News*, August 19, 2015.

in London refused to host the UK Jewish Film Festival, as it had done for the previous 8 years. An initial demand from the Tricycle's board to be allowed to view in advance all the films made with Israeli backing was rejected on the grounds it was censorship. Indhu Rubasingham, the Tricycle's artistic director, had insisted that the JFF refuse funding (£1,400) from the cultural section of the Israeli embassy, offering to fund the shortfall. In her words: 'Given the present situation in Israel/Palestine, and the unforeseen and unhappy escalation that has occurred over the past three weeks including a terrible loss of life, the Tricycle cannot be associated with any activity directly funded or supported by any party to the conflict...' The Tricycle's offer to provide alternative sources of funding was rejected by the UKJFF, forcing them to find another venue, though the Tricycle's position was later reversed. The UKJFF was, in their own words, an 'apolitical cultural festival' showing 'a diverse programme of films, which present a comprehensive view of international Jewish life' with Israeli films conveying 'a wide perspective on the conflicts in the Middle East.'[1] Support for the Tricycle's decision came from activists within BDS, including the group 'Jews in Britain against Genocide'[2], Artists for Palestine UK and many others within the BDS movement.

The issue here was not the rights or wrongs of the conflict in Gaza. It was the outrageous double standards on display. As Nick Cohen correctly observes:

> The Tricycle hosted London Asian film festival, which received funding from an Indian government guilty of systematically abusing human rights in Kashmir. The Tricycle itself takes money from the British government, which fought a war in Iraq [that] one of the Tricycle's own board members and writers condemned as "illegal," and which led to appalling civilian casualties.[3]

There was no suggestion that Rubasingham was antisemitic or even a hardened anti-Israel activist. Nor was the Tricycle hostile per se to Jewish culture, given its previous record of hosting the UKJFF. But events in Gaza,

---

[1] Hannah Ellis-Petersen, "Tricycle theatre refuses to host UK Jewish Film Festival while it has Israeli embassy funding," *The Guardian*, August 6, 2014.

[2] "Letter to the Artistic Director of the Tricycle," bdsmovement.net, August 9, 2014, https://www.bdsmovement.net/news/letter-artistic-director-tricycle, accessed November 30, 2025.

[3] Sunny Hundal and Nick Cohen, "Was the Tricycle theatre right to ask the UK Jewish film festival to 'reconsider' its funding?," *The Guardian*, August 9, 2014.

with all the pressure from the BDS movement, led to an outcome that was discriminatory for a UK Jewish institution. And as Cohen says elsewhere, racism is about 'demanding behaviour from a minority you would never dream of demanding from your friends,' namely 'forcing them to accept standards or privations because of their race.'[1]

7. Israel is a white supremacist state suppressing people of colour

The resurgence of identity theory and the polarising debates about race have helped spawn another narrative of political antisemitism. There is a view that Israel's alleged transgressions of international law stem, not from the perceived wickedness and misguided policies of her leaders, but from its identity as a 'white supremacist' state. Essentialized in this way, Israel merely reproduces the battle lines of contemporary western politics whereby powerful white elites are accused of suppressing and demonising people of colour. It is another example of how an anti-Zionist narrative reflects the deepest anxieties and preoccupations of contemporary society, as well as offering a safety valve for western guilt.

Since the rise of black nationalist groups like the Black Panthers, there has been a growing trend to identify Israel with the 'world system of white hegemony and colonial power' and Palestinians as a people resisting imperialism. As early as 1964, Malcolm X had 'articulated a consciousness of the Arabic population in historical Palestine as being dispossessed and as being a people under colonial occupation.'[2] There was also a strong hint of the same idea at the end of a booklet produced by the Student Non- Violent Co-ordinating Committee shortly after Israel's victory in the Six Day War. After slamming the Zionist movement for its allegedly illegal and criminal behaviour, the author stated that Israel was now in a position to 'help the United States and other white western countries to exploit and control the nations of Africa.'[3] In the 1980s, Jesse Jackson highlighted the connections

---

[1] Nick Cohen, "Anti-Semitic double standards: the arts and the Jews," *The Spectator*, August 6, 2014.

[2] Fabiola Cineas, "Palestine and BLM: The long history of Black solidarity with Palestinians and Jews," *Vox*, October 17, 2023.

[3] "The Middle East Crisis," Student Non-Violent Coordinating Committee, August 15, 1967, https://www.crmvet.org/docs/670815_sncc_palestine.pdf, accessed September 20, 2025.

between Israel and South Africa, adding a biting racial dimension to the critique of the Jewish state. Fast forward to today and the accusation has gained traction following the murder of George Floyd.

Naomi Dann has argued that there is a sense in which Israel's alleged policies of nationalism and ethnic exclusion help to inspire the 'white nationalist vision' of white supremacists like Richard Spencer. She has also written of 'the disturbing alliance between Zionists and white nationalists in the White House,' something that is no coincidence because, in her view, both sides have 'a shared bedrock of anxiety about demographics and racist and Islamophobic fear of "Arabs."'[1] Her analysis is similar to that of the anti-Zionist Jewish Voice for Peace. For JVP, 'settler colonialism' and 'white supremacy' are the 'right, holistic frame with which to understand Israel and Palestine, as well as the U.S.' They have described early Zionists as 'willing agents of white supremacist colonialism' in their attempts to build a state and 'internalized the same white supremacist hierarchy which had been used against them.' The idea that the Zionists had little choice but to win support from colonial powers like Britain and France is deemed irrelevant. The new Jew, JVP argues, was also 'blond, blue eyed, healthy and muscular,' as opposed to the shtetl Jew who was 'small, dark, hunched over, religious, an embarrassment.'[2] In other words, Zionism appropriated the colonialist belief in white supremacy but with a heavily Teutonic flavour. This analysis extends naturally to all those who dare to support and advocate for Israel. Thus, the 2017 issue of Tufts' disorientation guide described the campus organization Hillel as one 'that supports a white supremacist state'[3] and, doubtless, the same accusation would be extended to any other pro-Israel group.

Following the murder of George Floyd, some chapters of the BLM movement attempted to blacken Israel by linking Floyd's death with the Israeli state, adding to the incendiary suggestion that Israel was on the wrong side of the civil rights fault line. Some weeks after the attack, the British actress Maxime Peake declared: 'The tactics used by the police in America,

---

[1] Naomi Dann. "Richard Spencer Might Be The Worst Person In America. But He Might Also Be Right About Israel," *The Forward*, August 17, 2017.

[2] "Settler colonialism, white supremacy, and the "special relationship" between the U.S. and Israel," *Jewish Voice for Peace*, https://www.jewishvoiceforpeace.org/2015/03/10/settler-colonialism-white-supremacy-and-the-special-relationship-between-the-u-s-and-israel, accessed September 20, 2025.

[3] Seth J Frantzman, "Calling Israel 'white supremacist' perpetuates Western antisemitism," *The Jerusalem Post* September 10, 2017.

kneeling on George Floyd's neck, that was learnt from seminars with Israeli secret services.' The source for her story was an article in *The Morning Star* from 1 June 2020, which stated: 'At least 100 Minnesota police officers attended a 2012 conference hosted by the Israeli consulate in Chicago, the second time such an event had been held.' It went on to claim that the attendees 'learned the violent techniques used by Israeli forces as they terrorize the occupied Palestinian territories under the guise of security operations.'[1] Peake later retracted her support for the view, admitting that she was 'inaccurate in (her) assumption of American Police training & its sources' and expressing her abhorrence at antisemitism. The article was shared 40,000 times and spawned headlines in other publications. One piece in *Middle East Eye* spoke of the 'two decades of Israeli-US police cooperation' and was headlined: 'Knee-on-neck, mass surveillance and protest suppression: How Israel shaped US policing.'

Refutation

Any visit to Israel will immediately dispel any notion that Israel is a white supremacist state or, as some claim, a nation of white Europeans. In fact, the largest Jewish ethnic group in Israel are the 'Mizrahi,' meaning Eastern in Hebrew. These are Jews who hail from the Middle Eastern nations, among them Iraq, Iran, Syria and Yemen. Ashkenazi Jews form less than 32% of the Jewish population, those from the USSR form approximately 12% and a further 3% come from Ethiopia. The final 7.9% of Jews are from mixed backgrounds.[2] The issue is complicated even further by the groups that do not easily admit classification into the tripartite model (Ashkenazi, Sephardi and Mizrahi), such as the Bene Israel, Jews from the Indian subcontinent and the Jews of Central Asia.[3] There is no Jewish ethnic homogeneity in Israel and those classified most as white (European, Ashkenazi and Russian) are less than half the overall Jewish population.

---

[1] Georgina Lee, "Did Israeli secret service teach Floyd police to kneel on neck," Channel 4 News Factcheck, June 26, 2020, https://www.channel4.com/news/factcheck/factcheck-did-israeli-secret-service-teach-floyd-police-to-kneel-on-neck, accessed September 18, 2025.

[2] Noah Lewin-Epstein & Yinon Cohen (2018): 'Ethnic origin and identity in the Jewish population of Israel, Journal of Ethnic and Migration Studies.' Journal of Ethnic and Migration Studies. 45(11), 2118–2137. https://doi.org/10.1080/1369183X.2018.1492370.

[3] David L Graizborg, " Israel's mosaic of Jewish ethnic groups is key to understanding the country," *The Conversation*, November 30, 2023.

There are certainly historic issues of discrimination that affect the country's Jewish community, as much as there are a plethora of issues that affect the country's non-Jewish minorities. From the early years of the state, Ashkenazi Jews came to dominate Israel's political establishment, in large part because the early waves of immigration, and the wave that directly preceded the establishment of the state (1945-8), was from Russia and eastern Europe. The Ashkenazim also felt a sense of cultural superiority, reflecting the differing levels of education, technological awareness and knowledge, as well as political advancement they had experienced in their native countries. It produced a significant socio-economic gap between the two communities, one which exists to this day. In addition, the historic injustices meted out to the Yemenite Jews upon their arrival in Israel, and, to a lesser extent, those from some North African countries, remain a stain on the country's early history.[1] But this form of discrimination was not based on skin colour so much as cultural background, with all the terrible prejudices that entailed. If there is any issue of discrimination based on skin colour, it is that which affects Jews of Ethiopian origin, a community that has complained about discrimination and violence from wider society.[2]

If we now observe the Arab population of Israel and the ethnically indistinguishable Palestinians of the West Bank and Gaza, one finds that classifications based on race are also problematic. Are Arabs generally considered white? According to the US government, they are though this does not match the perception that most Arabs have of themselves.[3] The whiteness of Arabs has to be considered 'contested' and it is not clear why this does not apply to those living in Israel.

If the conflict between Israelis and Palestinians is predicated on a black v white racialized identity, that would presumably make Israelis easy to spot for their 'oppressed' neighbours. Indeed, that would tend to be the rule in such conflicts. In apartheid South Africa, each side could easily enough pick out the vast majority of those to whom they were opposed, just as southern states

---

[1] Miriam Samsonowitz, "Sephardim and Ashkenazim: Closing the Gaps?" *Jewish Action*, Fall 1999.

[2] Raffi Berg, "Israeli teachers' racist WhatsApp chat caught by pupils," *BBC News*, March 13, 2023.

[3] Neda Maghbouleh, Ariela Schachter and Rene D. Flores, "Middle Eastern and North African Americans may not be perceived, nor perceive themselves, to be White," *Proceedings of the National Academy of Sciences of the United States of America*, February 7, 2022.

imposing Jim Crow laws knew those to whom their noxious laws applied.

But Israeli intelligence operations in the Arab world, as well as the West Bank and Gaza, rely on the ability of Israelis to 'blend in' with their environment, to appear native while collecting valuable data on imminent threats to their country's security. One must ask how this would be possible if one side was white and the other a people of colour. Israelis do not need to 'black up' in order to enter the land of neighbouring territories, most often because they originated from those countries and thus have an unextinguishable link with their populations through ancestry. There is no racial bar that separates Israelis and Palestinians, even if far right Israeli racists racialize their opponents. Thus, labelling Israelis and Palestinians as white and people of colour respectively is a misleading attempt to shoehorn both peoples into a 'white-black' conflict to which they do not belong. As one journalist says of anti-Israel activists who racialize the conflict, they 'could not tell the difference between most Jews and Arabs in Israel if just confronted with photos of faces.'[1]

Finally, it is worth dismissing the notion that Israel was somehow indirectly responsible for the murder of George Floyd. The idea that Israel teaches 'neck kneeling' as a technique of control has been dismissed by the national spokesman for the Israeli police, Micky Rosenfield. On June 9, 2020, he tweeted that 'There is no procedure that allows an officer of the #Israel police dept to carry out an arrest by placing a knee on the neck of a suspect.'[2] It is true that there was a training event at the Israeli consulate, which focused on information sharing and explosive disarmament training. There is no evidence that neck restraints were taught at that conference. Moreover, as even The *Morning Star* admitted, it is not clear if any of the officers involved in the George Floyd killing were present at the conference. Indeed, two of the officers (J Alexander Kueng and Thomas Lane) could not have been as they only joined the force in 2019. Nor is Israel alone in providing training sessions for American officers, with many law enforcement officials travelling to Germany and many other European countries.[3]

---

[1] Frantzman, "Calling Israel 'white supremacist' perpetuates Western antisemitism."
[2] Micky Rosenfeld, "There is no procedure that allows an officer of the #israel police dept to carry out an arrest by placing a knee on the neck of a suspect," X, June 9, 2020.
[3] Georgina Lee, "Did Israeli secret service teach Floyd police to kneel on neck?" *Channel 4 Face Check*, June 26, 2020.

Moreover, an independent fact check revealed that the Minneapolis Police were using neck restraints from long before that training, possibly as early as 2002 and certainly in 2010. In the section on the use of force, it is stated that employees who have received MPD training are allowed to use the 'non-deadly force option' of 'compressing one or both sides of a person's neck with an arm or leg, without applying direct pressure to the trachea or airway (front of the neck).'[1] The Minneapolis Police did not need any Israeli training to use this technique. In addition, there are other controversial incidents of neck kneeling among other police forces, such as Pittsburgh (1995) and San Francisco (2009). Thus, in the absence of any evidence, this antisemitic conspiracy theory can be dismissed with the contempt it deserves.

8. Israel targets Palestinian children

Charge

Another charge often made against Israel is that its military forces ruthlessly and deliberately target Palestinian children. Israel stands accused of showing a reckless disregard for the rights and lives of young civilians who live in combat zones, and breaching the rule of distinction, one of the most fundamental laws of armed conflict. The rule states that parties to a conflict must 'at all times distinguish between the civilian population and combatants and between civilian objects and military objectives and accordingly shall direct their operations only against military objectives.'[2]

The UN has often thundered against Israel in this regard. Following the 2009 Gaza war, Israel was accused in the Goldstone Report of deliberately targeting civilians. In point 46 of the executive summary, the Mission found that the conduct of the Israeli armed forces constituted 'grave breaches of the Fourth Geneva Convention in respect of wilful killings and wilfully causing great suffering to protected persons' and accused Israel of 'the direct targeting and arbitrary killing of Palestinian civilians' which was 'a violation of the right to life.'[3] Judge Goldstone, who later recanted some of his accusations, observed that the Israeli action constituted 'a deliberately disproportionate

---

[1] 5-300 Use of Force - City of Minneapolis (archive.org)

[2] The principle is codified in Article 48 of Protocol Additional to the Geneva Conventions (Protocol I), 1977.

[3] "UN mission finds evidence of war crimes by both sides in Gaza conflict," United Nations, September 15, 2009, https://news.un.org/en/story/2009/09/312502, accessed May 10, 2024.

attack designed to punish, humiliate and terrorize a civilian population.'[1] More recently, in its report on Children and Armed Conflict (2024), the organization said that it was 'appalled by the intensity of grave violations against children in the Occupied Palestinian Territory and Israel.'[2]

During the Second Intifada, one of the most telling images was that of Mohammed al-Dura, a young child who was filmed cowering behind his father while shots rang out around him. Eventually, the cameras appear to have shown his dead body after he had been struck by a bullet allegedly fired by an Israeli marksman. The coverage from some western media outlets was unsparing in its narrative of responsibility. For Time Magazine, Al Dura did 'everything in his power to shrink his slender frame behind that of his cowering father' but pleas for Israeli soldiers to stop firing were 'answered with a fusillade of bullets.' The *Guardian* reported that Israeli gunners 'from their concrete fortress...inflicted the death that has become the symbol of these days of blood and rage.'[3] These and other accounts fed into a narrative in which an innocent Palestinian child was targeted and killed by merciless and murderous Israeli soldiers. In one of his columns for *The Independent*, Johann Hari slammed Israel's hypocrisy in condemning rocket attacks while it 'has been terrorising civilians as a matter of state policy.'[4] The *Financial Times* has often accused Israel of 'collective punishment' and acting illegally to harm civilians.[5]

In a BBC News TV programme in July 2023, former Israeli prime minister Naftali Bennett spoke about the counter-terrorism operation in Jenin which had begun the previous day. During that interview, presenter Anjana Gadgil used a statement put out by UNICEF in which it was claimed that 'at least three children' were killed in Jenin as the basis for accusations concerning what she framed as the illegitimate targeting of

---

[1] Rory McCarthy, "UN Gaza Report accuses Israel and Hamas of war crimes," *The Guardian*, September 15, 2009.

[2] "Children and armed conflict – Report of the Secretary-General (A/79/878-S/2025/247)," *United Nations*, June 17, 2025, https://www.un.org/unispal/document/children-and-armed-conflict-report-of-the-secretary-general-a-79-878-s-2025-247, accessed May 10, 2025.

[3] All the quotes above are taken from Stephanie Guttman, *The Other War* (San Francisco: Encounter Books, 2005), 48-50.

[4] Johann Hari, "The true story behind this war is not the one Israel is telling," *The Independent*, December 29, 2008.

[5] Robin Shepherd, *A State Beyond the Pale: Europe's Problem with Israel*, (London: Weidenfeld & Nicolson, 2009), 69.

innocent civilians. She asked Bennett: '…We now know that young people are being killed, four of them under 18. Is that *really* what the military set out to do: to kill people between the ages of 16 and 18?' Following Bennett's response that these were terrorists who had been targeted, she followed this up with the comment: 'Terrorists…but children. The Israeli forces are happy to kill children.'[1] Though Gadgil is not antisemitic, the implication was that Israel was a trigger-happy nation that was callously targeting the most vulnerable in society, regardless of their military affiliation.

In 2023, Israel found itself at war with the terrorist army of Hamas following the October 7 massacre. The regrettably high death toll in the war led to such headlines as 'Israel's war against Gaza's children' (*Al Jazeera*),[2] 'Damning evidence of war crimes as Israeli attacks wipe out entire families in Gaza' (*Amnesty*)[3] and 'The War turns Gaza into a graveyard for children' (*The New York Times*).[4] Israel was accused of a genocidal campaign of ethnic cleansing against the Gazan population, with children bearing the brunt. It was the reason why AIPAC President Michael Tuchin was blasted 'a baby killer'[5] and why a group of British Jews who attended an antisemitism march were branded 'child killers.'[6]

In the aftermath of the Hamas atrocities, Israel allowed journalists to view a short compilation of clips that showed gruesome evidence of the murderous rampage. For anti-Israel obsessive Owen Jones, the purpose of the film was to 'remember those poor, injured, little boys crying for their dead father, and then to wipe away the horror and anguish we feel about Gaza's innocents.'[7] He was drawing moral equivalence between the planned, premeditated killing of Israeli civilians and the subsequent actions by Israel to defeat Hamas in

---

[1] Richard Percival, "BBC admits 'Israeli forces are happy to kill children' comment was not impartial," *The Jewish Chronicle*, September 5, 2023.

[2] "Photos: Israel's war on Gaza's children | Israel War on Gaza," *Al Jazeera*, December 28, 2023.

[3] "Damning evidence of war crimes as Israeli attacks wipe out entire families in Gaza," *Amnesty International*, October 22, 2024.

[4] "The War Turns Gaza Into a 'Graveyard' for Children," *The New York Times*, November 18, 2023.

[5] "AIPAC President: 'Baby killer:' Head of pro-Israel lobby confronted by angry protesters," *Times of India*, November 24, 2023.

[6] Richard Percival, "Police launch probe after man filmed calling attendees of London antisemitism march 'child killers' on train," *The Jewish Chronicle*, November 27, 2023.

[7] "I Watched The Hamas Massacre Film. Here Are My Thoughts," *YouTube*, November 27, 2023, https://www.youtube.com/watch?v=mc5iG3DX7ho, accessed May 20, 2024.

Gaza. Given his acknowledgment that Hamas had deliberately sought to murder civilians, his accusation against Israel could hardly be clearer.

Naturally, the idea that Israel lusts for the blood of Palestinian children has been a staple of Arab cartoons over the years. Israel has been represented as a wolf devouring Palestinian babies, and satiating itself on their blood. Netanyahu has been depicted as a butcher, with knife and fork in hand, feasting on dead Palestinian skulls.[1] On July 2 2013, the German paper *Sueddeutsche Zeitung* published a cartoon which depicted the Jewish state as a Moloch, a Canaanite god that is associated with child sacrifice. The hideous monster was lying in bed, knife and fork in hand, while being waited on by a woman (presumably representing Germany).[2] Lebanese cartoonist Stavro Jabra chose to represent Israel as the Grim Reaper, pouring blood down his throat while surveying the devastated Gazan landscape. This is as close to a literal reproduction of the blood libel as you can get. Such graphic, demonising images are commonplace across the Middle East today.[3]

Refutation

It is undeniable that children are victims of the Israeli-Palestinian conflict. On the Israeli side, this occurs because of targeted or indiscriminate attacks carried out by terrorist groups, such as Hamas or Hezbollah, the aim being to terrorize and demoralize the remainder of the Israeli population and force them into a position of submission and defeat. There is quite simply no legal or moral justification for such actions. It is a direct violation of the law of distinction that governs all iterations of armed conflict and is thus illegal and morally unconscionable. But when Palestinian children are killed, tragic as this is, the same argument does not apply. It is thus the foundation of a modern-day blood libel.

Several points are in order. Firstly, not all Palestinian child deaths are those of innocents, a point that was made clear by Naftali Bennett in his BBC interview in 2023. Describing the two-day counter terrorism operation carried out in Jenin, Bennett pointed out that the Palestinians who were killed (aged 18 or under) were terrorist combatants rather than innocents. Among those

[1] "Antisemitism in Arab Cartoons during the Israel-Hamas War: A Chronology of Dehumanization of Jews and Demonization of Zionism and Israel," *Anti-Defamation League*, December 21, 2023.

[2] "German newspaper apologizes for 'Moloch' drawing," *The Times of Israel*, July 4, 2013.

[3] Joel Kotek, "Major Anti-Semitic Motifs in Arab Cartoons," *The Jerusalem Center for Security and Foreign Affairs*, June 1, 2004.

aged 18 or under were Nour al Din Marshoud (16), Magdy Ararawi (17) and Ali al Ghoul (17), all members of the Palestinian Islamic Jihad, and Husam Abu Deibeh (or Theeba) (18), a member of the PIJ who was also claimed by Fatah as one of its operatives. This was the rationale of the operation, yet by the end of the interview, Gadgil suggested that Israel had simply carried out the operation to 'distract from the other things going on in Israel at the moment.' Other recent acts of terror committed by Palestinian youngsters included a January 2023 shooting of an Israeli father and son by a 13-year-old in Jerusalem and a fatal terror attack by another teenager in the refugee camp of Shuafat. All this explains why there are a significant number of Palestinian teenagers inside Israeli jails. Far from being the innocent victims of a brutal Israeli regime that enjoys tormenting youngsters for fun, they are dangerous individuals who pose a threat to Israeli lives.

The question should naturally be asked as to why so many teenagers are being enlisted in these armies of Palestinian terror. To answer this, one must understand how Palestinian culture actively encourages youngsters to be groomed for terror and leads them to believe that murderous violence offers the allure of reward in the afterlife. While it is tempting and glib to parrot the Fatah line about resistance to Israeli occupation and settlements, the reality is much darker. Palestinian children experience the PA's incitement against Israel, Zionism and Jews on social media platforms such as Tiktok and Instagram. The videos that circulate on social networks, showing Israeli bombings and Palestinian deaths without any nuance or context, have been dubbed 'terrorist porn.' Those same Palestinians also go through an education system that openly vilifies Jews and Israelis and emphasizes polarising narratives like the Naqba. Within wider Palestinian society, those who fall to Israeli bullets are declared martyrs and there are financial rewards from the PA if those same people are incarcerated by Israel.[1] The PA encourages children to believe that if they die in martyrdom fighting Israel, they will receive honour and popularity. Children see images of past 'martyrs' in PA/Fatah summer camps, television programme, sports stadium and public squares. It is a sickness endemic within Palestinian politics to which much of the world seems oblivious.[2]

Second, the trope of Israel lusting for the blood of civilians ignores the

---

[1] Yoni Ben Menachem, "The Phenomenon of Palestinian Teen Terrorists," *The Jerusalem Center for Security and Foreign Affairs*, February 19, 2023.

[2] Itamar Marcus, "How and Why the Palestinian Authority kills its own children: Special Report for UN World Children's Day," *Palestinian Media Watch*, November 20, 2022.

painstaking attempts that Israel makes to avoid harming non-combatants. Israel's military operates via the 'purity of arms,' a military doctrine according to which the IDF must cleave to Biblical values in ensuring that as much as possible is done to avoid harming civilians. There is emphasis placed on the principles of 'proportionality and limitation' and a 1977 protocol requires the military to give civilian populations advanced warning of attacks that may affect them, where this is possible, something that stems from an ancient rabbinic military law.[1] In recent conflicts, those advanced warnings have included so called 'roof knocks,' leaflets dropped on a Palestinian area which warn of an impending attack and messages sent to mobiles in an enemy area.

Colonel Kemp has said that the IDF 'does more to safeguard the rights of civilians in a combat zone than any other army in the history of warfare.' Kemp is worth quoting at length. Speaking of his experience of observing the IDF in 2014 he wrote:

> The IDF took extraordinary measures to give Gaza civilians notice of targeted areas, dropping millions of leaflets, broadcasting radio messages, sending texts and making tens of thousands of phone calls. Let me repeat that. The Israelis called Gazans on their cell phones and told them to leave their residences and move to safety. Never in the history of warfare has an army phoned its enemy and told them where they are going to drop their bombs.[2]

It would be truly extraordinary for an army embodying such principles and using such methods to target civilians in a war zone. Moreover, it is hardly in Israel's interests to deliberately kill civilians, children or otherwise, even were it minded to do so. Every time there are civilian casualties from an Israeli air strike, it encourages Israel's enemies to ramp up the outrage and disseminate libellous falsehoods to an all too gullible western media. In turn, this leads Israel's allies in the west, doubtless under pressure from both domestic and international opinion, to hasten an end to Israel's military operations. This was certainly the case in 1982 when Ronald Reagan's horror at the carnage in Beirut curtailed Israeli operations in Lebanon.[3]

---

[1] Noam Zion, "Purity of arms: the ethical guide for the Israel Defense Forces," *JNS.org*, March 2, 2016.

[2] "Israel: The World's Most Moral Army," Prager U, https://www.youtube.com/watch?v=tN1MkAGuVyY, accessed October 1, 2025.

[3] Bernard Weinraub, "Reagan demands end to attacks in a blunt telephone call to Begin," *The New York Times*, August 13, 1982.

The third factor, following on from the above, is that the trope of Israel, the child killer nation, ignores the extent to which Hamas deliberately embeds its terrorist infrastructure in the heart of Palestinian civilian communities, making it likely, even certain, that vast numbers of innocent children will die. Hamas has implemented what has come to be known as 'the dead baby strategy' in their recent conflicts with Israel. In essence, Hamas stores and fires its deadly weapons from within the heart of Palestinian civilian society - from within mosques, hospitals and schools - with the express purpose of killing or terrorising Israelis but also with the intent of encouraging an Israeli response that will kill Palestinian civilians. In turn, they seek to exploit the outrage that such Palestinian deaths cause but with the certain knowledge that the western ire and concern will be directed towards Israel, not towards Hamas. By showing images of dead Palestinian civilians uncritically, aided by Hamas talking points, media outlets are serving as mouthpieces for the vile Islamist regime. They show pictures of dead bodies without pointing the finger of responsibility at the party that has put them in harm's way. As Alan Dershowitz points out, 'It's a win-win strategy for terrorists and a lose-lose strategy for democracies.'[1]

This is also true in Operation Swords of Iron. American intelligence revealed that Hamas had a command-and-control centre under Al Shifa hospital and had been stealing fuel that was intended for generators. Israel also provided video evidence of weapons in the basement of Rantisi hospital in north Gaza. In the words of National Security Advisor Jake Sullivan: 'Hamas does use hospitals, along with a lot of other civilian facilities, for command-and-control, for storing weapons, for housing its fighters.'[2] Israel's claims were also backed up within the EU. The European Union released a statement which condemned Hamas for using 'hospitals and civilians as human shields' in the enclave.[3]

But if one wants further proof, one can listen to the words of Israel's own enemies. Hassan Nasrallah admitted before the 2006 war that his fighters 'live in their houses, in their schools, in their mosques, in their churches, in their

[1] Alan Dershowitz, "Hamas' dead baby strategy," *Washington Times*, January 16, 2009.
[2] Jake Tapper, "Hamas has command node under Al-Shifa hospital, US official says," *CNN Politics*, November 13, 2023.
[3] "Statement by the High Representative on behalf of the European Union on humanitarian pauses in Gaza ," November 12, 2023.

fields, in their farms, and in their factories.'[1] In February 2008, Hamas representative Fathi Hamad told the Palestinian Legislative Council that his people had 'created a human shield of women, children, the elderly and the Jihad fighters against the Zionist bombing machine.'[2]Another Hamas spokesman, Sami Abu Zuhri, advised his people in Gaza not to heed Israeli warnings to leave their houses. He said: 'The policy of people confronting the Israeli warplanes with their bare chests in order to protect their homes has proven effective against the occupation...We in Hamas call upon our people to adopt this policy, in order to protect the Palestinian homes.'[3]

Civilian structures, which have protected status under the Geneva Convention, have been militarized by Hamas and turned into a part of their military apparatus. The civilians inside are effectively cannon fodder, pawns in a terrorist strategy that Hamas knows it is likely to win. It is the fact that one side is prepared to sacrifice its children in such a barbaric and illegal fashion that should cause outrage in the west.

---

[1] Joshua Muravchik, *Making David into Goliath: How the World Turned Against Israel*, (Encounter Books, 2014), 217.
[2] *Al-Aqsa TV (Hamas)* Feb. 29, 2008
[3] Patrick Worrall, "Factcheck: Does Hamas use civilians as human shields?," *Channel 4 News*, July 24, 2014.

Conclusion

How should we deal with antisemitism?

Much of this book was written in the three months following the October 7 attacks that convulsed Israel in 2023. During that period, antisemitic incidents skyrocketed around the world. The US based Anti-Defamation League reported that from October 7 to December 7 2023 there had been a 337% increase in the number of antisemitic incidents. The 2,031 recorded incidents included one fatality, 40 physical assaults, 337 incidents of vandalism, 905 rallies with antisemitic rhetoric and 250 antisemitic incidents specifically targeting Jewish institutions such as synagogues and campus Hillels.[1] During the same period, there was also an enormous rise in antisemitic crimes reported in the UK, according to the Community Security Trust. Between 7 October and 13 December, they recorded 2,093 incidents across the country, an increase of over 500% from the previous year.[2] A similar pattern was observed in France[3], Germany[4], Austria[5] and many other countries around the world. 'Pro-Palestinian' rallies held in these countries often featured placards and chants that supported the elimination of Israel, celebrated or excused the 7/10 attacks or called for genocidal jihad. Many of these events were planned on 7th October itself, a day in which Hamas terrorists had just carried out a murderous pogrom killing nearly 1,200 people

---

[1] "ADL Reports Unprecedented Rise in Antisemitic Incidents Post-Oct. 7," *Anti-Defamation League*, December 11, 2023.

[2] "Antisemitic incidents – 13 December update", *Community Security Trust* , December 13, 2023, https://cst.org.uk/news/blog/2023/12/13/antisemitic-incidents-13-december-update, accessed January 5, 2024.

[3] "Antisemitism surges in France after the Hamas attacks on Israel," *The Economist*, November 9, 2023.

[4] Ashifa Kassam, "Rise in antisemitism 'brings Germans back to most horrific times,'" *The Guardian*, October 24. 2023.

[5] Anthony Mills and Vianey Lorin, "Austria sees rise in anti-Semitic attacks against backdrop of Israel-Hamas war," france24.com, accessed March 9, 2024.

in Israel, almost all Jews, and were still inside Israeli communities butchering people.

One should never lose sight of the fact that antisemitism is a phenomenon of long standing, waxing and waning depending on the trajectory of historical events. It is called the world's oldest hatred for a good reason: old as in ancient. It is therefore a problem for which there are very few quick fixes or simplistic solutions. This is particularly important for modern critics of Israel who declare, in somewhat glib fashion, that only an end to the occupation or a changed policy towards the Palestinians will protect Jews from the scourge of hatred. Typical in this regard is the veteran political activist Tariq Ali. In one rally he declared: 'Every time they bomb Gaza, every time they attack Jerusalem – that is what creates antisemitism. Stop the occupation, stop the bombing and causal antisemitism will soon disappear.'[1]

Former Liberal Democrat politician Jenny Tonge also had form in this regard. In 2016, she responded to a Home Affairs Select Committee report on antisemitism, pointing out that the rise in anti-Jewish prejudice reflected a 'disgust amongst the general public' for 'the way the government of Israel treats Palestinians.'[2] When a neo-Nazi fanatic murdered 11 Jews at the Tree of Life synagogue, she condemned the 'absolutely appalling' act but followed up with a question: 'Does it ever occur to Bibi and the present Israeli government that it's (sic) actions against Palestinians may be reigniting anti-Semitism?'[3] The killer did not reference Israeli conduct towards the Arab population nor is it likely that he would have cared.

This attempt to rationalize anti-Jewish hate as the outcome of 'malign' Israeli policy is a classic form of victim blaming. In effect, it is saying that it is in Israel's gift to stop antisemitism and that attacks on Jews stem from the victims' own conduct. Apart from the intellectual short sightedness of this, it is effectively telling antisemites that they have no moral agency of any kind, that they cannot be held to account for their own morally reprehensible behaviour. Naturally, one heard a completely contrary message after both the 9/11 and 7/7 attacks. After those barbarities, it was repeatedly stated, and quite justifiably so, that Muslims should not be harmed or intimidated because of

---

[1] Lee Harpin, "'Jews are Christ killers' banner at anti-Israel protest," *The Jewish News*, May 22, 2021.

[2] David Hirsh, *Contemporary Left Antisemitism*, (London: Routledge, 2018), 23.

[3] "Anti-Israel UK lawmaker who blamed anti-Semitism rise on Jewish groups retires," *Times of Israel*, February 7, 2021.

their more radical co-religionists. A firewall was drawn between jihadis and non-jihadi Muslims, and between Islamism and Islam. Progressives everywhere baulked at the idea that Muslims could be held responsible for the fanatical terror of groups like al-Qaeda. The same thinking must be applied to Jews, even though Israel is unlike any iteration of Islamist terror. If people do not like Israeli policies, they are free to protest, demonstrate (peacefully), write to their MPs and confront Israeli policymakers. Antisemitism is obviously a choice, whether that comes in the context of opposing Zionism or blaming Jews for Covid.

1. Recognize the hatred

The first step in dealing with antisemitism is to recognize it. But what is crucial is that the stereotypical antisemitism of the far right, the one that comes dressed in swastikas, skullcaps and SS insignia, is but one manifestation. It does not just involve physical attacks against Jews or the daubing of swastikas on buildings and cemeteries, reprehensible as these crimes are. Nor does it just involve hatred expressed towards 'Jews,' as some like to think. Antisemitism has a unique vocabulary of hatred and prejudice, much of it dressed up in cyphers and coded language. It is about questioning the loyalty of Jews when they express support for Israel. It is about asserting Jewish or Zionist control over the media, the business world, the banks or popular culture. It is about singling out the Jew, or Jewish institutions, for special and unfair treatment, a staple of the BDS movement. It is about trivialising the Holocaust or claiming that Jews are behaving like Nazis. It is about telling Jews that they are the cause of the hatred they face, rather than blaming the perpetrators of antisemitism. It is about words like 'globalists,' 'Rothschilds,' 'puppet masters' and 'Christ killers,' which are sprayed around so casually. There is an entire vocabulary which is both visual (endless memes) and literary that is associated with the hatred of Jews.[1] Antisemitism is a conspiracy theory, the world's oldest and most malign, which asserts that 'the Jew' is at the heart of all wrongdoing, evil and chaos that affects mankind. Whether it is as a killer of God, the betrayer of prophets, the slayer of innocent

---

[1] The term 'globalist' is a coded attack on people who are perceived to be promoting international interests and institutions at the expense of national identities. Racists use the term in an antisemitic sense because they believe that Jews are at the forefront of controlling the world economy in their own interests and not those of their 'host' countries. Attacks on the Rothschilds follow the same logic.

children, the grand conspirator, the subversive revolutionary or the greedy manipulator, the Jew is a figure who cannot be trusted and is always tricksy and deceitful. You can be an antisemite without consciously hating Jews. Buying into recognized antisemitic tropes and canards is enough.

One tool that would help in recognising antisemitism is the definition offered by the International Holocaust Remembrance Alliance (IHRA). It is important, following on from this, that national governments, local authorities, civil society organizations and sporting clubs sign up to the IHRA definition.

There should also be honest reporting of antisemitism, with no attempt to pigeon hole all of its manifestations as a far-right phenomenon. Modern antisemitism is a tripartite phenomenon that enervates three distinct political groupings: the nationalist far right, the far left and radical Islam. While they are ideologically poles apart on many issues, they are united by their paranoid, obsessive loathing of the Jews. Yet there remains a tendency on the part of left-wing commentators to isolate the far right as the greatest danger to the Jews, ignoring leftist anti-Zionism, while those on the nationalist right purely emphasize the hatred of the left and Islamist teaching. Each can be purposely blind to how their own side contributes to the scourge of antisemitism.

Recognising antisemitism can be aided by speaking to the people who know it best: the Jewish community. As a general rule, anti-racism does not proceed by assuming that the investigator, who comes from a neutral background, is better informed about a specific prejudice than the communities that are affected by it. The term that is often bandied about is 'lived experience,' by which is meant that the victim of racism can personally testify to the pain and raw suffering that this prejudice brings – what racism actually feels like. While they do not offer a definitive judgment on whether an act is racist, they need to be consulted and their testimony heard with respect.

In general, that means that the mainstream organizations that represent any minority community are the ones best equipped to understand the tropes and imagery of racism, not fringe voices that have been cast out from the mainstream community. This was the mistake made by Jeremy Corbyn when he befriended groups such as Jewdas for a Passover seder.[1] It is the same

[1] "Labour anti-Semitism row: Corbyn defends appearance at Jewdas event," *BBC News*, April 3, 2018.

mistake that anti-Zionists make when they proclaim their undying friendship with the Neturei Karta, an ultra-orthodox sect that declares secular Jewish nationalism to be sinful. Groups such as these are no more representative of Anglo-Jewry than the conservative commentator and conspiracy theorist Candace Owens is representative of the African American voice.

Crucially, we should recognize that antisemitism is not just like every other form of racism and that dealing with it requires a non-generic approach. Too often, investigations into this form of prejudice lapse into more general ones with a broader remit: to investigate antisemitism and other forms of racism, one example being the 2016 UK Labour party investigation that was chaired by Baroness Chakrabarti. To be clear: it is as important to counter prejudice against Jews as it is to counter that against any other minority. The consequences of anti-black hate, anti-Muslim hate and homophobic hate are potentially just as severe and corrosive to the interests of the group in question. These forms of hatred and bigotry tarnish and disfigure society in just the same ways as antisemitism has always done. But the broad-brush anti-racism approach potentially misses a great deal more than it clarifies. The central problem with the Chakrabarti report was summed up well by one commentator: 'She failed to describe or define antisemitism, how it operates and what it looks like. She failed to go through the incidents, explaining why they were antisemitic. She focused on a few bad apples, not the problem with the barrel.'[1] The reason why the culture of anti-Israeli hatred remains core to the problem of modern political antisemitism is that this form of hatred has long metastasized, regurgitating ancient tropes and cyphers to fit new situations of social crisis. This perennial problem of mutating racism needed to be spelt out and condemned, with recommendations for how to confront it. Generic anti-racism will not do that job. Of course, the converse is also true. Society should understand all the rhythms and cadences of anti-Muslim hate or the prejudices against black people or the Roma community by carefully examining the histories of those forms of racial prejudice.

2. Social media

At the heart of conspiracy thinking is 'an instinctive hostility towards traditional gatekeepers,' requiring 'a binary worldview that divides societies

[1] David Hirsh, "The Chakrabarti report failed, again and again," *The Jewish Chronicle*, July 7, 2016.

between corrupt elites and the pure people.'[1] Social media channels have become fertile sources for the dissemination of conspiracy theories, some of which bleed into or encourage antisemitic attitudes. In recent years, there has been an explosion of conspiracy theories relating to the Covid vaccine, the policy of lockdown, the New World Order, the 5G rollout, the Illuminati and QuAnon. All of these have been shared on channels such as Google, Telegram, TikTok, Reddit and 4 Chan. Younger people, so the evidence tells us, are more prone to believing conspiracy theories than adults. The Centre for Countering Digital Hate (CCDH) found that 60% of 13-17-year-old Americans who were surveyed agreed with four or more harmful conspiracy statements – compared with just 49% of adults. This figure rose from 60% to 69% for teens who spend four or more hours a day on any single social media platform.[2]

There is a considerable amount of evidence that a younger generation trusts these channels as news sources more than conventional media outlets. A study by the UK based media regulator OFCOM found that for 2021-22, Instagram was the most popular news source among teenagers (used by 29%), followed by TikTok and YouTube. BBC One and BBC Two had been knocked down to fifth place with only a quarter (24%) using these as news sources. A younger generation is less likely to get their news from reading a newspaper or watching a mainstream news outlet than from scrolling though their phone. By contrast, television news remains the most trusted outlet for adults.[3] Studies of young Americans merely confirm this trend. A statistical analysis of news consumption among young Americans aged 18 to 24 shows that some 45% use social media on a daily basis as opposed to online news sites (17%), network news (13%) and national newspapers (6%).[4] A survey from February 2023 found that whereas 17% of Australian respondents from Gen Z used television as their primary news source, some 43% stated that social media was their main news outlet.[5] In Canada, Gen Z respondents are 'more likely to assign credibility to content from social media experts (23%)

---

[1] "Antisemitism in the Digital Age: Conspiracy ideologies, Covid 19 and antisemitism," *Belltower.News*, accessed November 4, 2021.

[2] Kari Paul, "Teens much more likely to believe online conspiracy claims than adults – US study," *The Guardian*, August 17, 2023.

[3] "Instagram, TikTok and YouTube teenagers' top three news sources," *Ofcom*, July 21, 2022.

[4] "Frequency of using selected news sources among millennials in the United States as of August 2022," *Statista.com.*

[5] "Main news sources used by consumers in Australia as of February 2024, by age group," Statista.com.

and general social media content (23%) than their baby boomer counterparts (7% and 4%, respectively).'[1]

It is arguable that conspiracy theories about 5G, Covid or Princess Diana serve as a 'gateway drug' to wider antisemitism, itself a potent set of conspiracy theories about a shadowy elite that manipulates and controls the rest of society for its own nefarious purposes. Not surprisingly, antisemitism is rife on social media channels as one recent report from campaigning group Hope not Hate has revealed. They showed that content posted with the hashtags #rothschildfamily, #synagogueofsatan and #soros had been viewed 25.1 million times on TikTok in half a year. The antisemitic video The Lost Battle, a 12 hour documentary from 2017 about European Jews' alleged undue influence, received 900,000 views on BitChute. A study found that antisemitic comments on Facebook had tripled from 2007 to 2017 and that 'the number of antisemitic comments on selected German media channels on Facebook increased from 7.5 to 30.1% of the whole volume of comments.'[2] The site features an array of antisemitic motifs and various forms of hostility ranging from anti-Judaism to modern conspiratorial thinking, and Holocaust denial to anti-Zionism. There has been specific correlation too between coronavirus conspiracism and antisemitism. In the wake of the October 7 attacks, TikTok has become a prime forum for the spread of antisemitic conspiracy theories and misinformation. One can find plenty of hateful material on these sites, including virulent images of Jews that would not be out of place in Der Sturmer.[3]

Given this plethora of evidence, social media companies must train content moderators to become aware of the multiple manifestations of antisemitism, something best done by adopting the IHRA definition. They need to ensure that there are clear and transparent policies for flagging up hateful material and make it easy for users to report it. Those moderators then need to remove antisemitic content quickly instead of allowing it to proliferate with the risk that it will be seen by impressionable people. They should adopt community standards indicating that free speech precludes antisemitic

---

[1] "Young Canadians are Increasingly Trusting News Broadly Shared on Social Media," *Kaiser & Partners*, November 15, 2023.

[2] "Antisemitism in the Digital Age: Online Antisemitic Hate, Holocaust Denial, Conspiracy Ideologues and Terrorism in Europe," *Hope Not Hate*, 2021, https://hopenothate.org.uk/wp-content/uploads/2021/10/google-report-2021-10-v3.pdf, accessed September 22, 2025.

[3] "Sliding Through: Spreading Antisemitism on TikTok by Exploiting Moderation Gaps," *Anti-Defamation League*, November 20, 2023.

discourse and remind users that they will be denied access if such standards are violated. Finally, such companies should appoint a dedicated liaison officer to work directly with Jewish community institutions. This would enable the company to be better informed about the community's concerns and foster greater mutual understanding and respect. Tackling this conspiratorial content on social media matters a great deal for one particular segment of the population.

3. Teach critical thinking to debunk conspiracy theories

Tackling conspiracy theories is no easy matter, especially for those who have become convinced believers. Not only do they believe that hidden forces secretly control the course of events, manipulating the rest of society into sheep-like conformity and submission, but they also see rational critics as part of the conspiracy. Conspiracy thinking has an allure and appeal that effectively immunizes such beliefs from refutation, giving them the sheen of certainty that they do not deserve. Ideally, one should debunk misinformation before it is disseminated, a tactic of pre-emptively warning people against adopting a belief that is often called prebunking. Crucial to this is the teaching of critical thinking skills to young people. Students should be encouraged to check the person making a claim about the world. They should be told to ask questions about the source they are viewing – its provenance, its tone and language, its purpose and the credentials of the person likely to be making it. They should be encouraged to question a theory that seems impossible to refute or which regards all criticisms as proof of the theory. Armed with such skills, students will be better able to identify conspiracy theories and the antisemitism that so often accompanies them. Evidence shows that online games in which players enter a fictional social media environment and follow the activities of a fake news creator are 'less susceptible to future exposure to common misinformation techniques.'[1] It is suggested that social media companies, governments and educational institutions develop similar programs to inoculate people from believing harmful forms of fake news, including antisemitism.

---

[1] Jon Roozenbeek, Sander Van Der Linden and Thomas Nygren, "Prebunking interventions based on "inoculation" theory can reduce susceptibility to misinformation across cultures," *Misinformation Review*, February 3, 2020.

Schools should also encourage students to meet their fellow Jews, among members of other faith communities. Jews are a small minority in almost all the countries in which they live in and, taking the UK as an example, form just 0.4% of the overall population. The vast majority of students will have had no contact at all with British Jews. Even in the US where there are 6 million Jews, the community numbers only 2% of the population as a whole. Outside of major cities (New York, Chicago, Washington and LA), most young Americans will probably not encounter many Jews in their local area. Thus, interfaith events have some value in creating bonds and friendships, dispelling misunderstandings and expanding the circle of empathy, all of these a valuable antidote to the racist narrative.

Above all, schools and universities should use the vast array of educational materials that are available from groups such as the Anti-Defamation League. The ADL's No Place for Hate programme is about creating diverse student committees that reject prejudice and which are designed to create the leaders of the future. It is one of the anti-bias programmes that this organization spearheads and which reaches thousands of educators every year. The UK based Solutions not Sides aims to tackle the racism experienced by both Jews and Muslims while contextualizing the suffering of the Arab-Israeli conflict. There are countless initiatives from other organizations, including ones from B'nai B'rith, the AJC and the Simon Wiesenthal Centre. Their experience and resources are critical in the fight against antisemitism and racism more widely.

4. Celebrate Jewish identity

One must recognize a startlingly obvious point: antisemitism is merely one facet of the Jewish experience, admittedly the darkest. Jewish history is certainly about pogroms, concentration camps and expulsion but it is also a story rich with eminent scholars, rabbis, lawyers, writers and artists. Jewish people have enriched every country they have lived in and enlarged every culture they have encountered. The Jews are not just a people of the book but a people of art, dance, music, film, food and song. There is a positive story to tell about the role Jews have played in various countries and the indelible impression they have left on their nations' institutions.

One can take the UK for starters. Certainly, England was the first nation to expel its Jewish population (in 1290) and the first nation to introduce a blood libel. It was a nation whose literary canon was saturated with antisemitic motifs of a Chaucerian, Shakespearean and Dickensian kind. Yet Anglo-Jewish life was not one marked just by the unceasing woe of Clifford's Tower, Shylock or Fagin. England also reinvited Jews to enter the country in the 1650s and, over the next three centuries, reaped the benefits of Jewish immigration. It produced such luminaries as Benjamin Disraeli, Britain's first ethnic minority Prime Minister, actors like Peter Sellers, Stephen Berkoff and Stephen Fry, the philosophers Sir Isaiah Berlin and Sir Alfred Ayer, figures in the fine arts like Lucien Freud and Sir Jacob Epstein, musicians such as Myra Hess, Lord Menuhin and Benny Green, a plethora of famous writers, among them Harold Pinter, Arnold Wesker and Will Self and a vast number of lawyers and judges. Many British high street stores, including Marks and Spencer and Tesco, were founded or co-founded by Jewish entrepreneurs. Thus, the idea of a British Jewish History month is long overdue and should be welcomed by the community.[1] It is a chance to see another side to the Jewish community other than as victims of racism. The US based Jewish American Heritage Month similarly aims to foster a sense of belonging, shared civic values and an understanding of the nation's rich cultural heritage, and speaks of the many contributions that American Jews have made to national life.

By the same token, there is much more to Israel than the sum of its conflicts with neighbouring countries. It is a land of invention and entrepreneurship, a place that has generated medical devices, scientific breakthroughs and high-tech achievements affecting the entire globe. For all its faults, it remains a stronghold of democratic values in a region beset by autocracy and illiberalism. It is not just a conflict zone of endless belligerence and occupation. It is a people, a land and a historic civilization.

5. Understand Israel better

For many progressives, it is easy to identify antisemitism when it comes from the far right. But that is not the principal vehicle for today's Jew hatred. The twenty first century has seen an explosion in anti-Zionist hatred, which is aimed at turning the Jewish state into a de-normalized, pariah nation that deserves no place in the civilized world. Ancient tropes of antisemitism have been regurgitated to fit a political zeitgeist, ranging from deicide (Israel sacrificing the Palestinian Jesus), the blood libel (Israel lusting after

---

[1] The first British Jewish culture month in the UK will be held in May-June 2026.

Palestinian blood), bestiality (Israel as a Nazi state), dual loyalty (Israel supporters betraying their countries through their support for the country), the all-powerful Jewish lobby (now a Zionist lobby) and avarice (the colonialist state greedily usurping the land of others). The imagery that accompanies such malevolent discourse, especially in an Arab world that has little regard for polite notions of anti-racism, takes crudity to extremes. It depicts the Jewish state in animalistic terms, directly reproducing the most virulent tropes of Nazi hatred, such as the octopus and the spider. In the West, progressives fetishise Palestinians to such an extent that they liken them to characters in a wild west morality tale – a group of noble warriors resisting an all-evil aggressor.

But such cartoonish representations, which naturally segue into anti-Jewish hatred, are easily avoided. Israel is a normal, but imperfect, country that has found itself at war for many decades with a host of enemies. There are certainly legitimate criticisms to be made of Israeli policies and leaders over the years, and much to be said about the current state of Israeli democracy. The Palestinians have suffered injustices too and, despite many being self-inflicted, their plight cannot be ignored.

Non-racist critics tend to focus on a number of issues: that Israel's behaviour in the West Bank is harsh or counterproductive; that the measures that Israel takes to defend itself, such as the security barrier and the checkpoints, impose too high a cost on Palestinian civilians and incentivize support for Hamas; that Israel's settlement policy is a barrier to peace and is a provocation to the Palestinian population; that the far right in Israel has created a toxic atmosphere of racism and extremism injurious to minorities; that there is social discrimination in Israel against the Arab population; that the presence of ultra-orthodox parties in Israel's system of proportional representation ensures that parties with narrow agendas hold the balance of power in the political system and translates into support for politically unsustainable policies; that Israel's leaders have not gone the extra mile for peace and that they are prepared to acclimatize their nation to an unending conflict. These criticisms can all be countered in various ways and are far from being beyond reproach. Yet they all focus on public policy and are an attempt to engage with the record of governments, past and present, in terms of commonly understood areas of concern. They do not denigrate the entire country or its population, nor do they demonize Israel's founding ideology

(Zionism). They are also the kind of criticisms that one might read in some of Israel's own newspapers.

Israel is not the Satanic state that Islamists and leftists like to imagine. By the same token, the Palestinians must be imbued with moral agency. When their leadership incites hatred against Jews, offers financial rewards for acts of terror and rejects meaningful steps to resolving the conflict, it is bad conduct that must be called out. When Palestinians commit egregious acts of terror, they must be condemned, regardless of the sympathy one might have for their right to self-determination. Palestinians are not puppets; they are actors.

One of the best antidotes to this thinking is to visit the country, not just its predominantly Jewish areas like Tel Aviv, but mixed cities and towns, such as Haifa, Acre, Jaffa and Jerusalem. Here one can see a real, living, breathing nation, with all its faults and curiosities, rather than a made-up entity. Here one can witness Arabs and Jews live cheek by jowl, eating in the same restaurants, travelling on the same buses, working in the same hospitals, studying in the same universities and walking on the same streets. There is more to be done when it comes to integrating Arabs into the population and overcome prejudice but, and this is the crucial point, this is happening.

6. Cultivate allies

Finally, we should remember that antisemitism is not a problem that Jews alone should be tackling. Throughout history there have been non-Jews ready to show solidarity with their Jewish friends and neighbours in times of adversity. Their willingness to ally with Jews against the hatred that engulfs them is something to be welcomed, admired and celebrated. Among the Islamic organizations that have taken a brave stand against this hatred are the UK based Muslims against Antisemitism, the Council of Muslims against Antisemitism, the Quilliam Foundation, the German based Muslim Alhambra Society and the Islamic Network Groups.

There are also important relationships between black and Jewish groups in America. The Black Jewish Entertainment Alliance was launched 'to bring the two communities together in solidarity, to support each other in their struggles, and to better understand each other's plight and narratives.' The AJC's Atlanta Black/Jewish Coalition brings together black people and Jews for the purposes of education, outreach and advocacy. Such organizations give hope that the common cause between Jews and black people more than a century ago can continue to be renewed in future generations. There are also many Christian groups around the world that actively oppose antisemitism, with Christians United for Israel being one prominent example, and examples of co-operation between Hindu and Jewish community organizations. Antisemitism primarily affects the Jews but it never ends with them. Those people who show allyship and solidarity with the Jewish people deserve recognition and gratitude for taking a stance for decency and justice, often in the teeth of unrelenting hostility.

Confronting antisemitism is one of the critical battles of our age, requiring an ongoing struggle with an ever-mutating form of hatred. In this struggle, each person can and should make a difference, no matter how small. One vital step is to call out and refute the lies, myths and canards of anti-Jewish hatred, exposing their absurdity, illogicality and malignity at every opportunity. If this short volume has made a contribution in that regard, it will have served its purpose.

Index

Q

R

S

T

www.ingramcontent.com/pod-product-compliance
Lightning Source LLC
LaVergne TN
LVHW011338110826
845153LV00014B/459/J

* 9 7 8 1 6 8 0 5 3 3 9 0 3 *